Chrétien de Troyes

Jean Frappier

Chrétien de Troyes
The Man and His Work

**Translated by
Raymond J. Cormier**

Ohio University Press
Athens, Ohio

Library of Congress Cataloging in Publication Data

Frappier, Jean.
  Chrétien de Troyes, the man and his work.

  Translation of: Chrétien de Troyes, l'homme et l'oeuvre.
  Bibliography: p. 191.
  Includes index.
  1. Chrétien de Troyes, 12th cent.–Criticism and interpretation.
I. Cormier, Raymond J., 1938-   . II. Title.
PQ1448.F713   841'.1   81-9475
  ISBN 0-8214-0603-5   AACR2

To My Wife

Contents

Illustrations

The illustrations are taken from illuminations for *Yvain ou Le Chevalier au Lion* found in the Princeton University Library Garrett MS 125. Permission to reproduce has been generously granted by Princeton University Library. For further detail, see R.L. McGrath, "A Newly Discovered Illustrated Manuscript of Chrétien de Troyes' *Yvain* and *Lancelot* in the Princeton University Library," *Speculum* 38 (1963):583-94. (—Translator.)

Translator's Preface

Open the pages of any recent study in medieval French literature and you will find Jean Frappier's name and scholarship cited with respect, a prestigious name indeed, which, since just before World War II, became synonymous with that area of comparative literature known as Arthurian studies. Such a reputation for excellence is hard won.

First, in the late 1930s, he published his major edition and critical study of *La Mort le Roi Artu* (the former he saw through its fourth edition in 1968). Just as these were hailed at the time as vital to the pioneering research on the Vulgate Cycle and its related erudite subjects, Frappier began and continued to turn out enduring "hautes vulgarisations"—in the popular Classiques Larousse series, for example, and, more recently, a careful modern French rendition of Chrétien's *Chevalier de la Charrette*. And his commitment to a wider audience is apparent in the present work.

One need only browse through his bibliography, prepared for the homage volume, *Mélanges Frappier* (2 vols., Geneva, 1970), to retrace his pride of major articles, widely considered as profound, judicious, and comprehensive; among these, many would agree to mention at least: "Littératures médiévales et littérature comparée: problèmes de recherche et de méthode"; "Vues sur les conceptions courtoises dans les littératures d'oc et d'oil au XIIe siècle" (1959); "Remarques sur la structure du lai: Essai de définition et de classement" (1961); "Structure et sens du 'Tristan': Version commune, version courtoise" (1963); "Remarques sur la peinture de la vie et des héros antiques dans la littérature française du XIIe et du XIIIe siècle" (1964).

Numerous other superlative studies, some of which are more polemical (but always generous) in nature and range, deal with Grail criticism and date from the 1950s and early 1960s. Frappier's varied interests, in the epic cycle and late medieval writers, or in philology, lexicography, and versification, for instance, led him to publish important monographs and articles treating in detail very technical matters (such as an exhaustive review and analysis of an edition of Marie de France's *Lais,* 1969). Frappier's contribution to the expansion of Arthurian studies is immeasurable. He was the most important European *arthurisant* of his time. In the years immediately following World War II, the need was felt for some control over the incipient but burgeoning Arthurian bibliography. Almost singlehandedly, Frappier launched the incomparable *Bulletin Bibliographique de la Société Internationale Arthurienne (BBSIA/BBIAS)* in 1949, and was instrumental in founding the association (the seeds of which were planted in the late 1920s). Frappier remained president of the society for eighteen years, during which time the *Bulletin,* through his tenacity and perseverance, increased in funding (from UNESCO), in size and in scope, and, of its type, it is now one of the most strategic yearly *mises au point,* or recapitulations, for research in medieval French literature (usually, but not always, exclusive of epic and non-Arthurian romance). In 1948, at the second Triennial Arthurian Congress in Quimper, attended by some twenty scholars, when asked if the society would be popular, Frappier reportedly smiled and exclaimed: "O, ce ne sera pas un mouvement de masse!" (It won't be a mass movement!) Now, more than thirty years later, the cohorts are impressive: the society lists well over 1000 members throughout the world, of which a record 400 attended the twelfth Triennial Congress at Regensburg, in 1979, with over 80 papers scheduled on the program. Professor Emeritus of the Sorbonne Frappier continued to work and campaign, taking stock to the delight of admirers with such projects as reediting his critical studies of *Yvain* (1969) and *Perceval* (1972), or collecting several of his major articles into one volume. The author died in 1974.

Frappier's method is distinguished by the key words *nuance* ("discrimination") and *mesure,* ("harmony"), full qualities not particularly relished by New Critics, but then, at least, he is not guilty of soliciting the text (i.e., asking of it unanswerable questions), nor of imposing a jargon-filled or obscure prose on the reader in order to appear profound. Less abstractly, Frappier's argument in the book at hand doubts

Chrétien's interest in symbolism, insisting rather on his lucid, skillful handling of psychology and characterization. Typical of Chrétien's own eclectic endeavors in the "open"–and dazzling–twelfth-century Renaissance, Frappier attempted to synthesize the enormous critical output on the author since the late-nineteenth century. By remaining open to but never absorbed by newer methods and interests (e.g., in the areas of psychoanalysis, sociology, and even structuralism), Frappier has in many instances here (unknowingly perhaps at elaboration) prophesied the direction of New Criticism on Chrétien de Troyes.

Simultaneously a handbook and synopsis, a precocious work, then, a harbinger of research, and now an historical document, *Chrétien de Troyes: L'Homme et l'oeuvre* appeared in 1957 (3d ed., 1968) in the respected series directed by the eminent René Jasinski, Connaissance des Lettres (which includes other single volumes, for example, *Stendhal, Baudelaire, La Chanson de Roland, Virgil Molière,* and *Le Roman de la Rose;* of these, the first three have already been translated into English). Drawn from his Sorbonne lectures in the late 1940s and early 1950s, the logical offspring of *Le Roman breton* (published first in four separate mimeographed fasciculi, now out-of-print and considered rare items by medievalists), Frappier's imponderous volume maintains the high quality of the series, as well as offering, in the historico-biographical mode, a scholarly, balanced, and mature survey of mid-twelfth century intellectual history: "Le Livre de l'Etudiant," a readable little masterpiece, is included in every important Arthurian bibliography.

Chrétien de Troyes is a canonical name in French literary history and certainly one of the most illustrious in Arthurian literature. An inspired, colorful storyteller and master verbal craftsman, Chrétien was primarily interested in his characters and in the technique of writing. More than a link in the chain from Geoffrey of Monmouth's *History of the Kings of Britain* to Sir Thomas Malory's *Morte d'Arthur* and beyond, Chrétien was the principal articulator of the Arthurian legend and wrote the oldest known French Arthurian romances.

Active during a great cultural florescence (ca. 1160–90), he tells us–only through his works–that after a debut adapting Ovid into Old French, he wrote a version of the Tristan legend (not extant), then in succession five romances: *Erec et Enide, Cligés, Lancelot* (which tells the original version of the knight's daring love for Arthur's spouse,

Guenevere), *Yvain,* and *Perceval* (the original Grail story). Modern readers find solace in their plots of chivalry and of love, and, in their heroic displays of social awareness, inner freedom, and self-discovery, a kind of irresistible, happy wisdom.

My students tell me that Frappier's longish first chapter provides an ideal critical introduction to medieval French literature. In addition to social backgrounds, it assesses the whole rich Arthurian tapestry available for Chrétien's labors by ca. 1160. Each of the subsequent chapters offers a summary, commentary, and critical study of the romance under discussion. The last chapter—the most sensitive and pervasive—analyzes for the most part Chrétien's style and expression. The selective bibliography should prove to be a useful guide for further reading.

A condensed version of this book appeared in English as chapter 15 of Roger S. Loomis's collaborative survey, *Arthurian Literature in the Middle Ages (ALMA)* (Oxford, 1959). Professor Frappier informed me that it was based on a short, working copy (from which he had elaborated this book in the early 1950s), and that it was this digest which the late Roger Loomis and his wife had translated for inclusion in the encyclopedic *ALMA.* Since I have not seen the original précis, to comment on the quality of the translation would be perilous. It is only fair to note that I have sporadically purloined certain of its turns of English expression or phraseology—sometimes even inadvertently—because they seemed right to me. But knowledgeable readers will recognize the differences between that chapter (in places, manifestly extreme as regards the Celtic hypothesis) and Frappier's essentially literary exposition here. For instance, Frappier neither specifies Brittany alone as the territory whence Celtic minstrels presumably circulated tales and poems heard by Chrétien, nor accepts without qualification the Celtic origin of the Grail legend. Now we are all indebted to the "Dean of Arthurians," Roger Sherman Loomis. But Frappier's influential views, with all their original values and emphases, have never appeared in unaltered English before.

Not unprecedented, then, my effort nevertheless has had as guiding inspiration the general appeal and interest of the book for students of literature, criticism, and history, and, of course, for any educated person wishing to learn about Chrétien de Troyes and the genesis of

Arthurian romance. To gloss Frappier's "vulgarization"—for the wider audience without French—has been my aim. One of the striking features of the volume is its artlessness, by which I mean that it manages, without skirting controversy, to grapple with the issues unpedantically. (One need only read a few of the early reviews to understand just how many questions remain moot regarding Chrétien, his dates, his sources of inspiration, his use of irony, etc.) Without being a testy zealot of a single theory, Frappier has contributed to Arthurian studies in this modest work a compilation of impressive arguments on behalf of the *celtisants* and for Chrétien's stunning originality—a compromise that should conciliate the baffled spheres of influence, the heretics, iconoclasts, and reactionaries.

Besides *ALMA*, as noted, I have drawn on diverse Arthurian publications in English for matters of usage like proper names; for example, R.S. Loomis, *Arthurian Tradition and Chrétien de Troyes*; Lewis Thorpe's translation of Geoffrey's *Historia regum Britanniae*; and J.D. Bruce, *The Evolution of Arthurian Romance*. Grateful acknowledgement is extended to Oxford University Press for permission to quote from Loomis's *Arthurian Literature in the Middle Ages* and to E.P. Dutton Publishers for permission to quote from *Arthurian Romances by Chrétien de Troyes*, translated by W. Wistar Comfort, an Everyman's Library Edition.

If my translation somehow survives the scrutiny of reviewers, it will redound only to the memory of Hans Wolpe, my first teacher of stylistics. For sympathetic and enthusiastic support, I am grateful to A. Micha; to E. Vinaver; especially to Professor Frappier, as well as to Rowe E. Portis; to Malcolm Craig for a patient, critical reading of the manuscript; and to Robert T. Corum and Douglas Kelly for assistance with the bibliography. I also wish to record my debt to René Jasinski for his animated confidence in the project, so long promised, herewith fulfilled, and to James Travis for his suggestion that I write a few paragraphs on Frappier's role in the evolution of Arthurian Studies. Were it not for the secretarial aid of Judi Halli, Lucilla Jones, and Nadia Kravchenko, this translation might have never seen light. Professor Frappier's dedication to his wife I leave unchanged, as an act of marital affection

Chrétien de Troyes

to my "Enide" (whom I have sometimes treated harshly); but to it I feel constrained to join here a word of acknowledgement on behalf of Urban T. Holmes, Eugène Vinaver, and Jean Frappier himself, models of scholarly abnegation, whose generous forms, but not our memory of them, have sadly passed from us.

Introduction

It is no longer necessary to rescue Chrétien de Troyes from neglect, for today he is one of the great names in French literary history. Even though his importance was not immediately recognized—critics as prominent as Gaston Paris and Joseph Bédier were somewhat hesitant about him—numerous studies over the past 100 years or so on the man and his work have increasingly guaranteed his fame.

But like other great authors, he is deep enough and varied enough to deserve different stress from one generation to the next. More and more, as he is studied, we discover new aspects of his achievement. In order to arrive at a clearer understanding of Chrétien's position as creator, it is our intention here to examine more attentively the moral, intellectual, and esthetic preoccupations of the period, as well as his sources of inspiration. At least let us hope that this conviction will serve as an excuse for the perilous plan of presenting in a few pages a synthesis on the unique and diverse Chrétien de Troyes—poet, artist, portraitist, romancer, and moralist for a whole refined and civilized society.

Only the rich get richer; one has tried to enhance Chrétien more than once by calling him the "father" of Arthurian romance and (nearly) the inventor of the *matière de Bretagne,* "Matter of Britain." Such absolute praise miscarries; inaccurate and useless in terms of the poet's true value, it even risks doing him a disservice by leaving unexamined the real explanation of his originality. He no more created Arthurian romance *ex nihilo* than Corneille or Racine by themselves devised French classical tragedy. But he too raised a still new and uncertain genre to a high degree of excellence, and, if he did not alone conceive of the *matière de Bretagne,* he provided it with a fascination until then unknown.

Chrétien de Troyes

Chrétien's work is a junction at which the principal currents of his epoch meet. Before he began to write, around 1160 or 1165, French literature was enjoying a resurgence of some ten or fifteen years in duration. The romance had already flowered, happy offspring and rival of the epic, corresponding to both a change in attitude and in feelings among the nobility, to a moral and poetic elevation of woman (or rather of the "lady"), and to that complex alloy of elegance, refinement, and psychology of love epitomized by the terms "courtly" and "courtliness." The first courtly romances, those of the "Cycle of Antiquity," the *Roman d'Alexandre, Roman de Thèbes, Roman d'Enéas, Roman de Troie,* in which imitation of the ancients, of Statius, Virgil, and especially Ovid, guided inspiration and anticipated a truer originality, were characterized by a new narrative technique—octosyllables rhyming in pairs that replaced the epic *laisse.* The authors of these romances in the "antique" style (concerned with the heroes of antiquity) were also careful about craftsmanship; but their clever, artistic intentions were often accompanied by clumsy, bookish gropings, while a simultaneous desire to please and instruct nourished their aspirations to fame: these were all signs of a zealous and yet hesitant humanism. Elsewhere, troubadour poetry, artfully infused with love meditations, offered more suggestive stylistic models than the manuals of poetic rhetoric *(artes poeticae).* Finally, to incite hearts and fire imaginations, there was Geoffrey of Monmouth's brilliant and dramatic Arthurian fiction *(Historia regum Britanniae, The History of the Kings of Britain)* as translated by Wace into brisk octosyllables *(Roman de Brut),* the spellbinding *Tristan* legend, arranged into a northern French romance toward the middle of the century at the latest, and, lastly, spread by minstrels, the Celtic lays and tales. All these diverse models were at Chrétien's disposal during his years of apprenticeship, and although that diversity brought him the risk of spreading himself thin, the influence of each of them left its mark on his work. His trial efforts were almost certainly Ovidian and in the "antique" style. Later, when his talent had matured and his principles were established, he settled his choice on the *matière de Bretagne.* But if, through its inspiring subject matter, Chrétien profited considerably from the *matière de Bretagne,* it too was prosperous in his hands. Arthurian romance became a superior form of courtly narrative, a personal embodiment in which he blended moral illustration, imitation of Latin poets, a legacy from the *chansons de geste* and from the romances with heroes of antiquity, and, finally, a charming, sparkling, and fluid series of myths. He knowingly arrayed and harmonized these elements, almost always imposing upon them a unity of conception and of style. He thus fashioned a world of his own, where fantasy was wedded to reason. His originality consisted in setting the limpid spirit of Champagne and of France to the classic task of endowing old materials with a more exquisite flavor, a clearer meaning, and broader human values.

Jean Frappier

Chrétien de Troyes

Chapter 1

The Background and the Work

Very little is known about the life of Chrétien de Troyes. In this sense he is a typical medieval author. Conjectures or hints regarding his character are divulged only through an examination of his works. We are sure of one single fact, that of his relations with the courts of Champagne and of Flanders. The dedication of his *Lancelot (The Knight of the Cart)* shows that the poem was composed for Countess Marie de Champagne, daughter of Louis VII of France and Eleanor of Aquitaine. The work is dated after 1164, since Marie ("my lady of Champagne," as Chrétien calls her) had married Henry I of Champagne in that year.[1] The prologue of *Perceval* (or *The Story of the Grail*) furnished a second date because it was dedicated by Chrétien after 1168 to Philippe of Alsace, who became count of Flanders in that year. This unfinished work was begun, therefore, before Philippe's death at Acre, 1 June 1191, or rather before September 1190, the time of his departure for the Third Crusade.

The learned court of Champagne was held most often in Troyes, and judging from his complete name, the poet was probably a native, although it is not inconceivable that the mention of Troyes indicates only the town in which he resided for a time; it can hardly be doubted, however, that he was born in Champagne. His language, quite close to pure Francien, preserves certain traits of the Champenois dialect. Moreover, he used only once the complete designation Chrétien *de Troyes* at the beginning of *Erec* (line 9), his first Arthurian romance; the later poems

3

are simply signed *Chrétien*—perhaps an indication of his having already acquired a certain reputation. Does his dedication to Philippe mean that late in life he accompanied his patron to Flanders? Certain passages of *Le Conte du Graal* permit this inference, although Chrétien could have met this new patron without leaving Champagne, for Philippe of Alsace often visited the court at Troyes, and in 1182, in fact, he proposed marriage, though unsuccessfully, to the Countess Marie, widowed the year before.

It is not necessary to mention in detail the attempts made in determining Chrétien's biography. Gaston Paris's conjecture that Chrétien was a herald is without foundation. He has also been identified with a certain Christianus, canon of Saint-Loup at Troyes, whose name appears in a charter of 1173; but Christianus was not a rare name, and, if we accept this hypothesis, we must admit also that he was an ecclesiastic, which, at least in principle, would be difficult to reconcile with the mundane and secular spirit of almost all his works. Yet he possessed the culture of a cleric (Wolfram von Eschenbach called him "master," a title often given to clerics: "Meister Cristjân von Troys"). It was at the flourishing schools of Troyes or perhaps elsewhere that he studied the *trivium* and the *quadrivium*. Since in this period the notion *clergie* encompassed a network of ideas, Chrétien could have been a cleric without taking priestly orders and thus have acquired his knowledge of Latin.

In answer to the question whether Chrétien, in the course of travel, visited those Celtic countries where occur the adventures of his romances, Gaston Paris thought that he must have crossed the Channel because of the accuracy of the poet's geographical knowledge relating to Britain in *Cligés;* Stefan Hofer believed that he had traveled to Nantes; but the evidence for these theories is not altogether conclusive. Chrétien could have learned much of the great world at the court of Champagne or in the town of Troyes, where the two great annual fairs, at the crossroads of the eastern and western, northern and southern routes, brought from every corner of Christendom a crowd of merchants, *jongleurs,* and storytellers.

In the study of Chrétien, unless new documents about him come to light, there is little chance for a lavish biographical method. But we might find consolation in the thought that perhaps a more extensive knowledge of his life would not necessarily reveal the secrets of his fictional creations; doubtless we would even be disappointed by the man himself if we could confront him with one of his works behind whose characters he disappears. For he used these characters not so much to represent his day-to-day existence as cleric-poet in the service of the nobility, but rather to idealize his elegant and heroic conception of life.

However diversified his work, it is not known in its entirety. Chrétien listed at the beginning of *Cligés* (vv. 1–8) the poems already composed: *Erec and Enide; Les Comandemenz Ovide; L'Art d'amors (The Art of Love); Le Mors de l'espaule (The Bitten Shoulder);* a tale of *Li Rois Marc et Iseut la Blonde;* and the *Muance de la hupe, de l'aronde et du rossignol (The Change of the Hoopoe, the Swallow, and of the Nightingale).* But this order is not necessarily chronological. Three titles correspond to translations or imitations from Ovid: *Les Comandemenz* (perhaps the *Remedia amoris*); *L'Art d'amors (Ars amandi);* and his only extant Ovidiana, the *Muance,* more often designated *Philomena,* which is found in a late-thirteenth-century *Ovide moralisé.* In another work that does not survive, *Le Mors de l'espaule,* Chrétien may have told the story of Pelops (in spite of Gaston Paris's doubts assuming rather a Celtic provenance for it). The poem of *King Mark and Iseut the Blond* was evidently related to the celebrated Celtic legend. On the nature of this lost work hypotheses have abounded, but in all likelihood it was only an episodic tale. In any case there is no reason to recognize it as the primitive *Ur-Tristan,* the archetype from which seem to derive the various later versions. If not posterior to *Erec,* Chrétien first used the *matière de Bretagne* in his tale of King Mark. One notable supporter of *Erec's* anteriority in relation to the Ovidiana was Stefan Hofer. But this is an ill-contrived conjecture since *Erec* cannot pass for the work of a beginner; it is more artful and personal, and the author seems more talented and more confidently mature than in *Philomena.* It is most probable that Chrétien practiced his romancer's apprenticeship with translations of Ovid before succumbing to the charm of Celtic materials.

After *Cligés* there followed three works uncontestably his, signed with his name and genius: *Lancelot,* or *Le Chevalier de la Charrette (The Knight of the Cart), Yvain,* or *Le Chevalier au Lion (The Knight with the Lion),* and *Perceval,* or *Le Conte du Graal (The Story of the*

Grail). He left *Lancelot* to a collaborator for completion, Godefroi de Lagny, and died before finishing *Perceval.* If to the list are added two lyric poems of uncertain date, one in the manner of Bernard de Ventadour, we have enumerated all of Chrétien's authentic works. There is the debated attribution of the non-Arthurian *Guillaume d'Angleterre (William of England),* an adaptation of the Saint Eustace legend. The critics are divided on whether or not to ascribe it to our poet. Though the name Chrétien appears in the first line as that of the author, this does not argue peremptorily for Chrétien de Troyes's authorship, for, if it is by him, it would come after *Cligés,* in whose prologue it is not cited. But *Guillaume d'Angleterre,* however interesting, lacks the turn of mind, style, and subtlety of the author of *Lancelot, Yvain,* and *Perceval.*

The difficult problem of Chrétien's chronology has been studied most recently by Stefan Hofer and Anthime Fourrier. Certain reflections of contemporary events and personages seem to place the date of *Erec* at 1170, that of *Cligés* ca. 1176. Between 1177 and 1179 or 1181, Chrétien probably worked alternately on *Yvain* and *Lancelot,* and after 14 May 1181 he began *Perceval* for Philippe of Alsace. Thus Foerster's datings have been moved forward considerably.[2]

Courtly Literature

Beyond these meager biographical facts, there is no better method to understand Chrétien the man and the author than to reconstruct his work, as much as possible, in terms of the period and society in which he lived. And, for a variety of reasons, his era was one of renaissance and of humanism.

Toward the middle of the twelfth century, the appearance of courtly literature in northern France corresponds to a shift of events in medieval civilization. By widening horizons and creating relative prosperity, increased commercial trade enriched the style of daily living, at least for the privileged classes. From the Orient, products of luxury, spices, incense, ivory, pearls, silks, and dyes were imported in greater quantity after the First Crusade. On the other hand, as feudal society became more hierarchical, the mightiest lords collected lands and vassals around them; and, in Champagne, Flanders, Picardy, and elsewhere, a thriving courtly life thus developed. As the etymology indicates, it was precisely under these circumstances of court life that *courtoisie* ("courtliness," "courtesy") appeared. (At that time *cour* was written and pronounced with the final "t" retained, as in modern English, "court.") This courtly ideal was related to a transformation in the social structure of the nobility, a period called the "second feudal age," during which time the aristocracy moved towards enclosing itself as a hereditary class and tended to codify its norms of behavior. As Marc Bloch put it, "Courtliness was essentially a class affair."[3]

The term *courtois* ("courtly") was a complex one. It was sometimes used more widely to qualify chivalrous actions and elegant, cultivated politeness (i.e., "courteousness"), while with its more precise meaning it designated a refined art of love inaccessible to common mortals. Thus constituted, "courtly love" formed an embellishment upon love's desires and fashioned the disciplines of passion. "Courtly" can even apply to forms of style and versification, for example, to the learned techniques of the Provençal lyric *canso*, or the *chanson d' amour* ("song," "song of love").

The highest qualities of the epic hero were preserved in the courtly hero: he had prowess (from *preux*, "brave") and was *courtois*, two characteristics often associated in the twelfth- and thirteenth-century romances. All this implied pride of lineage and control of self. But to these must henceforth be added other qualities, suitable to a more sophisticated social life, for example, refinement of language, manners, and clothing, a scrupulous loyalty in battle, *largesse* ("liberality," "generosity")—"lady and queen who illuminates all virtue," as Chrétien declares in *Cligés*—physical beauty, and similarly, strength and courage. Perfect courtliness also involved respect for the actions and feelings of others, however disconcerting; this in turn inspired a predilection for moral nuances on the part of those rare individuals, the elite who elevated themselves above the common order by dint of their inbred nobility or through their generous yet hidden thoughts. Not unexpectedly, the new ideal was matched by the increasing importance of woman in feudal society; nothing makes clearer the role played by *la dame* in all this social propriety than another distinctive trait of the courtly hero: he is not only amorous, he *must* be in love. Without love his claim to courtly perfection is in vain. "He needed a noble lady to serve...," states one troubadour's biography. In the presence of the *dame,* even at the thought of her, an exalting *joi* penetrates the courtly lover, and, in order to show himself worthy, to merit her, he sets out to win honors and fame in tourneys and adventures.

Certainly one of the boldest and most original of medieval creations was courtly love, or *fine amor* ("fine, perfect love"). Felt to be out of accord or incompatible with the concept of marriage, it included the "service of love" which was based in a way on feudal homage and on the services of a vassal toward his lord, because very often the beloved was of a higher social order than her devoted lover. Although its form appears as an absolute feeling, the courtly love experience is not simply blind or irresistible passion; it is based on choice which involves the use of will or reason, especially since the lady is freely chosen for her physical and moral beauty, for her "value." Imposed also on *fins amants* ("fine lovers") is the law of secrecy, and while not necessarily chaste (far from it indeed according to some texts), courtly love is in principle a "distant" love, strengthened by absence and obstacles. It was later codified into a doctrine with canons and etiquette to regulate, in Stendhal's words, "The official advancement of lovers."

The courtly style and ideology first burst into bloom in southern France, meaning of course that vast group of provinces called the Midi, where Provençal, or *langue d' oc* was spoken, including not only Provence and Languedoc, but also all of Aquitaine, Limousin, Poitou, and Gascony, as well as the regions of Toulouse and Auvergne. Courtliness of the Provençal type, whose cradle appears indeed to have been the Limousin-Poitou area, rapidly radiated and then, before 1150 but especially afterward, infiltrated the northern, *langue d' oil* domains. This was accomplished under the influence of important women like Eleanor of Aquitaine and her two daughters, Marie of Champagne and Aelis of Blois. But there were more profound reasons for this diffusion: an essential similarity existed between social and psychological conditions within the feudal classes in both north and south. In some ways the courtly ideal responded to similar polite aspirations, whether manifest or latent. And in passing to the north, a distinctive softening of the ideal is noticeable.

However, to the literature in *langue d'oil* we owe the creation of the romance form, which became, soon after its genesis, the courtly romance.

With less rigor and fewer subtleties than in the south, the northern conception of courtly love was more relaxed; it encouraged the refinement of emotion and resistance to impulsive desires. Through the potential of this ideology, the romance genre gained an advantage by subsuming at once plots woven of adventure and inquiries on the meaning of life; it thus tended toward much more character description than the subjective, static lyric *canso*. A second significant innovation was the personal adventure of the Arthurian hero, nearly always unrelated to that collective effort in which the epic hero participated.

As models to mirror and embellish the courtly ideal, the Knights of the Round Table likewise represented meaningful values. In the fictional universe of romance, the skillful mixture of marvels and realism offered the "second feudal age" nobility both a means of escape and the possibility of recognizing their own image, that is, of seeing themselves as they fancied themselves—if not as they really were. Courtly and Arthurian romance inaugurated a literature of escape both for those many fiefless knights, reduced to court service and to the modest success of tourneys, who were all the more inclined to quibble over points of honor, and for those many ladies with pining hearts and exotic imagination—did not more than one Emma Bovary languish in the palaces? But the playful illusions do not seem to have deceived these people to the point of losing the taste for reality. The intellectual and esthetic formation of courtly romancers, the nature of both writers and their audiences (and even of their readers) had progressed sufficiently to permit them to distinguish without the risk of error the importance of the marvelous and that of reality. Marc Bloch rightly saw the romances of this period as the expression "of an era henceforth refined enough to distinguish simple descriptions of reality from pure literary escape." (Ibid., p. 309.) The enigmatic spell of Celtic themes and of extraordinary adventures did not keep Chrétien de Troyes from being a conscientious and sometimes mischievous observer of his contemporaries.

Clerical Learning

The modern French critic Albert Thibaudet has said that "the medieval romance consists of a cleric speaking and a lady listening." This epigrammatic definition is as succinct as it is true: the lady represents

9

the most elegant aspect of the courtly society for which romances were composed, but the author is a cleric. What exactly is meant by this? The cleric of the Middle Ages was an educated individual with a knowledge of Latin. As an ecclesiastic, he of course knew Latin, or at least he was trained by and for the church, which at this time monopolized education and culture. Under these conditions it may seem disconcerting to find prowess, adventure, and love exalted in courtly romances authored by clerics. It is necessary to explain that in the Middle Ages and during the Renaissance, the demarcation between the sacred and profane was no doubt less sharp than after the Counter Reformation. But, especially, besides secular priests and regular priests, there existed clerics who were not priests, who had only taken minor orders, or just the tonsure. A few did not even possess the first orders of the ecclesiastical hierarchy. In order to gain access to culture and learning, however, as a rule, at the beginning of their studies, they were destined for the church. Their course of study included theology, a knowledge of Scripture, the liberal arts *(trivium, quadrivium),* and Latin literature. This "clerical" fringe was quite diverse and even embraced social pariahs, such as groups from which were enlisted the *clerici vagantes* ("wandering clerics"), or Goliardic poets. But apart from these vagabonds, at a time of considerable freedom, moderation, and decorum were observed by most clerics. With their culture and learning, they entered the courtly world because, through personal distinction or through the favors of chance, they were welcome in the royal, seignorial courts. It seems very likely that it was clerics of this type who read to noble ladies, and who, most probably, were the authors of courtly romances in the second half of the twelfth century. More men of letters than men of the church, such clerics in a way were also humanists. Ideally, they saw themselves responsible for the heritage and the transmission of Latin and even of Greek poetry. Ever mindful of the advice in the *Liber Sapientiae* (*Book of Wisdom,* attributed to Solomon in the Middle Ages), they sought to cultivate and never conceal man's divine gifts—knowledge and wisdom. Thus, a scriptural text justified their lofty desire for glory and linked them to traditions of antiquity.

Consequently, in their works the courtly clerics endeavored to imitate the ancients. Of course, an abundant output of "neo-Latin" poetry had already preceded and prepared their efforts, yet simple imitation of

Virgil or Ovid's language ran the risk of pastiche; the imitator or adapter never realizes his creative potential fully except by using his mother tongue. Arising from the study of Latin, the innovation of the courtly romancers was to imitate the ancients—in Old French. Although these clerics did proclaim their literary principles by manifesto, they nevertheless achieved a defense and illustration of the French language some four centuries before the poet-scholars of the Pléiade.

The most direct result of the imitation of the ancients was the romance of antiquity, represented principally by three important works, composed between ca. 1150 and 1165, the *Thebes* romance, *(Roman de Thèbes)*, the *Eneas, (Roman d'Eneas)*, and the *Troy* romance, *(Roman de Troie)*. But these adaptations were not just limited to a borrowing of subjects and themes. From Latin authors the clerics also appropriated rhetorical and literary skills, e.g., control over plot and dialogue, methods of description and portraiture, the use of similes and metaphors, and other stylistic procedures. All these conventions of composition had been codified and were diligently practiced in the schools. While such preparation posed certain dangers, at least it taught and required craftsmanship in style. Moreover, it did not inhibit subjective readings of the ancients, by which the formal character of conventional rhetoric could then be attenuated or renewed; in fact, within ten years or so, there is a noticeable change between the still quite obvious conscientiousness in *Thebes* or *Eneas* and the more thoughtful and contrived manner of Benoît de Sainte-Maure, Thomas of England, or especially of Chrétien de Troyes.

In spite of their nascent humanism, the courtly romancers were decidedly indiscriminate in the choice of models: Statius was hardly distinguishable from Virgil. But they were partial to Ovid—often seen as the most modern of the ancients, and in spite of a certain artificiality, it was he who captivated the medieval mind with his appealing style and spirited wit. In line after line of the *Amores*, the *Heroides*, and the *Metamorphoses*, he appears as an incomparable artist of passion. The didactic side of his *Art of Love* also attracted the clerics who never completely abandoned scholastic descriptions of love. Was this not after all a paradoxical encounter, between the old cleric Ovid and the promulgators of courtly love? Indeed, Ovid's libertinism and tactical advice for erotic gallantry differ considerably from the cult of the lady and

11

the poetic raptures of troubadour and trouvère. But it is also true that a certain Christian and ecclesiastical misogynistic tradition (also apparent in the courtly romances) was perpetuated, if we consider the behavior of those wily coquettes so well described by Ovid. Not only did Ovid help solve the mysteries of the heart, but his works offered a series of images and metaphors as well as a frame of reference for deliberative monologues, suitable to interiorized meditations and fitting for the expression of dramatic sentiments. And, finally, a compendium of fabulous and captivating tales was transmitted by the *Metamorphoses.*

Chrétien de Troyes underwent such an Ovidian formation, first evident in his appropriation of subjects dealing with the stories related in his Ovidiana, works of his youth most likely. But the influence continues in *Cligés* and even in the later romances, as the comparisons and metaphorical developments reveal. More subtly, however, Chrétien seems to have derived from his Latin model the vivid turn of expression, the narrative elegance, the artful and restless musical beauty of his verse. Perhaps too he was swayed by Ovid when he transferred the interplay of metamorphosis to a psychological level: Chrétien's characters evolve affectively and glow more and more in variegation as their adventures unfold in reciprocal interrelationships.

Chrétien's Formation

Among the qualities displayed by our author, the most significant is his clerical learning; along with imitations of Ovid and Virgil and his acquired literary craft, he combined a predilection for the feats of dialectic. But more important is his humanistic mental attitude. At the beginning of *Erec* (vv. 23–26), he asserted his faith in the value of his work and his assurance of long-lasting fame; in the prologue to *Cligés* (vv. 24–44), he celebrated earnestly the alliance of learning and chivalry and their glorious migration from Greece to Rome and from Rome to France. Though the theme of the *translatio studii* was a scholarly commonplace with a long past, there is no mistaking the pride in Chrétien's tone. It is noteworthy that for Chrétien the legacy from antiquity consisted of not only the transmission of culture but also the union of learning and chivalry. Such a synthesis is fundamental to twelfth-century humanism, a form of civilization at once ideal and real, whose image Chrétien projects into antiquity. To read this passage in *Cligés* as simply a fleeting thought would be incorrect, for it contains one of the most important concepts of the time. Let us recall that it was further symbolized in *Erec* (vv. 6736-93) by the allegorical figures representing the arts of the *quadrivium* embroidered on the coronation robes of the hero. The union of learning and military prowess was apparently incarnated in the person of Chrétien's protector, Henry I of Champagne.

Medieval admiration for pagan antiquity did not, of course, exclude a familiarity with Holy Scripture. Though Chrétien's romances revolve about psychological situations and moral problems in secular life, he drew surprisingly little from the Bible; yet we can nevertheless perceive its influence in the adaptation of religious imagery to a profane context. Indeed, in the prologue to *Perceval* (vv. 47-50), Chrétien translated powerfully and with moving simplicity a verse of Saint John (inadvertently attributed to Saint Paul).

Nor is symbolism absent from his work. This principle, based in part on biblical exegesis, attached spiritual meanings to tangible objects. Precious stones, animals, colors, and numbers: all had a "hidden sense," a *senefiance.* In reading texts, the duty of scholars and poets was to *gloser la lettre,* as Marie de France says in the prologue to her *Lais;* or again, to "moralize," i.e., to discover a religious significance, even in fabulous pagan narratives. Symbolism was deeply embedded in the medieval mind, especially before the rise of Aristotelianism. But though this habit is perceptible here and there in Chrétien's romances, in certain subtleties of composition and in correspondences between concrete details and the conduct of his characters, it was limited in his work by a strong feeling for psychological realities (Chrétien was especially gifted in his portrayal of characters), and by a turn of mind which favored rational motivation. He was neither a Dante nor the author of the mystical *Quest of the Holy Grail (Queste del Saint Graal).*

To the *chansons de geste,* to Wace, to the romances of antiquity, Chrétien owed something in the way of names, motifs, and technique, but his main debt lay elsewhere. The elaborate and formal troubadour

13

lyrics (which could be called a kind of "modern Parnassian poetry") were his source for conceptions of courtly love, to which he added his own reflections. Even more powerful was the impact of the prevailing and ubiquitous *Tristan* legend, not just restricted to his lost composition on Marc and Iseut. In *Erec,* in one of his lyric poems, and above all in *Cligés* (which has been called an "anti-*Tristan,*" a "hyper-*Tristan,*" a "neo-*Tristan*"), he reveals a will to oppose and surpass the famous love story. Whether for reasons of personal morality or for the sake of courtly values, Chrétien endeavored to substitute another pair for Tristan and Iseut. Even in *Lancelot* and *Yvain* the influence of the legend is felt, and only in *Perceval* was he released from this real obsession. Chrétien was at the same time fascinated and irritated by the *Tristan:* it was something like his shirt of Nessus.

Arthur of Britain

The generally recognized attraction of the *Tristan* raises a much larger question—the influence of the *matière de Bretagne.* If we exclude *Guillaume d' Angleterre,* of uncertain authorhsip, and *Cligés,* whose action takes place partly in Greece and Germany, all of Chrétien's romances deal with adventures localized entirely in Celtic areas, Great or Little Britain (i.e., Armorica), in the far-off days of King Arthur. When *Erec* was being written, tales of the Round Table were already circulating, and Arthur was becoming the poetic focal point of an immense and diverse *matière de Bretagne.* Sovereign of glory, of adventure, melancholy, and hope, more a spiritual than a temporal monarch, the legendary King Arthur was possibly in part historical (a Roman chieftian, *Artorius,* who was, it has been suggested, changed into a Celtic hero by a kind of epic transformation). Some years later, Dante would only record a long-time literary truism when he admiringly designated the romances of the Round Table as *ambages pulcherrime Arturi regis,* "the majestic and convoluted narrations of King Arthur." Of these narrations, Arthur rightfully became the eponymous hero.

But how did the tales of Britain and the stories of Arthur originate? How shall we explain their popularity during the second half of the twelfth century if not earlier? There is no doubt that a certain learned tradition, illustrated by Geoffrey of Monmouth in his *Historia regum Britanniae (The History of the Kings of Britain)*, completed in 1136, was well known to Chrétien and his contemporaries. In that work, this Welshman or Armorican (i.e., Celt) by birth, amplified in an exceptional way the few bare facts which he had found in previous works, such as Gildas's *De excidio et conquestu Britanniae (The Destruction and Conquest of Britain)*, the Venerable Bede's *Historia ecclesiastica gentis Anglorum (The History of the Church of the English People)*, the *Historia Britonum (The History of the Britons)* attributed to Nennius, and William of Malmesbury's *Gesta regum Anglorum (The Deeds of the Kings of England)*. Basing himself on these and other sources, Geoffrey set about to relate in Latin prose a supposed history of the British kings, in twelve books, from Brutus's odyssey and landing in Great Britain (three generations after the fall of Troy), to the death of King Cadwallader, A.D. 689, and the end of British independence. Arthur dominates Geoffrey's boundless amalgamation—he is the son of Utherpendragon and Ygerna, born under imaginary and marvelous circumstances (for which Geoffrey happily reproduced the old legend of Jupiter, Alcmene, and Amphitryon, bestowing the role of go-between upon Merlin the prophet)—though his power and glory are celebrated only in books nine and ten.

History of the Kings of Britain

With a keen sense of style and with a few rich episodes, Geoffrey sets forth the events of a portentous reign. King at fifteen by reason of his valor and generosity, Arthur welds together the whole British nobility. His first task is to reconquer Britain in a war of liberation against the Saxon invaders. Not only did the Britons have their revenge in this undertaking, it was also a vindication of Christendom over the forces of paganism. Just before the battle of Mount Badon (Bath), Archbishop Dubricius utters a harangue animated by an epic-like religious inspiration. When Arthur is about to throw himself into battle, his armor is described, fusing bits of Celtic, Latin, and Christian traditional elements: dressed in a splendid cuirass, he wears a gilded helmet decorated with Utherpendragon's war emblem, a symbolic dragon; on his shoulder is his shield Pridwen, painted with an image of the Virgin Mary. Girt at his side is his sword Caliburn, forged in the Isle of Avalon, and in his right hand he holds the lance, Ron. These proper names, Avalon, Pridwen, Ron, Caliburn (Escalibor in the French romances) are in all probability of Celtic origin; and if, regarding the sword of Avalon, Geoffrey was reminded of the *Aeneid* and of the swords of Aeneas or Daunus, forged by Vulcan at Lipari, he was doubtless also aware of the Celtic tradition telling of magical isles where fairies produced arms for heroes. Victorious over the Saxons, Arthur in turn fights the Scots and the Picts, whom he quickly defeats. After organizing his newly conquered lands, he marries a young girl of noble Roman stock, the most beautiful woman in all Britain, Guenevere.

Arthur then seizes control of Ireland, Iceland, and the Orkneys, after which a twelve-year peace ensues and the young sovereign's fame spreads throughout the world, his court setting the tone in elegance and courtesy for all of Europe. But the continental monarchs are troubled and provoked by so much prestige. Learning of their hostile coalition, Arthur endeavors to anticipate their strategy: he subdues Norway, then sails to Gaul, with an elite Gaulish guard in his services. There he besieges Paris, to which had retreated the tribune Flollo, governor of Gaul in the name of the Roman Emperor Leo. On an island in the Seine, the two leaders fight a single combat, and with Escalibor Arthur splits open Flollo's head, Paris surrenders, and at the end of nine years Arthur becomes master of all Gaul. Normandy is given to Bedevere, the cup bearer, and Anjou to Kay, his seneschal. More obviously in this section of the book than elsewhere, Geoffrey took curious historical liberties that are continually turned to the greater glory of the Britons.

Ruler of a vast empire, Arthur returns to Great Britain where he convokes an assembly of vassals to celebrate his coronation at Whitsuntide; it will be held in the City of the Legions. This was the famed *Urbs Legionum* in Latin, *Carilegeion, Caerlion, Caerleon* [or *Kaerusc*] in Welsh, so named during the Roman occupation when the second Augustan legion was quartered there. This wealthy city was situated near the Severn River estuary, its palaces adorned with golden gables; with its venerable churches, its monastery for nuns, its college with two hundred augurs and learned men, the city was a match for the splendor of Rome. With his usual gift for creating proper names, Geoffrey then enumerates the most illustrious guests, after which the double coronation of the king and the queen takes place, similar to the rites in use in the twelfth-century French and British courts. The feast draws to a conclusion after a magnificent banquet and games–tourneys, military exercises, and draughts. Notable is the early date (1136) of the courtliness with which Geoffrey tinted this passage; it suggests that as early as the first half of the twelfth century a certain psychological and moral refinement, originating in Poitou, Limousin, and Aquitaine, was already widespread in the north of France and even in Britain. It is not just a broadly defined courtesy, or politeness and elegance in manners; it is not simply the practice of wearing clothes and armor of a single color. For already in process of definition is the conception of an accord between individual knightly valor and the experience and inspiration of love. In this wise, Geoffrey affirms optimistically, no one was worthy of love unless victorious at least three times in jousting: "In this way the womenfolk became chaste and more virtuous and for their love the knights were ever more daring." (Thorpe trans., p. 229.) Thus, early in the twelfth century, in the hands of Geoffrey of Monmouth, Arthur's court becomes a focus of civilization, a trend that diverges from pure Celtic tradition (represented for example by the Welsh romance *Culhwch and Olwen*), and which was followed by French authors, including both his translator Wace, who lightened this episode's courtly hue, and, even to a greater degree, Chrétien de Troyes, who also praises Arthur's court. (Cf. *Cligés*, vv. 144–53; *Yvain*, vv. 33–41.)

Amidst the celebration on the fourth day, as Arthur lavishes gifts upon his vassals, suddenly there appears, bearing olive branches, a majestic retinue of twelve messengers. From Lucius Hiberius, procurator of the Roman Republic, they deliver the Roman demand for tribute to Arthur who is summoned to yield, in Rome, to the will of his masters. The alternative is war. Arthur immediately calls together his council which accepts the insolent challenge of the Romans. Both sides mobilize: Arthur assembles the kings of the West, and Lucius Hiberius those of the East. At the approach of the Kalends of August, Arthur confers the regency of Britain upon his nephew, Mordred, Gawain's brother,

17

and to his wife, Queen Guenevere, then sets out for Barfleur, the harbor of Cotentin, where his armies will converge. At Mont-Saint-Michel, he defeats a giant whose monstrous embraces had caused the death of a young girl, Helen, niece of Duke Hoel of Armorica. With his forces arrayed, Arthur heads for Autun; the Roman encounter with the British army is in a region vaguely associated with the area where Caesar had defeated the Gauls. After various intervening episodes—noble products too of Geoffrey's fancy—a great battle is fought somewhere between Langres and Autun, on the mysterious plain of Saussy (Soissie, Siesia). Rallied by the exploits of Arthur and Gawain, by routing the Romans and killing Lucius Hiberius, the British win the day, suffering, however, the loss of Bedevere and Kay.

Arthur's ascendancy is now at hand. The limit would be the capture of Rome, but that far Geoffrey dared not go. He devised, on the other hand, a fine dramatic twist by immediately causing his hero, resplendent with victory, to come in for a reversal of fortune through bitter betrayals, which brings about the cosmic collapse of Arthurian dreams and British hopes. Arthur's story concludes as a tragedy of destiny, a notion Geoffrey might have borrowed from Welsh tradition: a passing allusion to it is made in the tenth-century Welsh annals *(Annales Cambriae)*.

The valorous and munificent Arthur was, in fact, ready to march on Rome when he was rewarded with the double treason of his nephew and of the queen. Mordred, in order to assert his authority over the kingdom, had dared to appeal to the hateful Saxons, Picts, Scots, and Irish; and Guenevere had collaborated and become the usurper's consort. At the beginning of book 11, Arthur entrusts the government of Gaul to Hoel, then crosses the Channel to punish the traitors. In three battles the fate of Britain is determined. With superior numbers, Mordred tries first to breast the debarkation, but is thwarted and retreats. In the struggle Gawain dies. Guenevere takes refuge in a monastery. Arthur then pursues and meets Mordred at Winchester, defeating him a second time. The perfidious nephew doubles back to Cornwall where the major battle is staged, on the banks of the Camblam. After a bitter struggle, he is run through by Arthur, but the king, mortally wounded, is transported to the Isle of Avalon, *ad sananda vulnera*, "for the healing of his wounds," in the year A.D. 542.

The *Historia regum Britanniae* is clearly a work of fabulation and of mystification. In his critical study and edition, *La Légende arthurienne,* Edmond Faral successfully and almost continuously caught Geoffrey right in the act of deception. His powerful imagination was apparently kindled by an ardent erudition. Able to build a tall story from one sentence in Bede or in the *Historia Britonum,* and benefiting from his imaginary chronological scheme, Geoffrey exploited the resources of his clerical education. Familiar, of course, with the Bible, and a student of the Latin poets, Virgil, Ovid, Lucan, and Statius, Geoffrey had access to still other sources: Pliny the Elder, Pomponius Mela, Saint Jerome, and Isidore of Seville, the Roman histories of Paul the Deacon and of Landulf, not to mention the vernacular *chansons de geste* or the Alexander romance. Sometimes, in relating the bygone days of the first British kings and of King Arthur, he also recalls matters contemporary to the twelfth century. But why, one might ask, such an imposture? If his especial hope was to illustrate his people's past, we can also surmise a more immediate and ulterior political motivation (given its accord with the social situation in Great Britain around 1136). This attitude would have led him to direct at the Norman conquerors his plea on behalf of the British cause—they were, after all, the oldest inhabitants of the island—and to discourage support for the still-hated Anglo-Saxon invaders of yesteryear, conquered, of course, in their turn.

In the Middle Ages, the very successful *History of the Kings of Britain,* as such, deceived and beguiled masses of people, for Geoffrey was commonly considered an uncontestable authority, even though his forgery was denounced early by a few defiant or observant readers. Nevertheless, Geoffrey's hoax was to a degree poetic. By conferring upon his fiction a semblance of historical truth, was he not following Virgilian tradition? Was he not writing—as rhetorician and sometimes gloomy entertainer—in a sense a British prose *Aeneid?* Nor could an average writer envision the fall of Arthur's exploits and brilliant reign as a final, unexpected, and immediate collapse. The end is all the more gripping because Geoffrey himself draws no moral lesson for the victors, rather it is presented as a natural catastrophe, not as a consequence of pride or excess. British patriotism doubtless kept him from allowing God to condemn a leader who had brought so much glory to his country. Moreover, in two short sober lines he tells of Arthur's translation to the Isle of Avalon. Poetically rich and strong are his suggestive, covert words that adumbrate a possible survival of the "mortally wounded" king: they break the circle of doom in which Geoffrey himself had circumscribed the last days of Britain's most glorious reign. The open-ended myth of British hope is thus forged, ready to be pursued and reborn again and again. Vanished like his empire, a victim of blind fate, Arthur took solace and vengeance in the company of the fairies: the story of his terrestrial fall does not, then, seal forever the destiny of the British peoples. Such an original and beautiful conception it was that Arthur's marvelous death ransoms whatever banality and bombastic splendor taints Geoffrey's narrative of the hero's conquests.

Wace's Brut and the Matière de Bretagne

Since in Latin the *Historia regum Britanniae* could not reach a wider, nonclerical audience, Geoffrey's extravagant chronical was translated to celebrate the past for the benefit of French-speaking lords and ladies, and in particular for the Norman and Angevin court of England. Wace, a Norman cleric, a native of Jersey, authored the principle translation or paraphrase, the *Brut*, which he completed in 1155 and probably dedicated to Eleanor of Aquitaine, wife of Henry Plantagenet. Wace himself called the work *Geste des Bretons (The Deeds of the Britons)*, but the generally adopted title is *Le Roman de Brut*, the *Romance of Brutus*, or simply the *Brut*, in line with the eponymic legend that Brutus founded the British kingdom. But the term *Brut*, borrowed even by the Welsh, also serves to designate similar works derived more or less from Geoffrey's *Historia*.

Wace's work survives today in twenty-four manuscripts, not all of which are complete; even though that is much smaller than the number of extant manuscripts of the *Historia*, it does indicate a thriving success: his *Brut* soon eclipsed all previous translations. Before Wace, at the request of the noble Constance, wife of a Fitz-Gilbert, for whom he was chaplain, Geoffrey Gaimar had exploited the *Historia* for a condensed chronicle of Great Britain. Only part of this *Estoire des Engleis (History of the English)* survives, dating from 1147-51. Probably from the same period, there is also the fragmentary Munich *Brut,* and, in the British Museum, a manuscript containing an incomplete rhymed translation of the *Historia.* Finally, it is likely that Wace's poem was amplified at some point before 1205, as may be inferred from the Anglo-Saxon *Brut* by Layamon who cites Wace as his principal model; but many episodes are added, doubtless derived in part from an expanded intermediary source.

Moreover, about sixty Welsh *Bruts* survive in manuscript, which are by turns translations, paraphrases, or adaptations of the *Historia.* In light of recent research, however, it seems that, while generally consistent with Geoffrey, the redactors interpolated names, facts, and details from native Welsh legends. A collation of the Welsh versions with the complete manuscript tradition of the *Historia* might possibly permit us to reconstruct a Welsh proto-*Brut.* But no conclusion to this problematic and still quite complex question has yet been reached.

Although he dilates, develops, and adds picturesque details, all in all Wace left unchanged the material taken from his predecessor. Hardly an obedient translator, he rethinks and refreshes the Latin text with agile and lively octosyllables, still powerful enough for epic breadth, though not without humor. No doubt Wace believed ostensibly in the general authenticity of the *Historia,* but he wrote especially as a poet and artist, enjoying the depiction of scenes in all probability observed in reality: the maneuver of a ship, the disembarkment of an army or its return to harbor. Where Geoffrey shows us nothing, Wace adds a multiplicity of concrete details, excels in describing the retreat of an army or the agitation of a crowd rejoicing—animation of a piece with his narrative of the coronation feast at Caerlion. His masterful quality of movement is highlighted by the accumulation of terms and the precipitous rhythm of sentences. Wace's favorite stylistic procedures are anaphora, or the repetition of words and expressions, sometimes stressed by antitheses or chiasma, a simple but clever and model rhetoric that served Chrétien de Troyes well in his *Erec* and *Cligés.*

Also, for those names which Geoffrey most often simply enumerates, Wace exchanged a highly original series of psychological sketches, not portraits, but pithy identifications that condense the dominant quality of a character. Thus a variety of ancient British kings prance in review, appearing and disappearing quickly: one is a great drunkard prince, another a famous hunter before the Lord, another the victim of luxury, another of unequaled nobility. To illustrate, two examples from the Arthurian section of the *Brut* will suffice. Queen Guenevere, Geoffrey dryly states, surpassed in beauty all the women of Britain: *totius insulae mulieres pulchritudine superabat*. She clearly retained this privilege in the *Brut*, but Wace adds: *Mult fu large et beune parlier* ("She was generous and wise in speech," v. 9655). Thus, in passing, Wace individualizes the traits of Guenevere, so frequently praised in Arthurian romance for her largess and elegant language. With Gawain, this device is even more obvious. By means of playful words addressed to Cador, Duke of Cornwall, who has just praised war—the only means, he thinks, of rescuing the barons from the dangers of idleness—Gawain, always fervent in the presence of ladies and damsels, is sketched as a kind of courtly Don Juan, a trait soon adopted by later Arthurian romancers: "'Sir Count,'" says Gawain, "'truly, you are troubled for no reason; fair is the peace that follows war, and the land is improved and beautified thereby. There is value in pleasant words and the exercise of gallantry: it is for love and for their ladies that knights perform their chivalric deeds'" (vv. 19765-72). It would be useless to search in the *Historia* for an analogous passage.

Finally, certain additions by Wace have considerable bearing on the origins of the Arthurian cycle. More inclined than Geoffrey to advance the fraudulent dignity of Britain's pseudohistory, he does not hesitate to note legendary traditions and popular "fables." While in the text of the *Historia* the British belief in the survival and possible return of Arthur remains latent, in the *Brut* it is stated explicitly, and ironically commented on.

> Unless the chronical lies, Arthur received mortal wounds, and he had himself transported to Avalon to heal them. He is still there and the British await his return, if we believe their stories and interpretations which tell of his return, for he may still be alive. Maistre Wace, who wrote this book, did not wish to assert more about Arthur's demise than what the prophet Merlin says: about Arthur, he declared (and he was right) that his death would be uncertain. The prophet told the truth; since then there has been

no end to the doubting and, in my view, doubts will persist as to whether he lives or is really dead (vv. 13275-90).

Not a word did Geoffrey whisper about that notorious Round Table which became the center of all adventures in Arthurian romance. Wace is the first to mention its existence and to relate the origin of its institution (vv. 9747-60). For the purpose of avoiding quarrels of precedence among the "noble barons," each of whom claimed to be the best—and not one of whom could be known as the least good—"Arthur established the Round Table about which the British recount many fables." At Arthur's table, his vassals sat in perfect equality so that none of them could boast that he sat higher than his peers.

Close upon this passage dealing with the Round Table, another alludes to strange stories about Arthur, "marvels" and "adventures," spread by professional storytellers (*Brut,* vv. 9785-98). Their rapid growth worried Wace, but while he accorded no belief to these "fables," he noted in them some fiction and some truth: "It is neither pure lie nor pure truth, neither total folly nor complete wisdom. To embellish their tales, so much have storytellers told and inventors of fabulous stories contrived that they have given a fabulous appearance to everything" (*Brut,* vv. 9783-98). In disdain, Wace mentioned them only collectively, and in skepticism, he did not report a single one of the familiar fables. Yet his very reservation leaves intact his valuable witness, should a demonstration be necessary, that around 1155, independent of any erudite influence from the fraudulent *Historia regum Britanniae,* Arthurian stories and tales were in circulation.

Even more significant in this regard is the Norman poet's bemused confession in another poem, the *Roman de Rou,* or *Romance of Rollo.*[4] Intrigued by the celebrated forest of Broceliande where, he states, "if the Britons tell the truth, fairies and many other marvels are seen" (*Rou,* ed. Holden, vv. 6387-89), Wace was especially fascinated by the fountain of Barenton which made it rain when water from it was poured on the "block," a huge stone near which the water rises from the ground (this folkloric motif is also found in *Yvain*). Wace wanted to set his mind at ease in this matter and decided to visit this corner of Armorica. But he declares he saw nothing: "I was in search of marvels but found none. I came back just as foolish as I had gone" (*Rou,* ed. Holden, vv. 6395-98). This positive-minded Norman was not deluded by the Briton mirage. He bears witness, however, to the fact that many were beguiled by its seductive, poetic character. Why doubt the veracity of the assertion? Since the marvelous tales of Britain amused but also bothered Wace, he is in no way suspect of promoting them, rather he simply recorded their actual vogue.

Chrétien and the Matière de Bretagne

Even though he followed the learned tradition apparently created by Geoffrey of Monmouth alone, Wace throws light on the practices of Briton storytellers and on their tales. Taken alone, his testimony might seem fragile and perplexing. But many other arguments lead us to think that the *matière de Bretagne* did not arise uniquely from the enigmatic *Historia regum Britanniae;* its deceptions alone cannot explain the legendary themes, myths, marvels, and adventures of Arthurian romance. An enormous hiatus separates the Arthurian legend, as we have defined it according to Geoffrey and Wace, from the fictional world of Chrétien de Troyes. What, in the final analysis, do his romances, *Erec, Lancelot, Yvain,* or *Perceval,* owe to the *Historia* or to the *Brut?* However much closer to their bookish and pseudohistorical inspiration, is the debt of *Cligés* any greater? A few character sketches, notably of Gawain, a courtly hue, the notion that the Arthurian court is a brilliant, civilizing focal point, a model of nobility and chivalry. That is about all; Chrétien's Arthur is not the glorious conqueror who humiliated the arrogant Romans or the still-heroic, sudden victim of treason and doom. He is transformed into a composite figure that combines the qualities of a loyal, just, and generous sovereign; he is slightly fantastic and disturbingly strange—natural for high-born kings of marvelous tales. Geoffrey's influence alone cannot explain the rise of the romances of the Round Table. Clearly, the relationship between the *Historia* and the *Brut* and Chrétien's romances is not analogous to the one between the *Aeneid* and the *Roman d' Eneas,* nor to the bond between Statius's *Thebaid* and the *Thebes* romance, nor even to that between Dares the Phyrygian's epitome and the Troy romance.

Both Geoffrey and Wace's true function was especially to confer upon the Arthurian legend an appearance of authenticity, advancing and guaranteeing its fame; for now, without question, poems could feature Arthur, just as they had Charlemagne and Alexander. But it was not to the *Historia* or to the *Brut* that Chrétien and other poets turned for subjects during the second half of the twelfth century. Yet another, later generation, at the beginning of the thirteenth century, during the period of prose romances, was significantly influenced by Geoffrey: it was in his prestigious work that Robert de Boron and his imitators unearthed the character of Merlin, and from his work also was derived the dramatic theme of Sir Thomas Malory's *Morte d'Arthur*. Though too fabulous to be acceptable as history, the *Historia* was not romantic enough to inspire the mysterious adventures and sentimental affairs in which Chrétien deals.

To maintain that Chrétien alone invented the poetic world of the *matière de Bretagne* would be to commit a major error of oversimplification. Certainly it was enriched considerably when he took it beyond the stage of simple "adventure tales." In his hands, the *matière de Bretagne* is furbished with flashes of style, and in the depiction of characters his originality seems nearly absolute. But from a rich Celtic legacy, Chrétien's inheritance was variegated: a mythical fund of resources that Celtic storytellers and minstrels had begun to diffuse in the West, probably as early as the end of the eleventh century, after the Norman Conquest of Britain. In this way, the *matière de Bretagne* first reached the world of romance. The close association between poetry and music seems to have characterized the minstrels' repertory; to the accompaniment of small harps, the *rote* (a Celtic word), they recited or sang their "lays" (another word of Celtic derivation, cognate with Irish *laid, lóid,* "a piece of music, song, or poem"). A plausible hypothesis suggests that, preceding the musical or lyrical lays, a short, probably prose explanation was given, i.e., a summary which always told of a marvelous or sentimental adventure and which could have been the nucleus of the many oral tales of professional storytellers as well as the basis of the narrative lays authored by Marie de France and others. The double and triple titles of a few of Marie de France's lays seem to indicate that the Welsh and perhaps also Armorican *jongleurs* or minstrels were trilingual, or at least were able to declaim their lays in the three languages then spoken in Britain, Anglo-Norman French, English, and

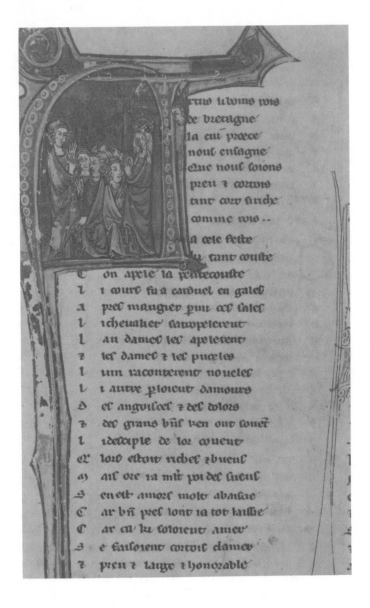

1. Kay Scolding Calogrenant.
   (Princeton University Library, Garrett MS 125, fol. 40r.)

Brythonic. These storytellers would thus be the successors and emulators of the *filid,* "poet-reciters" of early Ireland. Without yielding too much to retrospective illusions, Irish myth can be considered the grandfather or great-grandfather of Arthurian romance.

Geoffrey of Monmouth himself was perhaps not as ignorant or disdainful of the legendary oral traditions as might suggest the noble tone and productive erudition of the *Historia.* The names of Arthur's shield, lance, and sword are probably borrowed from native sources; the infidelity of Queen Guenevere, whose name seems to mean originally "white phantom" (i.e., a fairy), may be related to the myth of her abduction by an otherworld character, Melwas or Maheloas (Meleagant in the *Lancelot*). However timid and sober an allusion, the mysterious motif of Arthur's final departure for Avalon was probably not original with Geoffrey—but even to a rational mind, it is quite revealing. And what should be said of the giant Retho (Rion in the French romances), that peculiar collector whose mania was making fur coats from beards, trophies of defeated kings? He had dared ask King Arthur willingly to send him his own; Arthur, responding to the challenge, ended the duel victoriously.[5] The Welsh were no doubt much amused by this story, but it is quite interesting that Geoffrey interpolated it in his pompous narrative of the episode at Mont-Saint-Michel, where Arthur triumphs over another giant. If we assume that Geoffrey would not have invented so absurd and tasteless a fable, then the image of a mythical Arthur is not altogether lacking in the *Historia:* the tale of Retho can only derive from an earlier Arthurian legend. Even if Arthur were not a purely Celtic hero, even if his "historical" ancestor were the Roman chieftain Artorius, his fantastic exploits would still controvert the notion of *Arturus miles, dux bellorum* ("Arthurus, soldier, leader in wars"). In all likelihood, the Britons had already fancied him as a marvelous king, who attracted to his own orbit, through the well-known phenomenon of centripetal concentration, a number of disparate characters and tales.

From about 1150, more frequent and more precise indications converge to certify the existence of Celtic storytellers, even though the widely recognized corroboration of Wace has been unsubstantially subverted or denied (most notably by the Arthurian scholars J.S.P. Tatlock and Maurice Delbouille). In his references to the host of Celtic "fables" and to their inextricable blend of falsehood and truth, Wace was recalling perhaps certain chapters from the *Historia Britonum (History of the Britons)* or a sentence in the *Gesta regum Anglorum (The Deeds of the English Kings)* where William of Malmesbury deplored how foolishly the Britons told "bits of nonsense" *(nugae)* about Arthur. (This skepticism proves also that popular traditions about Arthur were circulating as early as 1125, the date of the *Gesta*, or even, in the light of several Welsh saints' lives, from 1100.) But nevertheless, Wace uses the present tense ("the adventures *are* told") and, when he speaks of storytellers and of "fabulators," he certainly is not alluding to a text of the *Historia Britonum.* Further, it is very doubtful that by "adventures" he meant the battles Arthur had fought against the Saxons. *That* was history, or pseudohistory which, under the circumstances, was the same thing, and not *adventures,* i.e., chivalric quests or undertakings. It is also unlikely that by the word "marvels" Wace was simply referring to the oddities, especially geographical, topographical, or monumental, recorded in the *Historia Britonum,* in the chapter *De mirabilibus Britanniae (On the Marvels of Britain).* These curiosities he described in his own particular way, still following his model Geoffrey, while, justifiably and with Norman prudence, he withheld any mention of the swarming "fables" or "adventures."

Indeed, the association or the proximity of the two words "adventures" and "marvels" here has a literary nuance in perfect harmony with the themes of the known lays by Marie de France and others. The passage in Wace is elucidated more by reference to the circulation of these lays than by a laborious collation of scattered texts. Likewise, regarding the Round Table, although its origin remains uncertain, it is hardly convincing to insist that Wace would have fallaciously attributed its invention to Arthur simply because he needed a rhyming word, or only because of a conjectural misunderstanding of the particular text of the *Historia* used by him. Must we unreasonably accuse of falsehood or total innovation his declaration that "Arthur made the Round Table of which the Britons tell many tales"? If so, hypercriticism runs the risk of negating logic, all the more because Wace's affirmations must not be isolated from the analogous testimony which confirms them. In good faith, Marie de France reinforces the idea that the Britons had made lays about the very "adventures" which she relates. In the prologue to his first Arthurian romance, Chrétien de Troyes reproaches "those who live from the profession of storyteller" for mangling the story of *Erec*, the son of King Lac. Thomas of England and Beroul, each of whom composed a version of the *Tristan*, also mention the activity of storytellers whose widespread tales recounted—with variations—the most celebrated of Celtic legends. Obviously, neither Wace, nor Marie de France, nor Chrétien de Troyes, nor Thomas of England, nor Beroul made these declarations in order to give an account of nonexistent tales or storytellers.

The Onomastic Argument

It is again the writings of Chrétien de Troyes—two passages in his first romance, *Erec*— which furnish the final proof that the *matière de Bretagne* had reached an important development outside of the tradition represented by Geoffrey of Monmouth and Wace. When Enide, Erec's fiancée, enters the room where Arthur and his companions are seated, all rise to honor her. Chrétien, taking advantage of the opportunity, enumerates the Knights of the Round Table (Foerster, ed., vv. 1682–1750; Roques, ed., vv. 1662–1706). The list reads like an index of proper names; one might say that the author, in an effort to exploit the *matière de Bretagne*, wished to introduce his audience to the repertory of Arthurian characters and to construct a kind of personal fund from which he could borrow at will.

Gawain must come first, for he was *first above all good knights*. Was this primacy Chrétien's invention? Did he feel the need to create an ultimate paragon of chivalry? Or was Gawain already considered the leading knight of the Round Table? It seems probable that his eminent and superior role was lifted from the *Historia* and the *Brut*, in which texts, as the benevolent nephew of Arthur, he is both the foil of the maleficent nephew Mordred and the most distinguished of all those associated with the king. In the totality of Chrétien's work, however, he is accorded a somewhat banal perfection, and, even though Chrétien is apparently sympathetic toward him, he never gave him an extensive role (with the exception of his adventures in *Le Conte du Graal*).

Second place falls to the hero of the romance under discussion, Erec, in no way slighted as Gawain's subordinate. Third is Lancelot du

Lac, a flattering position which suggests that already Chrétien had his eye on him. Possibly a similar explanation suffices for the fourth, Gornement de Gohort, the aged, experienced knight who, in *The Story of the Grail,* teaches the code of chivalry to the young hero. Perceval is noticeably absent from the list (which, by the way, according to the author, is not exhaustive), but he is mentioned in a slightly earlier passage, along with Kay the seneschal and Lucan the butler, and it may be surmised that, within the outline of his literary syllabus, Chrétien gave him some thought, but not necessarily in relation to the Grail adventure, about which he undoubtedly did not know until later through the so-called "book" of Philippe of Alsace.

Several more are enumerated: Beau Couard ("Fair Coward"); Laid Hardi ("Ugly Bold"), an amusing antithesis; Meliant de Lis (who also turns up in the *Perceval*); Mauduiz li Sages ("Accursed Sage"); Dodinel le Sauvage ("the Wild") and Gandeluz. After these Chrétien breaks the numerical order, and about twenty more names follow one upon the other, perhaps forty or so: depending on the manuscripts, the list varies both in length and onomastic content. But at least considered canonical are Yvain, son of Urien, Yvain li Avoutre ("The Bastard"); Bleobleheris; Caradoc Briebras; Caveron de Roberdic; Yder du Mont Dolereus; Gaheriez; Giflet (Girflet), son of Do; Loholz, son of King Arthur; Sagremor le Desrée ("Quick Tempered"); Bedoier the constable; King Lot; Galegantin; and two or three more.

Whence derive these characters? From the *Historia* and the *Brut* come only a few names: Gawain; Yvain, son of Urien; King Lot; Kay; and Bedoier. Geoffrey and Wace mention nowhere Erec or Lancelot du Lac, nor Gornement de Gohort, Dodinel, Giflet, Sagremore, Galegantin, Perceval, or several others—present that day at Arthur's court. Shall we attribute all of them solely to Chrétien's imagination? Certainly we should admit that he himself was in a sense the creator of this list of names, and allowances should be made for fantasy and humor. By varying the strange names as a diversion, he probably invented a few amusing characteristics. But most of these characters, not mentioned in Geoffrey or Wace, he found in all likelihood in an antecedent Arthurian tradition. A few among them bear names that are French: Beau Couard, Laid Hardi, and, according to Foerster's edition, the Chevalier au Cor ("Knight of the Horn") and the Valet au Cercle d' Or ("Squire of the Golden Circle"). More precisely, some are designated with a paraphrase alluding to a significant detail or adventure, and evidently several of them were confected by Chrétien in search of a rhyme. Could they not have originated, however, in some of the lays related by trilingual storytellers? And if these examples are not accorded conviction, shall we presume that Chrétien would have created, while working on his list, imaginary, legendary pedigrees which are implied by names like Lancelot du *Lac* and Perceval le *Gallois?* Only the most scrupulous would deny that these epithets were already functioning to particularize well-known, traditional characters. Likewise, the etymologies cited by Chrétien assure a nonchimerical, Celtic origin for a few names.

Now it is true that side by side with them subsist certain doubtful cases, for example, the handy but not altogether certain Welsh equivalents proposed for Gawain or Lancelot. Perplexities of this kind are not surprising because, in passing from one language to another, many names obviously would be distorted beyond all phonetic laws. If, as a result, the bases are missing or too obliterated, rather than hazard conjectures and unscientific assimilations, we should yield to ignorance. A conscientious quest for euphony and sometimes symbolic intentions appear to influence the proper names of French Arthurian heroes, removing them from their Celtic counterparts. Thus, for example, the aptly modified, half-invented name of *Perceval* (otherwise *Perlesvaus* in a thirteenth-century prose romance) kept only the first syllable of the corresponding Welsh name, *Peredur.*

But, this said, the list of the Knights of the Round Table contains names which are indisputably Celtic: Erec (variation of *Guerec, Weroc*), an Armorican name whose Welsh form is *Gereint;* Meliant de Lis (cf. Welsh *llys,* "court, seignorial lodging"); Bleobleheris; Giflet and Do; Loholt. Caradoc Briebras or Briefbras (*Caradawc Breich Bras* in Welsh) is a very revealing surname resulting from a curious error made in the Welsh *Vreichvras,* or *Breichbras* ("arm strong"), an epithet analogous to that of the French epic hero William *Fierebrace. Bras* was interpreted as "arms," and *breich* as "short, brief." Thus Caradoc "with large arms" became Caradoc "of the short arms," an amusing case of popular etymology, and a name that Chrétien could not have devised. Etymological research of this sort on the *Erec* would also cover other examples of Celtic origin, like the names of Evrain (or Eurain), king of Brandigan;

Mabonagrain (in the "Joy of the Court" episode); Nut, father of Yder; Gawain's horse, Guingalet (cf. Old Welsh *guin-calet,* "white-hardy"); among others. Likewise, in the *Lancelot* or *Le Conte du Graal* or *Yvain* there is a profusion of Celtic names. None was inserted into these different contexts simply to confer upon them an artificial, Celtic coloring. Their true origin proves the existence of Celtic substrata or background in the Round Table romances, inasmuch as they could not have reached Chrétien autonomously or without being embodied within lays and tales in a poetic or narrative setting.

No less interesting is the second list in *Erec* that enumerates "the counts and kings" invited to Erec and Enide's sumptuous wedding feast (Foerster, ed., vv. 1932-2014; Roques, ed., vv. 1882-962): Brandes of Gloescestre; Menagormon, the lord of la Haute Montagne ("High Mountain"); the count of Treverain; count Godegrain; all of whom arrive in state; Maheloas, a rich baron and lord of the Isle de Voirre where reigns an everlasting spring; Graillemer (Greslemuef, or Graislemier) de Fine Postern (i.e., Finistère), with his brother Guigamor (or, Guigomar, Guingamar), lord of Avalon and lover of Morgain la Fée ("'twas verily so"); David of Tintaguel; Garras, king of Corque (probably Cork, modern Ireland), escorted by five hundred knights in full dress; Angusel (Anguisseaus), king of Scotland; King Ban of Gomerest, with a retinue of young, beardless companions, all gay and elegant, each one holding a falcon or sparrowhawk on his fist; Kerrin, the old king of Riel, followed by his hoary centenarians, beards hanging down to their belts; Bilis, the tiny dwarf king of the Antipodes, whose brother Brien is a half foot or a full hand taller than any knight in the kingdom; finally, two other dwarfs, Kings Grigoras and Gleodalen. Here again Chrétien no doubt delighted in composing a playful parody, a humorous pastiche of princely parades so frequently enumerated in the literature of his time. As the list continues, the guests become more and more bizarre, concluding with two cacaphonous patronymics. However, Chrétien's mischief is not continually mystifying; if, in order to sort out his variegated onomasticon, we put aside the products of verbal fantasy, the "serious" names remain. Chrétien owes in all few names (only one, in fact, Angusel) to the *Historia-Brut* tradition, and it is manifest that he has borrowed more from an Arthurian legend of another provenance. To this category of authentic, but distorted,

Celtic derivation belong both: *Brien,* an Armorican form for the Welsh *Bran* (cf. Bran the Blessed, a pan-Celtic hero whose name reappears as Brandes, Ban, and again in Brandigan, King Evrain's "castle"), and: *Bilis,* an Armorican name, *Beli* in Welsh. Since this dwarf was represented by Chrétien as the king of the *Antipodes,* a fabulous country whose tradition seems to derive ultimately from Isidore of Seville's *Etymologies,* the term Antipodes has been emphasized, and the name *Bili* has been neglected (seen as an imaginary character disguised by a Celtic name), while *Bili* itself, simple and modest, is much older, and the term Antipodes is in fact the imaginary, disguised part. *Maheloas,* Welsh *Melwas* ("prince of youth"), lord of the Isle de Voirre, like Avalon, a region in the otherworld. Graillemer (the correct form is *Graelent Muer,* from the Celtic *mor* or *muer,* "great"), a semi-legendary king from Armorican Cornwall and the hero of the anonymous lay *Graëlent,* (or, Guigomar), another Celtic name and again a character—in the anonymous lay *Guingamor.*

That the last three names—Maheloas, Graillemer, Guigamor—follow one upon the other in the list is worthy of our attention. Chrétien here hammered out an uncommon medley of sheer folk stuff, for the three legends are related through an essential theme common to Arthurian romance and Celtic myth, that of a mortal's visit to the joyous regions of the otherworld, sojourn of the dead or of the fairies. Overly skeptical critics might attribute this medley to pure chance, or claim that Chrétien could not have perceived the analogies sufficiently to be able to associate and classify diverse and already extant tales. It would be a contradiction to maintain that he alone created the entire subject matter, for we would then have to explain how he was capable of inventing a singularly pagan mythological structure. A more reasonable assumption would recognize rather his capacity to contemplate upon the *matière de Bretagne* in an intelligent, serious, and methodical way. We do not mean that he necessarily tried to understand the primitive significance of the material; no doubt the immediate meaning of the sources would have been already mutilated or at least disjointed. Chrétien was certainly no twentieth-century mythographer. Yet, as the late medievalist Albert Pauphilet pointed out regarding the "Marvelous Castle" episode in *Le Conte du Graal,* Chrétien seems to have divined in a way the ancient meaning in the fables: "He relates at one stage that Gawain meets an old queen during a strange adventure.... And finally he learns that it was King Arthur's mother, dead for twenty years! Chrétien thus understood that the legendary tale he was using treated of the hero's voyage to the otherworld. But such indications are rare.[6]

The two lists of *Erec,* then, are all the more invaluable for literary history. Because of their serious scope, we should not be misled by the humorous and offhanded tone. Chrétien was plainly smiling as he recounted the love of Guigamor for Morgain la Fée ("for 'twas verily so"), but it would be absurd to conclude on that basis that his episodes about Maheloas, the Isle de Voirre, or Avalon were pure invention. Other revealing testimony bears him out and attests to the currency of the trend of storytellers—a tradition linked to Celtic transmission, as is shown by the etymology of a number of proper names that are free of any debt to Geoffrey of Monmouth or to Wace.

The Celtic Background

Unfortunately, beyond this last observation only conjectures will aid our search to unravel the genesis, development, and transmission to France of Celtic *mirabilia.* That none of the original lays or tales of the storytellers has come down to us is no surprise since oral tales by their nature tend to disappear. And the problem is complicated manifestly by the fact that the dates of certain indirect testimony remain disputed and that conditions for debate are often compromised by tenacious prepossessions: a given critic's potential "celtomania" is unparalleled except by another's "celtophobia." Nevertheless, opponents would be wrong to claim any decisive advantage from the clearcut impediments that plague the Celtic theorist in quest of lost intermediaries.

It is, however, probable (and *only* probable) that the celebrated *matière de Bretagne* came with the Norman Conquest and that, from the end of the eleventh century onwards, it was propagated on the continent. For this view the most favorable argument is a curious sculpture on the north portal of the cathedral at Modena, a resting place in Italy for pilgrims and *jongleurs* on the *Via Francigena* ("Frankish Route"). The scene on the archivolt appears to represent some primitive version of the abduction of Queen Guenevere; the names of the characters are engraved in the stone, ensuring their Arthurian authenticity: Isdernus (Ider), Artus de Bretania, Burmaltus, Winlogee (doubtless an archaic, Armorican form of Guenevere's name, Winlowen), Mardoc, Carrado, Galvaginus (Gawain), Galvarium, and Che (the seneschal Ké, Kay, or Keu). The whole difficulty, of course, lies in knowing to what precise date we should assign this iconographic evidence—one question, among others, on which the opinions of specialists, art historians, and Arthurian scholars are divergent. One group maintains the end of the twelfth century, another the beginning, a third the middle. Two other scholars, J.S.P. Tatlock and Stefan Hofer, both systematically adverse to the Celtic origin of Arthurian romance, have speciously argued that the names were added to the sculpture *post facto,* "at a later date." At the present stage of research, it cannot be determined whether the sculpture precedes or follows the *Historia regum Britanniae.* However, judging from the methodical and detailed studies on the question by the late Roger S. Loomis, an early date in the first half of the twelfth century seems more plausible. His demonstration may in part seem frail, but other evidence he produced is more conclusive, e.g., the fact that the names *Isdernus* and *Winlogee* are archaic forms, and that the scene on the Modena archivolt has no apparent relationship to Geoffrey's *Historia.*

One obvious consideration of critical importance to our inquiry is the state of Celtic literature during this period. First, since the traditional legends, lays, and tales of British Cornwall and Armorica never outlived the status of oral creation, no portion of them can be disinterred for our purposes (although conversely, there survives a rich tradition, especially in Cornish, of legendary place names). Extant, however, is an abundance of Irish and Welsh literary materials but in manuscripts that unfortunately very often postdate works like the *Historia regum Britanniae,* Chrétien's romances, and the *Lais* of Marie de France. Yet, in our pursuit of the beginnings of Arthurian romance, prudence dictates a methodical comparison with the Celtic materials, an examination that may reveal both their independence of Geoffrey and the French texts and their possible derivation from earlier, purely indigenous forms.

Ireland must come first, for the oldest Celtic traditions have been preserved in tenth-, eleventh-, and twelfth-century Irish manuscripts embodying a very dim memory of pre-existent themes of heroic narrative and myth. Cycles appear quite early: the Mythological Cycle; the Cú Chulainn-King Conchobar, or Ulster Cycle; and the Finn, or Leinster Cycle. However, upon the introduction of Christianity into Ireland in the course of the fifth century, and following the foundation of monastic schools, a literature of Christian inspiration grew up side by side with the old, persistent pagan tradition, which never really disappeared from the magical isle. Medieval Ireland remained at once the land of fairies and missionaries, of saints and scholars: most often paganism and Christianity were fused as early Irish myth became very slowly and only superficially Christianized. Classical culture, which had accompanied Christianity to Ireland, included a more or less extensive knowledge of Greco-Latin mythology, and in some cases narratives from antiquity mixed with Celtic myth. In medieval Ireland legends were always astir.

Prior to the twelfth century, when in France the *matière de Bretagne* and the Arthurian legend were becoming increasingly synonymous, Irish myths and tales had spread to other Celtic realms, principally Wales, with which Ireland remained in close contact, and where tales of all types began to converge around the figure of King Arthur. While Welsh literature absorbed Irish traditions, however distorted or transmuted in the process, it shows considerable originality. Its claim to fame is the *Mabinogion* (the plural of *mabinogi,* "literary apprentice, aspiring bard"), now accessible to both French and English readers in the excellent translations by Joseph Loth and G. and T. Jones.[7] These prose tales of wonder consistently maintain an epic quality and harmonize enumerations of patronymics, purely ornamental epithets, and somewhat exuberant descriptions. But each recounts at length an extraordinary adventure so that, in breadth, the tales are analogous to Marie de France's *Lais* or Chrétien's romances. The collection itself is truly a composite: only four of the tales are actually *Mabinogion* or, to be more precise, they make up the four branches of one *mabinogi,* a classical genre containing only traditional elements; nor do the four branches deal solely with King Arthur *(Pwyll Prince of Dyfed, Branwen Daughter of Llŷr, Manawydan Son of Llŷr, Math Son of Mathonwy.)* Of the others, traditionally associated with the four branches, but in a more personal, distinctive style, five are related to the Arthurian cycle.

The relationship of certain of these Welsh texts to Chrétien's romances raises complex and highly controversial issues, but, since at least three of the tales contain plots parallel to three of his works, they are worthy of our consideration; *The Lady of the Fountain* (or, *Owein and Luned*) corresponds in a striking manner to *Yvain; Peredur Son of Efrawg* is vaguely analogous to *Le Conte du Graal;* and *Gereint Son of Erbin* is clearly a doublet of *Erec.* Because the Welsh tales, which do not seem earlier than the beginning of the thirteenth century, obviously cannot have been among Chrétien's direct sources, several critics have simplistically concluded that Chrétien must have therefore been the model of the Welsh storyteller(s). An attentive comparison of the texts vitiates this view, for the differences are so manifest that direct imitation of Chrétien seems preposterous. Furthermore, in *The Lady of the Fountain, Peredur,* and *Gereint,* some clearly non-Celtic details of material and moral life suggest the influence of twelfth-century French civilization, an apparent anomaly that is explained most plausibly by lost Celtic-type sources common to Chrétien and to Welsh storytellers. Thus, it may be inferred that he was not the first to compose Arthurian stories in French. By his own admission, he did not invent the subject of his *Erec*: from an inspiring "tale of adventure," he proudly spins out, he says, "a coherent narrative," which it lacked— a coherence also lacking in the Welsh *Gereint.* To this delicate matter we will return later.

Two other *Mabinogion* corroborate the existence of Arthurian romance in Welsh literature independent of French models: *The Dream of Rhonabwy* and *Culhwch and Olwen,* about which tales the eminent Celticist Joseph Loth wrote:

> Arthur there reigns over a fantastic world of purely Celtic customs and traditions. His court resembles in no way that of the Arthur in the twelfth-century French romances. Here courtly love prevails, with its refined manners, elegant language and good behavior, all outstanding qualities of the Knights of the Round Table. There it is rather a disorderly assemblage of the most diverse characters, of enchanting and supernatural beings, culled here and there from assorted traditions and grouped artificially around a national hero famous for his enchanting nature. (*Les Mabinogion,* 1:35–36)

Chrétien de Troyes

While the thirteenth-century *Dream of Rhonabwy,* which still embraces
some very ancient traditions, postdates the *Historia regum Britanniae,*
most Celticists are in agreement today in dating *Culhwch and Olwen*
from the second half of the eleventh or from the beginning of the
twelfth century, i.e., anterior to Geoffrey's work. This opinion, as is the
case in all sensitive matters of chronology, is not universally accepted,
but it is by far the most widely held.

Nevertheless, *Culhwch and Olwen,* the most beautiful romance of
the *Mabinogion* and the masterpiece of Welsh Arthurian literature, relates how, with the help of King Arthur and his best knights, after a
long and difficult quest and some thirty-eight tasks to overcome, the
hero Culhwch succeeds in marrying Olwen, daughter of the giant
Yspaddaden Penkawr. This truly original tale of artistic inspiration is
characterized by a dramatic rhythm in the narration of adventures and
by an atmosphere of wonderful magic; it features a quickly paced
dialogue, a malicious vigor (sometimes in parody), and a slightly over-
charged use of colorful descriptions by itself evidence of the Celtic
genius clever enough to create a classic. Here, then, is Culhwch riding
on toward Arthur's court.

> Off went the boy on a steed with light-grey head, four winters
> old, with well-knit fork, shell-hoofed, and a gold tubular bridle-
> bit in its mouth. And under him a precious gold saddle, and in
> his hand two whetted spears of silver. A battle-axe in this hand,
> the fullarm's length of a full grown man from ridge to edge. It
> would draw blood from the wind.... And two greyhounds,
> whitebreasted, brindled, in front of him, with a collar of red
> gold about the neck of either, from shoulder-swell to ear. The one
> that was on the left side would be on the right, and the one that
> was on the right side would be on the left, like sea-swallows
> sporting around him. Four clods the four hoofs of his steed would
> cut, like four swallows in the air over his head, now before him,
> now behind him.... Never a hair-tip stirred upon him, so exceed-
> ing light his steed's canter under him on his way to the gate of
> Arthur's court.

And now here is Olwen:

> She was sent for. And she came, with a robe of flame-red silk
> about her, and around the maiden's neck a torque of red gold,
> and precious pearls thereon and rubies. Yellower was her head

than the flower of the broom, whiter was her flesh than the foam of the wave; whiter were her palms and her fingers than the shoots of the marsh trefoil from amidst the fine gravel of a welling spring. Neither the eye of a mewed hawk, nor the eye of the thrice-mewed falcon, not an eye was there fairer than hers.... Whoso beheld her would be filled with love of her. Four white trefoils sprang up behind her wherever she went; and for that reason she was called Olwen ['white track'].[8]

The Celtic Thesis

By what route, it may be asked, did the *matière de Bretagne* reach French authors? This also is a disputed question, for even if Ireland did preserve many Celtic legends, it is obvious that its geographical location would make difficult any direct influence on twelfth-century French literature. Celtic tales could have penetrated into Romance-speaking areas only where the Celts and the French were neighbors, for example, in the two contiguous areas: Great Britain (both Wales and Cornwall bordered on the Norman-French kingdom conquered by William), and on the continent, Armorica (which borders on Anjou, Maine, and Normandy). Repopulated from the sixth century on by Welsh colonists fleeing the Anglo-Saxon invasion of Great Britain, Armorica became the refuge and cradle of British hope (it may be recalled that, in Geoffrey's *Historia*, it was Armorican reinforcements who saved the day against the invaders). We are thus confronted by two theories: the "continental thesis," according to which Armorica played the essential, if not unique, role, and the "insular thesis," which recognizes as significant only Welsh and Cornish traditions.

Of course, each of these theories has determined, sometimes obstinate, partisans, but they are in fact complementary, not mutually exclusive. There is some evidence to support the continental side: (1) several of Marie de France's *Lais* are in close relationship with Little Britain; (2) the onomastics of Arthurian romance is partly Armorican; (3) from the first half of the tenth century onwards, the Bretons of Armorica were in contact with the Normans; (4) Bretons comprised a third of the effectives in William the Conqueror's army and, from that time, were established in Britain, doubtless accompanied by their own *jongleurs.* It was these latter, Armorican *jongleurs,* who reacted like a catalyst upon the transmission of Celtic themes to the French-speaking conquerors, and, more than the Welsh themselves, were inclined by a kind of nostalgia to regain their old native traditions. Traveling the length and breadth of Anglo-Norman Britain, twisting place names and inventing new ones, it was they who apparently created the extravagant topography of Arthurian story. This is the explanation advanced notably by the late R.S. Loomis, a hypothesis as ingenious as it is compelling, yet the supposed poetic pilgrimage, the adventurous return by Armorican *jongleurs* to their traditional past, is extremely difficult to prove.

To explain the transmission of Celtic materials, adherents of the insular thesis do not propose as complicated a circuit, rather they point to the Gallo-Norman border as the bridge for the *matière de Bretagne.* No doubt Gaston Paris was mistaken about the preconquest circulation of Celtic tales among the Anglo-Saxons. But it has been established that, after the conquest, almost immediately in Cornwall, and soon after in Wales, from the late-eleventh century on, distrust on the part of the Celts toward their new masters was checked by alliances and marriages which soon affiliated the Norman and Welsh aristocracy. Under these potent circumstances, the Welsh *jongleurs* could easily have begun to propagate their lays and tales in Britain, an explanation which (without our rejecting completely the rival theory), is all the more viable as the literature did, after all, have appeal in Wales.

It is hardly surprising that these traditional materials were carried from Britain to the Continent, for the splendid Norman court ensured their diffusion, as did later the Norman-Angevin kings, whose dominions were both insular and continental. In all probability, the goals of Henry Plantagenet's expansionist politics in Celtic territories and, even more, the personal role and literary patronage of the great Eleanor of Aquitaine, enhanced the prestige of the Arthurian legend. The *matière de Bretagne,* much wider in scope than the written tradition of Geoffrey of Monmouth or Wace, in this way reached authors like Chrétien de Troyes or Marie de France. Living in Britain Marie ostensibly had first-hand access to Celtic tales and lays. By what means they impinged upon Chrétien may seem less clear, but the difficulties are at least as ungrounded as one early hypothesis that he voyaged to Britain or Armorica. Harpers and *jongleurs* from across the Channel and from Little Britain were most likely drawn to the fairs in Champagne. The court of Troyes would have gladly received them, because even before Eleanor's daughter, Marie, had married Henry I the Liberal, the family of Champagne both maintained friendly terms with Anglo-Norman authorities and was, moreover, related to the Armorican rulers—a situation conducive to a double flow of Celtic tales towards Chrétien's native province.

But even without *jongleurs*, books could travel; by means of written texts, the *matière de Bretagne* also enjoyed a high circulation. In fact, misreadings account for certain graphic distortions of proper names. "Goirre," the kingdom of Baudemaguz and of Meleagant in the *Lancelot*, for example, is visibly a corruption of "Voirre" (cf. the *Isle de Voirre,* "Isle of Glass"). The outstanding philologist, J. Vendryes, has commented on such changes:

> Undifferentiated Welsh forms, *Owain* or *Yvain,* were used for a Latin-derived name, *Eugenius,* as the *y* shows, pronounced "i" [i.e., "e" as in *feel*], thus giving the graphy *Ivain,* current in French texts. ... The name *Kei* [Ké, Kay], derived from Latin *Caius* ..., is often written *Keu* in French texts ... so that the graphy *Keu* cannot be explained from French, but it is normal in Welsh because the diphthongues *ei* and *eu* are equivalent, the letter *u* representing a sound very close to "i," so close in fact that throughout Wales it is confused with *i*. ... The curious form *Guanhumara* (Geoffrey of Monmouth's rendering into Latin of the name of Arthur's wife) results from a mis-reading of *Gwenhwyfar* as *Guenhuiuar,* an old graphy read with an *m* instead of *iu*. Linguistic facts of this kind attest indeed to a bookish origin for the sources. (*Etudes Celtiques* 5 [1949] : 34).

Statements by the authors themselves are in essential agreement with such positive evidence. For example, in nearly all her allusions to sources, Marie de France mentions an oral tradition, yet she also affirms, at the beginning of *Guigemar,* that she is going to narrate "according to the text and the writing." She further refers to both an oral and a written tradition in the short prologue to *Chievrefoil:* "Many people have told and recited it to me, and I have seen [it] written down...".[9] Chrétien himself consistently disclaimed that he was the sole creator of his *matière.* We know by his own account that for the *Perceval* romance he used a "book" given him by Count Philippe of Alsace, and it is most likely that this book contained an "adventure tale" similar to the one used in deriving the "coherent narrative" *(conjointure)* of *Erec et Enide.* For many reasons, one can conjecture, as did Gaston Paris, that toward the middle of the twelfth century, Anglo-Norman authors were composing Arthurian tales in verse and perhaps also in prose. Though none is extant, one is known indirectly: Ulrich von Zatzikhoven's Middle High German poem, *Lanzelet,* dated between 1194 and 1203, which draws upon an Anglo-Norman original, and whose hero, Lanzelet, differs considerably from Chrétien's *Lancelot.* It seems most reasonable to speculate that *Erec, Yvain,* and *Perceval* and their Welsh doublets derive from lost common sources and would therefore belong no doubt to this very same category of Arthurian texts in Anglo-Norman. But whether we choose the *Lanzelet* or the "pseudo-*Mabinogion,*" brief comparison of them with the works of Chrétien demonstrates to what degree he raised the *matière de Bretagne* from the level of simple adventure tales, in which episode followed episode carelessly, without psychological coherence, to the higher plane of a *romance,* ingeniously conceived by the poet as an alloy of "narrative material" *(matière),* a "coherent narrative" *(conjointure),* and a dominant thesis (*sen,* "sense, meaning").

The Celtic Legacy

But however preponderant the Celtic substrata, the conclusion cannot be drawn that everything Chrétien treated was of Celtic provenance. His classical and Ovidian formation was responsible for much more than simple transcriptions of poetic rhetoric, for even in the *matière* of his Arthurian romances, Chrétien did not hesitate to use Latin authors. The Celtic background of most of the Round Table fictions is indisputable, a fact that cannot be dismissed by referring to clouded illusions, twilights, or obsessions. The onomasticon is a persuasive guide to research, and sufficient parallels exist between the narratives of Arthurian romance and ancient Celtic sagas, folktales, and legends.

But any attempt to measure out each of the intermediary steps would be useless, for the early Irish and Welsh materials that came to French authors were already in a state of debris. It would, moreover, be a gross exaggeration to impute all the exploits of the Knights of the Round Table to mythical combats between Irish "solar deities," Curoi ("the sun god") or Cú Chulainn ("the young sun"). Yet certain fundamental, recognizable themes remain, such as: the love of a fairy princess for a mortal, an adventurous quest for marvelous objects (e.g., magical armor and cups of plenty), encounters with the hospitable host, the constraints of *geis* (interdiction, "taboo"), boons rashly promised, strange metamorphoses, and voyages to the otherworld. This last, the conception of the otherworld, deserves special mention because it is inevitably imbedded in other themes and because it confers a special nuance to the Arthurian adventure and helps explain a number of curiosities in the French romances. The otherworld of the Celts—identified variously with Elysian Isles somewhere in the Western sea, or with an underwater paradise, or even with haunted mounds or underground palaces—included at once the land of the dead (or, more precisely, of those believed dead, but who are perhaps still living) and the dwelling of the gods, goddesses, and fairies; blissful regions, ageless, timeless, where one day lasts for a century. Its most striking feature was to permit the crossing of obstacles like a body of water, an ocean, river, or wall of fog by means of a separation from the terrestrial world. The real world could communicate with it only through navigation to a distant place, sometimes perilous, sometimes simple, or even by traversing an intermediary zone to hunt an animal, like a white stag or wild boar. The two worlds were also conjoined by a kind of seasonal solidarity, especially during the great fall and spring feasts. Yet, although humans could enter and leave the otherworld by dint of certain precautions, it was not open to everyone, for it was often as likely to vanish from sight as to appear out of nowhere. The otherworld adventure was reserved for the hero prepared to fulfill fearful and enigmatic tasks or for the man loved by a fairy princess ready to whisk away her privileged subject.

While these mythical elements are partly diminished and rationalized in Arthurian romance, they persist disguised within a feudal, chivalrous, and courtly setting. In the final analysis, it matters little if the primitive significance of most Celtic legend escaped Chrétien and his contemporaries, because, neither mythographers nor professional folklorists, their intention was rather to create typical works.

However, even if, in their view, it was no more commanding than were *Mother Goose Tales* for Charles Perrault, or more important than are the *Last of the Mohicans* or Indian stories for modern readers, the *matière de Bretagne* still would have had the power to transport the audience into an imaginary, extraordinary universe. Providing in fact more than local color and imagery, the *matière de Bretagne* revolutionized literature in the twelfth century and enriched it with a delightful fantasy and forceful allure, for which, in the proem to his *Chanson de Saxons,* Jean Bodel offered a characterization: "the tales of Britain are so vain and pleasing." It is indeed this enchantment, the wonders of Britain, that embodied the new Arthurian atmosphere, so unique, so sparkling, as if dilated in comparison to the mood of the *chansons de geste*, and which best explains why the "adventure" is the predominant theme of Round Table romances, why an individual and solitary quest for knightly exploits replaces the collective action of epic heroes.

While recognition of the Celtic legacy remains legitimate, Chrétien's share was not so large as to inhibit his freedom of invention. With a degree of independence, Chrétien treated the *matière de Bretagne* with light fingers, most often intentionally retaining the exceptional either to evoke curiosity or surprise, or to orchestrate humor and irony. His artistic sensibility was more readily captivated by the charm of these broken-down myths, filled with marvelous and delightful subjects, than by symbolic allegorization or the fabulations of the romances of antiquity. But a penchant for lucidity prevented his lingering in the Celtic maze, because to fantastic characters he preferred moral truths, though sometimes he strung out a double thread, like a sorcerer, doubtless amusing himself by evoking the extravagant and the relevant at the same time: his was a discreet and idealized didacticism. Finally, the legendary perspective of the Celtic materials lifted real heroes to a paradigmatic role, raising them somewhat above humanity, like the figures sculpted high on the tympanum of cathedral portals. In a word, Chrétien may be considered a kind of Ovid of Celtic myth—or of its reflections.

Chrétien's Esthetic

As a professional writer, Chrétien was eager for success, liberal in praise of his patrons, and scornful of the cruder efforts of other story-tellers. Far more important was his awareness of critical concepts, as is shown by his esthetic of the romance. Besides the fact that he seems to have been the first to designate a distinct genre with this term, no one determined or practiced its precepts better than he. *Matière, conjointure, sen;* with these words, found in the prologues of *Erec (conjointure,* v. 14*)* and of the *Charrette (matière* and *sen,* line 26*),* Chrétien discloses his key concepts. *Matière* is nothing more than the principal source of the work, the raw, narrative material of the story. It is to be organized by means of a *belle conjointure* ("coherent narrative," "well-ordered story") that transforms the overly exteriorized and basic action of the simple "adventure tale" to which notion Chrétien opposes the disorganized versions of the *jongleurs* which only added adventure to adventure. *Conjointure* ensures the internal coherence and unity of the subject, establishes a link between the continuity of events and the depiction of characters, and may even aim for a latent archetectonic structure in the romance. Chrétien speaks disdainfully of the professional storytellers who were accustomed to *depecier et corrompre* ("dismember and spoil") the story of *Erec: he* refuses to tell the adventure just for the sake of the adventure. Instead of mangling it, he seems to have purposely used a composite imitation and combined diverse narratives within a conceptual plan of the whole, a method effected by means of the *sen.* A word with didactic connotations, the *sen* is the dominant thesis of the work, the moral interpretation of the adventures, the ideal which they venture to illustrate, or simply their psychological and human importance. Unquestionably, the notion of *sen* is of clerical origin and is closely related to the term *sapientia* ("wisdom") of the scholastic philosophers. But Chrétien has in a way secularized the concept by transposing it to a courtly milieu.

Almost without exception, the title he chose for each of his romances summarizes the *sen.* Contrary to received opinion, he gave a double title to none of his poems. The only authentic titles are *Erec et*

Enide, Le Chevalier de la Charrette, Le Chevalier au Lion, Le Conte du Graal. *Erec and Enide* is the romance that unriddles the conjugal love of the couple as strengthened by tests. *The Knight of the Cart* (nearly a linguistic blend!) lays bare the knight Lancelot who, for his love, dared climb onto the cart of infamy. *The Knight of the Lion* is Yvain whose nobility and generosity gained him the friendship of a lion, the noblest animal of all. More enigmatic, the title itself, *Le Conte du Graal,* ought to be interpreted with the cryptic Grail vessel foremost in mind. *Cligés*'s title cannot be ascertained as such by the text, although two lines of the prologue do authorize it within Chrétien's canon: *"Cil qui fist d' Erec et d' Enide ... /Un novel conte recomance/D' un vaslet qui an Grece fu/Del lignage le roi Artu."* (·"He who wrote of Erec and Enide ... will tell another story now about a youth who lived in Greece and was a member of King Arthur's line."[10]

Chrétien applies his esthetic conception of the romance gracefully. Though he felt and exploited the spell of fantasy, he recognized the classic qualities of balance and reason. These were accomplished through the work of revision and artistic polishing, *la peine* ("effort, hard work") and *l' entencion* ("intention, intense concentration, careful attention")– the only part of the *Lancelot* (line 29) he proudly claims as his own. Though he learned and adopted some of the artificial precepts from the manuals of rhetoric, he quickly acquired a personal style, both finely tuned and, at the same time, natural, polished, yet picturesque, modelled on the rhythms of actual speech. The octosyllable lines carry the narrative vividly, without monotony; the phrases are euphonious, the words and images fitted to their task, sometimes luminous and precise, sometimes delicately tinted. Chrétien must be read or recited aloud, as he meant us to, in his native *langue d'oïl.*

Chrétien the Humanist

Yet he did not write solely to offer his audience a diversion. He wanted to please but also to instruct. Never losing sight of reality (he synchronizes the marvelous with ordinary social realities, the laments of exploited women workers, a riot in a commune), he still defends an ideal, not however simply to juxtapose reality with this ideal, but rather in the hope that reality would be enriched by an ideal vision. More than any of his contemporaries, except perhaps Thomas of England, Chrétien exemplified a rational striving for lucidity. The language may today seem trite, but it was an untried innovation in the twelfth century to seek to illuminate the mysteries of the heart and the conscience. We must not be blinded, even when he yields—for the fun of it—to precious overrefinements, as in Soredamors or Alexander's monologues in *Cligés;* we must not be impatient with the fastidious metaphors which, after all, are concordant with examinations of interior states. His depiction of love, on occasion injected with humor, sometimes star-crossed by fate, is generally imbued with elements both vigorous and velvety. He liked to enlace and unlace situations humanly significant, however latent or unusual. He defined and sought to solve current problems of conscience posed by the conflicting claims of love, morality, and knightly honor. His solutions blend an unforbidding clarity with that flexibility necessary for examinations of conscience and confessions of the heart.

Without contradicting the moral doctrines of the church, he taught (except in *Le Conte du Graal*) a somewhat distinctive and prescriptive code of worldly ethics. He did not reject the joys of this transitory life and yet, conceding nothing to baseness, demanded of his heroes greatness of soul while exalting the virtues of abnegation. Chrétien maintained an unyielding conception of chivalry.

What he condemned was futile excess and lack of balance. Interested of course as a psychologist in subconscious states, in the amorous obsession of Lancelot, in Yvain's folly, in the love trance of Perceval on seeing the three drops of blood on the snow, yet, in his consummate heroes, Chrétien combined lucidity and freedom. He preferred those characters *who make themselves,* who develop power and self-knowledge through trials. This same restraint and equilibrium led him (notwithstanding his adulterous, passionate, and idealized *Lancelot,* taken up at the dictate of Marie de Champagne) to criticize the extravagant side of the courtly doctrine and to depict the marriage of true love as the ideal type of union. In Enide, Erec's wife, mistress and lady *coexist:* she thus increases in value, keeps her social attractiveness, and wins esteem and honor. In our grasp here is the explanation of Chrétien's antipathy for the *Tristan* legend and his reticence toward fatal passion, uncontrolled and gainless. Optimistic and humanistic, his ethos of prowess and charity confidently turns outward, to man and his world.

Chapter 2

Early Works

Philomena

Philomena, a much more frequent medieval form than Philomela, is a poetic name for the nightingale. This "fable" (1468 octosyllables), Chrétien in his prologue to *Cligés* calls *The Change* [or Metamorphosis] *of the Hoopoe, the Swallow, and of the Nightingale.*

Philomena, whose theme is borrowed from the *Metamorphoses* (6: 426–674), Chrétien's only extant Ovidian adaptation, was discovered in 1884 by Gaston Paris in the late-thirteenth- or early-fourteenth-century *Ovide moralisé,* a ponderous poem, in which, following the translation of every tale from the *Metamorphoses,* there is a "moralizing" tag or commentary disclosing the allegorical and religious meaning embedded in mythology. For two tales the author used antecedent French versions, *Piramus et Tisbé (Pyramus and Thisbe),* dating from about 1150–1175, and, ostensibly, Chrétien's *Muance (The Change).* Although contested, the attribution is assured by two authorial declarations in the *Ovide moralisé,* before and after the *Philomena,* to the effect that he is reproducing, in this interpolation, the tale as "translated" by Chrétien. Moreover, it is certain, according to the prologue of *Cligés,* that Chrétien de Troyes adapted a story of Tereus, Procne, and Philomela, a coincidence which casts doubt upon conjectures that the "Chrétien" mentioned in the text of the *Philomena* was not our author.[1] Furthermore, the stricture regarding some slight revisions in vocabulary cannot seriously alter the paternity of the text inserted in the *Ovide moralisé* because a literary comparison, especially in matters of style and narrative tone, of the *Philomena* with Chrétien's accepted romances would demonstrate many similarities between them. As for the differences, they are clearly of the order which separates the insecure apprentice from the master, and one who has achieved his quest for originality.

The choice fable from the *Metamorphoses* was by itself sufficiently tempting for a devotee of the extraordinary, or one inquisitive about passionate love. Pandion, king of Athens, cherishes his two daughters, the younger Philomena, and Procne the elder whom he gives in marriage to Tereus, king of Thrace. After a somber wedding, foreboding evil, Tereus takes his wife to his kingdom, and a beautiful son, Itys, is born to them. At the end of five years, Procne wishes to see her sister again, and Tereus sails to Athens hoping indeed to keep his promise not to return without Philomena. But upon meeting the young girl, he is smitten with a senseless love for her. Pandion resigns himself, in great sorrow, to the departure of Philomena. Once the ships reach the Thracian coast, the still frenzied Tereus deceitfully leads his sister-in-law to a solitary house deep in a woods, where he begs in vain for her love. Insensitive to Philomena's pleas of indignation, he ravishes her, then cuts out her tongue to conceal his crime. The girl is abandoned in the house under the guard of a peasant woman, but Tereus returns home and strikes an afflicted pose by means of which he cunningly informs Procne of Philomena's death. In despair and mourning, Procne sacrifices a bull to Pluto for the repose of her sister's soul. Meanwhile Philomena has embroidered in a tapestry the story of her misfortune and manages to get this silent message to her sister. Procne understands everything, discovers Philomena, hides her in the palace, then takes vengeance upon her husband at dinner by serving to him a delectable meal—the decapitated body of her son, at which point Philomena appears and flings in his face Itys's bloody head. In this climax of horror, stripped of their humanity, the three characters are metamorphosed: Tereus becomes a hoopoe, Procne a swallow, Philomena a nightingale.

This brutal tale is clearly a brilliant school exercise, a youthful imitation following the Latin model, and should be judged as such. The author, naive and proud, obviously fresh out of school, had at his fingertips the principles of rhetorical composition, which he has diligently applied. The literary tyro is most evident in his portrait of the heroine at the moment when her beauty kindles Tereus's heart. In three hexameters, Ovid briefly compares her to nymphs, but Chrétien undertakes a methodical and complete description according to the rules taught at this time. First, he underlines the difficulty of his task, enough to cause Homer or Cato to hesitate. With no delusions of greater ability, he intends at least "to expend his effort" and produce something well-wrought. The resulting minute and careful portrait represents near-perfect banality. It is an automatic enumeration of the physical charms of a model of nature; Chrétien does not scruple to describe her in the traditional order, head first, body afterward, quite conscientious about ethical qualities and social talents. Given to joyful amusements, Philomena excels in chess and other games, is an expert in falconry as well as needlework, embroidery, and music. Finally, she has read the classical authors, knows grammar, and composes verse; the highest acclaim is that she could even "teach." This mythological princess is almost like a courtly high brow, someone who has passed through the *trivium* and *quadrivium:* her conversation with Tereus, in the dialectic mode, observes the methods of *disputatio* (vv. 275–319). The debate justifies all the more Chrétien's own later argument (vv. 392–448), a dissertation on the nature of love, set forth as a controversy with artificial queries and responses. In spite of its clumsy pedantry, this personal imitation shows some true merit; though following Ovid closely, Chrétien manifests a leaning for dramatic order and psychology. In his hands, the narrative is tempered, clarified, and riddled with frequent dialogues, characteristics at once more vivid and logical which reveal a flair for conscious control of characters. Chrétien's Tereus, for example, is described much more precisely and acutely than in the *Metamorphoses.*

It is hardly surprising or unusual that the representation of antique life is modernized, medievalized in the *Philomena,* for, in this way, Chrétien could expand upon short tableaus with felicitous simplicity (e.g., Tereus's navigation or the feast in Pandion's palace). As in *Erec* and *Cligés,* he is possibly undergoing already the influence of the brilliant descriptions in Wace's *Brut.* There are even other affinities between *Philomena* and the rest of Chrétien's work. He will effortlessly confer a certain complicity to his Arthurian romances, keeping the reader in suspense by holding off surprises, often by means of word play. In this sense, the strange and ingenious tale of *Philomena* doubtless appealed to him, apparent in the carefully detailed stratagem of the embroidery, or Procne's double talk during the horrible dinner scene. Ovid's seamless tale is here organized into two equal parts, connected by verse 734, in which *Chrestiien li Gois* is mentioned (one wonders if there is an authorial ruse in the signature here). A buoyant, elated Philomena is followed upon by a tragic one, a kind of bipartition similar to that of *Cligés* and *Erec* (although the latter romance seems rather like a triptych). But this observation is not altogether convincing; what better distinguishes Chrétien's style in the *Philomena* is a nearly ubiquitous easy elegance.

Finally, there is some justification in noting that Chrétien, without the advantage of proficiency in the art of *conjointure,* had difficulty joining his *sens* and *matière.* But at least he allows moral reflections to appear sporadically, now retaining, now rejecting the Ovidian theory of tyrannical, savage, and treacherous love. Chrétien finds equally reprehensible both the foolish and raging excess of Tereus whose base passion is opposed to the conception of *fine amor,* as well as any definition of true love as a renouncement of wisdom or reason. "'For, unless I'm wrong, love does not involve the surrender of one's reason'" (*"'N' est pas amors de forsener,'"* vv. 485-86). This moral reflection on the nature of love is in harmony with the doctrine defended in all Chrétien's romances, regardless of the overt monstrous passions in the antique legend itself.

Some critics place the composition of the *Ovidiana* after *Erec;* but to claim that this romance depicts love in a manner altogether independent of the Latin poet's example or teachings is to misunderstand artistic creation. Clearly, Chrétien could have already been familiar with Ovid's work and still have sufficient discrimination to shun its inspiration, especially if he did not find it in accord with one of his works. In any case, it is completely unlikely that *Erec* precedes *Philomena,* for, while the Arthurian romance reveals a masterful confidence, the latter imitation after Ovid is still more or less a scholarly exercise whose major import is to set in bold relief the auspicious talents of a gifted artist during his period of apprenticeship.

Two Love Poems

The amorous lifestyle of certain of Chrétien characters (like Cligés, Yvain, or Lancelot) in itself indicates both an awareness of Provençal poetry and, based on the positive attribution of two extant poems, that he was himself a lyric poet—perhaps even a prolific one.

His two poems attest to the influence of the troubadours and serve to place him among the first, if not *the* first, *trouvère* to introduce the courtly lyric into northern tradition. Although of uncertain date, they may have been composed as early as his *Ovidiana;* or perhaps they were written either concurrently with *Cligés* (which exploits the gallant vocabulary of the southern lyric) or with the *Lancelot* (which conforms most of all to the Provençal conception of love). What these two love poems lack in distinction is made up for in craftsmanship and charm. One is composed of six stanzas of eight heptasyllabic lines each, with the rhyme scheme *ababbaba,* followed by a final half stanza. The other has six stanzas of nine octosyllabic lines each, *ababbaaba.* In both, the stanzas are paired with the same rhymes. Chrétien does not seem to have been put off by a difficult technique.

As convention was the rule, the poems manifest little thematic innovation. The first, *"Amors tançon et bataille"* ("Love disputes and struggles . . ."), is a lament addressed to the god of love who is waging an unjust war against its "champion," its unrequited yet faithful servant. For the second poem, *"D' Amors, qui m' a tolu a moi"* ("Love, which has taken me from myself . . ."), Chrétien found inspiration in parts of Bernard de Ventadour's famous "Poem of the Lark" *("Quant vey la lauzeta mover,"* "When I see the lark move"*),* but without its throbbing or its artistic sparkle. With an abstract elegance, Chrétien elaborates and refines the commonplace that his lady's demands cannot keep him from being a faithful lover. Still, one persuasive stanza is enlivened with a personal note, formulating a rule of the heart that seems to echo a polemic, an antagonism between the courtly lover's will and Tristan's fatal, involuntary, spell-binding passion, caused by the philtre.

Never did I drink the drink
That poisoned Tristan,
But I love bitter than he
By my tender heart and free will.
Surely I ought to consent to this love,
For never was I forced into it,

Except this much, that I trusted my eyes,
And thus entered the path,
And from it I shall never roam nor abjure.

(vv. 28–36)

William of England

The edifying tale, *Guillaume d' Angleterre* (3366 lines), begins, with its frequent tests from on high, like a hagiographic legend; but thereafter, depending on the episode, it resembles either a romance of adventure or of morality, with a propitious fulfilment. The whole work is studded with moral developments whether of a devotional or an aristocratic bias.

Once upon a time, there was a king of England named William, praiseworthy for his piety, humility, and charity; his beautiful, high-born wife, Gratienne, was equally remarkable in Christian virtue. For six years they remain childless, but in the seventh year, to their great joy, Gratienne perceives that she would soon be a mother—at which point Providence oppresses them with unexpected tests. At matins one night, William, in his chamber, hears a thunderclap and is blinded by a brilliant light; a mysterious voice then orders him to abandon all his possessions and to go into exile. In great perplexity, the king takes counsel with his chaplain who advises him to distribute his wealth. Even when this is done, the divine message is repeated again and again. William then decides to obey and, one night, away from his castle in Bristol he steals, accompanied by the queen, whose own fate is linked to that of her spouse.

The couple plunges into the forest and there lives on wild fruit. One day, near the seashore, they take shelter in the hollow of a rock where the queen, seized by labor pains, gives birth to two sons. Unassisted, the king carries on as best he can, functioning as the midwife. With his sword, he cuts the two panels from his tunic to swaddle the newborn twins, then braces up, with his knees as a pillow-support, the head of his exhausted wife. Tortured by hunger, Gratienne is afraid she may not be able to resist eating one of the twins! Horrified, William is about to cut pieces of flesh *(braons)* from his thigh in order to nourish the distressed mother, but, touched by such resolve, she masters her discomfort and sends her husband to beg for alms in the vicinity.[2] A precipitous series of misfortunes fail to weaken William's faith in Providence. On the shore, he meets and brings back to the rock where the mother and the children are resting, some merchants who, overwhelmed by Gratienne's beauty, snatch her up and set sail. Thereupon, a wolf carries off one of the twins, while the other is missing from the small boat in which the father had left him. Finally, at the very moment when William is grasping toward the branch where is stuck fast the red purse (containing five gold pieces, thrown to him by one of the queen's abductors), it is torn from his hands by an eagle. The king considers this additional disgrace as a divine chastisement for his sin of greed.

Twenty-four years go by before the family is again reunited. William, wandering dejectedly in the forest, chances approaching some merchants who, in a clearing, are eating a late evening meal. At first they treat him as a dangerous outlaw or beggar, then agree to take him on their ship and bring him to Galloway *(Galveide),* a peninsula in southwest Scotland. Under the name Gui (i.e., "Will," from the first part of *Guillaume*), he there distinguishes himself as a devoted and patient servant of a rich but frugal townsman and ends up as the house steward.

Abruptly, the narrative then switches to the queen who, on the merchant ship, came to Corlink (probably Stirling, Scotland). Its overlord, Gleolaïs, once as valiant a knight as Roland but now doddering, takes Gratienne under his wing, falls in love with her, and, once widowed, wishes her to become "his wife and lover." But, remembering that she is a queen, that she cannot marry a lowly baron, intending also to remain faithful to William, Gratienne tries to put off the suitor by pretending to be a fallen woman, a debauched nun who fled the convent and lived seven years as a shameless wanton. Now Gleolaïs in his turn accuses himself of frequent error and, finding a very profound moral in the humble confession he has just heard, becomes more obstinate about his proposal. "God has now raised you up again high enough and He wished you to be my wife" (Wilmotte ed., vv. 1180-81). Disconcerted, the queen cries and reflects upon her desire to possess the land but not to wed its ruler. In the end, Gleolaïs promises her that their marriage will remain unconsummated for a year. The wedding is celebrated with display but not without ironic remarks from the guests. Yet, certain of becoming soon the lady of the manor after the imminent death of

Gleolaïs, Gratienne's sweet and generous character endears her to all those around her.

But what about the twins? The first, carried off by a wolf, fell from its jaws and was taken in by a merchant; the second was found on the small boat by another merchant. The adoptive fathers take them to "Quathenasse" (Caithness, an area in northeast Scotland) where they are baptized Lovel (the first, because of the wolf) and Marin. At the age of ten, they are the most beautiful, most courteous children of all, with no other formation but that of nature, always better than nurture. They are identical morally and physically, and, though ignorant of their relationship, a tender friendship unites them. Since both are repelled instinctively by a commercial profession (fur trading), and are thrashed by the incensed adoptive fathers, they go off together to seek adventure. In the forest, they kill a buck and, taken unawares by a guard, are brought before the king of Caithness, who, struck by their noble bearing and graceful manners, absolves and keeps them in his court, there to be initiated into the glorious arts of hunting and falconry.

Now we return to William. His master, the townsman of Galloway, rewards him for his loyal service with a loan of three hundred pounds. Now quite an expert merchant, the king goes from fair to fair, earning a good deal of money by buying and reselling furs, cloth, and colored goods. Accompanied on yet another trip by the townsman's two sons, and with a valuable cargo, he reaches Bristol, his kingdom, now governed by one of his nephews. While selling his wares at the fair, he sees, in the hands of a youth, his old hunting horn, a royal souvenir he buys dearly— for five pence. Then, nearly recognized by his former subjects, he rushes to embark.

The ship is swept by a storm to the land controlled by Gratienne, where custom demands a high toll tax. The lord, the lady, and the seneschal have the right to choose freely the most precious object from the cargo, after which merchants are permitted to carry on their dealings in complete security. Once the ship's arrival is announced, the lady first (she is a widow now), then the seneschal hasten to exercise their privilege. Gratienne, whose face is covered, is not recognized by William, but she shudders at the sight of the merchant and is beginning to guess the truth, having noticed both the horn suspended from the mast and a ring, once hers, which, as a token of their separation, William wears on his finger. Of all the merchant's goods, she requires only the ring, which William sadly surrenders, seeming to pull it not from his finger but from his heart. Gratienne then invites the merchant and his companions to the palace for a meal of thanks. The queen, lowering her wimple and uncovering her face, is recognized, but, seated next to her, William says nothing; they simply exchange polite words. Suddenly the sight of some dogs which enter the hall reminds the king of his grand old diversion, the joy of venery. Plunged in reverie, he daydreams about pursuing a sixteen-point hart in a forest. Half-awake, he cries out, "'Halloo! Halloo! Jack! The hart is bolting!'" (Wilmotte ed., v. 2573) Laughter and mockery ensue but Gratienne tenderly embraces him and offers to change his dream to reality.

To the woods they go hunting. In a clearing, the huntsmen find the sixteen-point hart and unleash the hounds. Then William and Gratienne, unable to feign another moment, cry tears of joy and reciprocally relate their destinies. She will permit him to pursue the hart provided he not cross the river separating her land from that of a disappointed suitor—a neighboring king who has waged war against her for some years. William promises to respect the interdiction, but in the arduous pleasure of the hunt he forgets everything and crosses the river to follow the hart. He has thus penetrated into the domains of the king of Cathenasse. Threatened with death or imprisonment by his own sons, Lovel and Marin, he evokes their pity by telling his life story. During the part about the purse (ripped away by the eagle), miraculously it falls from the sky with the pieces of gold. Then, the father and children immediately recognize each other; Lovel and Marin are now aware that they are brothers. They are also surprised to learn (as is the king of Cathenesse) that the woman they had been in rivalry with is their mother. The next day they meet with Gratienne whose personal anxiety is transformed into bliss. Providence has joined again what it had once sundered. Lovel and Marin send for their adoptive fathers to reward them generously. The greedy and clumsy townsmen are welcomed by the courteous queen who playfully bestows upon them precious garments as gifts. The land of Sorlinc is then presented in good will to the king of Cathenasse. William returns with the family to his kingdom in England and takes back the crown which his nephew gladly restores.

The author of this rather disorganized yet sometimes felicitous tale calls himself, in the first line, Chrétien, not so rare a name in the twelfth century and not sufficient proof that it was Chrétien de Troyes. Based on one reference, we are even tempted to believe the contrary, with Philip A. Becker—"Chrétien ...*relates*" (v. 18)—which can only refer to the profession of storytelling. The same is true for a final allusion (vv. 3364-66) to a "companion," Roger, who presumably transmitted the "matter" of an original story found in Suffolk, at Saint Edmund's monastery (vv. 11-17). These indications suggest that we are to group the author of *William of England* among those professional storytellers and *jongleurs* whom Chrétien de Troyes held in open disdain (cf. the opening of *Erec*). But what solid arguments can be drawn from this insufficient data?

To study the work itself, its inspiration and technique, is decidely the most likely method of solving the problems of attribution, although it will not unwind all the perplexities. The author was not uneducated; perhaps his original text already connected hagiographic and narrative themes which relate *William of England* to the Saint Eustace legend and to the story of Apollonius of Tyre, but his knowledge of Horace, Ovid, and occasionally Wace's *Brut* suggests a direct reading of sources (punishment of Tantalus, vv. 905-28; description of the storm, vv. 2294-2377). In many passages his literary talent is not unlike Chrétien's; his language is correct, the vocabulary slick, with remarkably precise technical terms, the rhyme artful and proficient. The narrative is quick and expressive, sometimes even peppered with caustic remarks. Although his manner does not approach the unified composition, the *conjointure* of *Erec* or *Yvain,* his boast of brevity, of "keeping to the straightest path," is justified (vv. 5-10); and he is clever enough to arrange the final meeting for all his characters. He does not pause to describe them, though he *can* describe. Despite the conventional rhetoric, his strokes for the storm scene are broad, forceful, and vivid; he does a pleasant little sketch of a corner of the forest where water from a stream flows upon the fine sand. The hunting scene is exact because of a masterly choice and sequencing of events and through the use of hunting terms, technical terms which are retained only to the extent that they stress the dramatic and psychological quality of the narrative; the hunt is so well shaded that it causes William to forget the queen's prohibition. A similar power of observation and even raw realism is apparent in the depiction of the rapacious merchants and in the animated, variegated scenes of the fairs, the harbors, and commercial activity. The final recognition scene between William and Gratienne is delicately etched, but nowhere does the author invent so graphically as in the symbolic and psychological treatment of the false merchant's return to his true royal character. Both the horn found at the Bristol fair, and hung on the ship's mast, and then the joyous passion of the hunt suggest and translate William's inner metamorphosis. Faithful also to Chrétien's manner is the daydreaming motif, when William, at the sight of the dogs, plunges into reverie so deep as to lose his feeling for exterior reality—just like the somnambulistic Lancelot and Perceval.

However, if we are dealing with an authentic work by Chrétien, where shall we place it in the sequence of his romances? Supposedly early in his career, since this tale contains neither Arthurian nor courtly conceptions. But *Guillaume* is not a piece of school work like the *Philomena* and it is not cited in the prologue to *Cligés,* where Chrétien carefully enumerated his previous creations. Such an omission might be explained by the forced admission that if *William of England* is in fact by Chrétien, it was composed after *Cligés.* In this perspective, the only plausible one, the problem of attribution changes importantly in aspect, because, in spite of the obvious affinities, there is little real harmony between a rather simplistic, weak work like the *Guillaume* and his stunning masterpieces, like the *Lancelot, Yvain,* and the *Conte du Graal.*

Of course, after completing *Cligés,* there was nothing to stop Chrétien from composing out of whim a non-Arthurian story, shorter by one-half than his other romances. Nor is there anything to stop us from conjecturing that he did not spend too much time or application on this lesser work. But it remains quite unlikely that of all the possible subjects available, he chose a tale unavoidably banal and simplistic. It is not so much that a religious theme could not be inspiring to him, for he handled one, quite unusually, in the *Conte du Graal,* to illustrate the value of charity, penitence, and faith in God. What a lack of balance there is between Perceval's dramatically human repentance on Good Friday in his uncle's hermitage and the shoddy hagiography of the *Guillaume,* whose miraculous machinery appears artificially determined. Clearly, the unimaginative episode showing the queen's hesitation about

59

eating one of her newborn, and the king's offer to sacrifice a piece of his thigh, cannot be blamed on the deft, inventive pen of Chrétien de Troyes, without the risk of insult.

An aristocratic morality or rather prejudice is benevolently expressed in *Guillaume d'Angleterre,* in contrast with the Christian virtue of humility praised in the beginning of the tale. Like a dogma, the superiority of the nobility over the churls (a scornful characterization of the townsmen) is stressed and justified by the privilege of birth. For nature, steadfast and untamed through nurture, has divided men for all time into two distinct classes, as the theoretical and involved development declares on the subject of Lovel and Marin, rebels against their role as apprentice merchants. A nobleman will remain so forever, and likewise, once a churl always a churl. This same absolute conception is bitterly reaffirmed in proverbial form: "Trust not an angry churl any more than a bear"; "a churl is a very silly beast" (Wilmotte ed., vv. 1458-61). Try as they may to prove their goodness, the townsmen, the twins' adoptive fathers, ridiculed or hated for their love of money, seem incapable of open generosity. Should this hostility toward the townsmen be offered as ground for attributing the *William of England* to Chrétien de Troyes? It is undeniable that he has aristrocratic leanings, that his Perceval, for example, illustrates the great force of natural instinct in a noble being. Still, the denigration of churls is a commonplace in the romances of the period, one which occasioned a kind of artistic flattery of the audience's feudal prejudices; it is not necessarily characteristic, then, of Chrétien's work. If, moreover, he playfully aims barbs in the direction of townsmen, he does so without the bitterness or gravity apparent in the *Guillaume.* The two are in fact opposed—in moral, not social terms—at the very beginning of the *Chevalier au Lion,* by means of a proverbial expression, "a dead courtier is worth more than a living churl," stated like a gloss to his melancholic observation that courtesy and prowess no longer flourish as they did in the days of King Arthur. And if, as noted by Philip A. Becker, the seneschal Kay is there described as a villein by Queen Guenevere, it is only because of his unpleasant character (*Yvain,* line 90.). In the final analysis, this scornful caricature of the burghers, or townsmen, in the romance *Guillaume d'Angleterre* suggests rather that it does not belong to Chrétien's canon.

2. The Marriage of Yvain and Laudine.
(Princeton University Library, Garrett MS 125, fol. 52r.)

The author's doctrine, furthermore, is not applied consistently. To Gratienne, claiming a churlish background, Gleolaïs answers that merit and virtue do not depend upon the coincidence of birth, a response that may only serve to portray the fatuous, senile lover. Yet at the conclusion of the story, this burgher of Galveide is rewarded; William makes of him a chief counselor, arms his two sons, and marries them to wealthy duchesses. These inconsistencies demonstrate a perfunctory design in the work, unlike the deliberation we associate with Chrétien de Troyes. Similarly, there are incertitudes and ruptures in characterization. In the earlier episodes, the royal couples' piety appears as a fundamental theme, only to be displaced—eclipsed—later by secular concerns. In point of fact, William and Gratienne are quite shallow, rigid even, as if controlled by Providence. There is no interior emotional or psychological conflict within them. William, who at first accused himself of cupidity for wanting to take the purse and the money reveals one fine day an amazing aptitude for business affairs, unscrupulous about his earnings from buying and selling. Still, he somehow remains a king even while becoming a merchant, a subtlety for which we should be more or less grateful. But, with Gratienne, the incongruities become hopelessly more serious in the episode when old Gleolaïs makes her a marriage offer. Even though the queen's duplicity seems somewhat necessary, it is hazardous to propose, as has been done, that under the circumstances (in a supposed desire to remain a "lady" but be neither wife nor mistress), she is obeying some highly spiritual conception of courtly love. Such an interpretation does not accord with the text, for Gratienne's behavior is in fact managed with a kind of loud vulgarity, quite at variance with Chrétien's well-known discriminating taste. Besides, the author of *Erec, Cligés,* and *Yvain* does not so much set in opposition the "lady," wife, and mistress, but rather prefers to combine all three in one person.

Other evidence also precludes attributing the *William of England* to Chrétien de Troyes: its precise geographical decor extending as far as Scotland, its numerous lexical particularities (listed by Philip A. Becker), and the fact that its manuscript tradition diverges from that of Chrétien's accepted romances.

Some doubt persists: possibly the Champenois poet dashed off here an inferior sketch, but probably *Guillaume d'Angleterre* is the work of a rather gifted imitator, one who lacked the master's clever ability.

Chapter 3

Erec and Enide

From a certain story of adventure which told of Erec, son of King Lac, Chrétien boasts of having derived a "pleasing argument," while the *jongleurs,* in the presence of noble audiences, can only mutilate and spoil it.

The introduction, called "the first part of my story," is an interlaced narration of two motifs, the hunt for the white stag and the joust for the sparrowhawk. It tells how one of the most brilliant Knights of the Round Table, Erec, satisfies his claim against Yder, son of Nut, who had permitted his dwarf to insult Erec; how he becomes engaged to Enide, the daughter of a simple vavasor. The hero then brings his fiancée to Cardigan, in Wales, where is assembled King Arthur's court and where the maiden's beauty, grace, and moral qualities evoke everyone's admiration. This unified prelude could stand by itself if Chrétien had wished simply to write a lay with a legendary, courtly theme; its two interwoven motifs cohere for the greater glory of Enide, the most beautiful of all women, and the narrative is so well trued as to deserve praise on its own as a most "pleasing argument."

But the action rebounds thereafter. At the court, a month-long celebration of Erec and Enide's marriage, with great ceremony and rejoicing, is concluded by the tournament of Tenebroc (Edinburgh) in which Erec is triumphant. So that his father, King Lac, and all the people may meet his wife, he decides to return home where the young couple is cheerfully greeted and then enjoy a blissful honeymoon. However, Erec's lovely felicity causes him to forget his prowess, to put aside his arms and lose sight of chivalry, behavior that disconcerts and distresses his companions. Enide is blamed for his *recreantise,* i.e., the abandonment of prowess and of his own self. Enide grieves in solitude, but as she contemplates him one morning while Erec is still sleeping, she can no longer keep from bursting into tears, then accuses herself and takes pity on him. Still dozing, Erec heard only the last part, a terse but troubled lament: *"Amis, con mar fus!"* ("'Unhappy thou!'").[1] He is aroused, demands an explanation, and thus learns of the invidious rumors circulating about him. Instantly he makes a decision: recognizing the accuracy of the reproach, like a true Knight of the Round Table, he will chance adventure. Normally, such a decision could hardly be considered unusual, except that he orders Enide alone, wearing her best dress, to accompany him, to post in front of him, forbidden to speak a word under any circumstances, unless and until he first addresses her. Erec's resolve is obviously not dictated solely by chivalrous honor; some doubts must have arisen in his mind that prompted a secret test of Enide's real feelings. Thus, a psychological drama, limned in half tones, intensifies the moral dilemma or conflict between love and adventure, marriage and prowess.

Still smiling, Enide obeys without protest. The two undergo a diverse series of adventures in which Erec's exploits are subtlely calibrated with the demonstrations of his wife's unwavering love, so devoted that she cannot *not* warn him of dangers, in spite of his command. Their adventures include attacks by thieving knights (who are brilliantly defeated); an ardent courtship of Enide by a vain, brutal count (who later repents); a desperate joust against a nobleman, of minute size but of unequaled fierceness, Guivret the Little (who afterward befriends the victor); a brief halt at Arthur's court after an encounter in the forest (where the king and his knights were hunting); the deliverance of a captive knight (from two giants); Erec wounded and falling faint near Enide (who believes him dead); in despair then, thinking of suicide, she is saved by the count of Limors (who immediately falls in love with her) and, when the falsely departed recovers, Enide is released from a forced marriage. In the end, the misunderstanding that had separated the couple is dispelled, and harmony reigns anew between them.

"Sweet sister mine," says Erec to Enide, "my proof of you has been complete! Be no more concerned in any wise, for I love you now more than ever I did before; and I am certain and rest assured that you love me with a perfect love. From this time on for evermore, I offer myself to do your will just as I used to do

before. And if you have spoken ill of me, I pardon you and call you quit of both the offense and the word you spoke."
Then he again kisses her and embraces her. Enide delights in her husband's embraces and the assurances of his love. "Rapidly through the night they ride, and they are very glad that the moon shines bright."[2]
It would seem that the tale is coming to a close, that Chrétien will soon have the reunited couple, Erec and Enide, return to the kingdom of Lac or to Arthur's court. But this is not the case. Wounded in error by Guivret, then healed by his friend's two sisters, Erec faces still another adventure, the most extraordinary and dangerous of all, the "Joy of the Court" (Foerster, ed., vv. 5367-6410; Roques, ed., vv. 5319-6358). As King Evrain's guest on the fertile island and at the castle of Brandigan, he enters into a marvelous orchard surrounded by a wall of air, a beatific yet frightening place, filled with flowers, fruits, rare plants, and melodious birds. But nearby are sharp stakes with helmets and with the heads of dead bodies on display, except for the last one, on which a horn is suspended. Erec then perceives a beautiful, well-dressed girl, lying silently in a silver bed, shaded by a sycamore. As he comes near, a gigantic knight, Mabonagrain, King Evrain's nephew, heaves in sight, who, acting on orders from his beloved—the girl on the silver bed—fulfills his love duty by fighting all those who dare to cross the pale of the enchanted realm. The battle is long and dreadful, but Mabonagrain finally avows defeat. Erec blows the horn, setting off a celebration, and all rejoice—Enide, King Evrain, and the entire populace—for the evil custom has been abolished. However much in love, Mabona-grain has no regrets over his release from a fatal confinement. Weeping at first for fear of losing forever her lover whom she wanted to mono-polize, then consoled by Enide who discovers her to be a cousin, the maiden of the orchard understands finally that she will enjoy a more rational comfort from love unshackled by romantic tyranny.
Crowned with knightly success, Erec and Enide, along with Guivret, make for Arthur's court. And upon the death of King Lac, the moral and social splendor of the privileged pair is hallowed by their glorious coronation on Christmas Day at Nantes.[3]

The existence of a *conjointure* in *Erec* has sometimes been questioned. It is, however, quite manifest that Chrétien carefully marshalled the episodic progressions of the work. But in addition to a certain geometric spirit equally proportionate in all Chrétien's romances (except for *The Story of the Grail)*, pervasive narrative subtleties in his works guard against an overly rigorous order. Medieval authors did not have access to our modern theories of unity. Even the notion of *sen* implied a method of multiple interpretations, prompting an educated cleric-romancer to harbor, on the level of linear simplicity, adumbrated, complex, and layered designs. In the *Erec,* Chrétien avoided the recondite and marked the development by degrees, organizing its structure in a triptych.

The "prelude," or *premier vers,* a short but vigorous idyllic romance, constitutes a whole, a psychological antecedent for what follows. With little analysis and by means of a few sober but significant gestures, the sketch of the characters is clear enough for an understanding of the projected conduct of the hero and the heroine. Erec is the elegant, courtly, and generous one, however proud, secretive and easily offended. Independent and a little ostentatious even, his impulsiveness is tempered by enough self-restraint to keep his composure. And he plays resolutely, to the very end, the dangerous game of "avenging his disgrace or increasing it."[4] His love is ardent, profound, and imperious for the young rose drawn from obscurity, Enide. She, on the other hand, a physical *and* moral beauty, is modest, submissive, devoted, and active around the house (making her adaptable to a dangerous life); yet she is a limpid soul, still passive, lacking the experience of life, and prepared to accept a tranquil, quiet happiness. Enide is deeply in love and full of gratitude and infatuation for this "king's son," Erec, her new fiancé. But Chrétien has carefully shunned here any suggestion of a misalliance, an omission tactfully achieved no doubt to retain his autonomy over the fine dramatic distinctions by which marital harmony is here tested, then reaffirmed. Though he may insist on Enide's poverty, he also extols the faultless equality between the two souls, united in a marriage of love. "A perfect match they were in courtesy, beauty, and gentleness. And they were so alike in quality, manner, and customs, that no one wishing to tell the truth could choose the better of them, nor the fairer, nor the more discreet."[5] To accord with the image of light and youth formed by the

ideal couple, in the first part of the romance—like a springtime overture—
there predominates a suggestion of the *premier vers* as *primavera.*[6]
But the euphoric interlude soon passes, for a pivotal, dramatic crisis
develops or rebounds, after which the account proceeds somewhat by
episodes. Even these are varied and well-arrayed, their symmetry evinc-
ing an artful, conscious subtlety. And in spite of the movement and
picturesque narrative, the psychological continuity is never broken.
One might even say that the accelerated cadence of the adventures
contributes to the moral verisimilitude of the test. The conclusion,
advancing yet inscrutable, is dominated by love's conflict, taking
exactly four days from the departure "for adventure" to the moonlit
reconciliation of Erec and Enide—a close-knit action in itself contribut-
ing to the *conjointure* of the romance.

However imminent the conclusion may seem, the poet prolongs the
story enough to allow Erec to try the mysterious adventure of the
"Joy of the Court," an experience undertaken with full consent, by an
act of will alone, in knightly virtuosity and for the sheer beauty of its
name, "joy." In this way, it differs from all earlier adventures and is
an innovation over the individual adventure—a splendid gamble—now
broadened to include a victory of collective utility, and now fulfilled
by the joyful liberation of a king and of his people. Lastly, this strange
marvel, the "Joy of the Court," echoes a fundamental feature of Celtic
mythology, the otherworld adventure, one which here acknowledges
the superiority of the Arthurian hero and reveals to himself and to
others the full measure of his achievement.

The tripartite structure, at once lithe and learned, first sets forth
an eminent knight and a love adventure with a happy ending; then, by
means of a psychological crisis, the narrative is launched in another
direction; in a much longer third part, the interior drama is gradually
moderated at the unfolding of each episode. Part three, then, restores
happiness once-threatened and is elaborated upon by means of a prodigious adventure which enhances the prestige of the hero in his quest
for perfection. Filled with surprises, swayed by an ascending rhythm,
the whole work embodies Chrétien's favorite theme, that of the self-
made hero who sets his own trials and reaches his full potential on his

own.[7] The "Joy of the Court" is not, then, just a bit of frosting, for through it are completed the portraits of Erec as well as of Enide. One might say that its *sen* lies precisely in the apparent redundance of it all.

In all likelihood, however, Chrétien did not construct *ex nihilo* the skeleton of his romance. What he no doubt did was to revive, in his own lucid way, a series of episodes from the "tale of adventure," a hypothesis bolstered by comparison of the *Erec* with the pseudo-Mabinogion, *Gereint,* as we shall see later. In any case, whether Chrétien followed an outline already sketched, or whether he was the first to associate originally disparate tales, it is clear that his *Erec* is a combination of elements from diverse sources. Certain legendary themes appear to be of Celtic origin. For example, in the opening scene, the hunt for the white hart is the traditional white animal hunted by the hero or the knight in the "forest of adventure" and sent by a fairy princess to lure her idol to herself in the otherworld (cf. the lays of *Guigemar, Graëlent,* and *Guingamor*). But its marvelous character is deemphasized by Chrétien: here the white hart does not attract the hero to a meeting with a fairy princess or with a beautiful woman, for Erec does not even take part in the hunt. The pursuit of the exceptional animal is rather transformed into the *custom* of the kiss given to the most beautiful woman, functioning then as a pretext for courtly play, a chivalrous ritual of gallantry, mindful not of primitive fantasies, but of diversions enjoyed (much later) in the Hôtel de Rambouillet.[8] Thus when the curtain rises on this Arthurian fiction, one has the distinct impression not of creativity but rather that Chrétien is following a familiar path; that without much ado he can simply report the presence of a certain white hart in the forest; and that this somewhat stale yet charming motif might profitably be embellished with a few niceties.

The mystery of the adventure is less blurred in the "Joy of the Court" episode. However skeptical, Chrétien was too talented a storyteller not to take advantage of its strange atmosphere, one for which Gaston Paris severely reproached him, saying that he rendered "an old tale poorly preserved ... even more unintelligible by trying to explain it."[9] Without the need for logical explanations, Chrétien had only to inject a psychological—and ethical—*sen* into a marvelous tale in which had coalesced two very distinct mythical elements: the visit to Bran's castle and the legend of Mabon liberated from captivity. We can recognize in fact the name Bran in Brandigan, castle of King Evrain, and the name Mabon in Mabonagrain (Mabon Irain, or Ivain, which perhaps became Ewrain, Evrain for Chrétien). With Bran the Blessed, King Evrain shares the characteristics of the hospitable host, dwelling on a lush island whose fertility and "joy" are possibly symbolized by the horn suspended from a stake in the enchanted orchard—if we accept Helaine Newstead and R.S. Loomis's idea that some confusion arose between *cor*, "horn," i.e., horn of plenty, a talisman owned by Bran, and *cor*, "horn," i.e., a wind instrument. The same critics have interpreted analogously the expression "Joy of the Court," a less convincing explanation than the first, one which in fact is corroborated by the curious words used by Chrétien himself to express the fervent joy felt by Erec after sounding the horn: "Erec was well sated with joy and well served to his heart's desire" (Foerster, ed., vv. 6190-91; Roques, ed., vv. 6138-39). Another interpretation is possible, as suggested by E. Philipot on the basis of the Lanpart episode in the *Bel Inconnu*, namely that Evrain's hospitality might simply be a courtly attenuation of the "forced hospitality" theme, which also turns up in the *Chastel de Pesme Aventure* episode in *Yvain:* he who enjoys its hospitality is obligated to undergo a dangerous trial.

The story of Mabonagrain, the "marvelously large" knight locked up in the orchard with his beloved, originally goes back to the one about the giant held prisoner by a fairy princess. Required to do battle with any who happened upon the forbidden scene, he, if victorious, would kill them, and, if vanquished, would himself be killed, then to be replaced by the victor who would take up with the fairy princess and play out the triple role of lover, captive, and guardian of a deadly custom. Chrétien's version is less harsh, retaining the heads of the dead planted on stakes while lending delicate sentiments to Mabonagrain; and it is more gracious, somewhat contradictory, amusing even, for the tyrannical enchantment imposed by the fairy princess is replaced by a chivalrous enthralment.

The background of this episode is unchallengeably Celtic, a tradition discernable without question in other adventures and motifs, in characters such as Guivret, the fantastic dwarf, in his sisters, and even in Gawain's horse, Guingalet. However courtly and perhaps of southern descent, the sparrowhawk contest also suggests a Celtic background. Some traces of magic subsist also in the character of Enide and even in the theme of Erec's *recreantise,* yet remain as if masked, making it appear likely that some part of the narrative was invented, without any basis in legend, by the author of the "tale of adventure."

It is also clear that the background of the adventures in *Erec and Enide* depends in no direct way upon classical antiquity or upon contemporary French writings, influences in any case that manifest themselves only in Chrétien's technique. The most obvious source is the *Brut.* Identical details and stylistic similarities suggest that two descriptions, one of Erec's marriage, the other of his coronation, are modeled in part on the brilliant tableau of the feasts at Arthur's coronation traced by Wace. It is less certain whether the scene of Enide's weeping was inspired solely by a passage in the *Brut* in which the tears of Brien awaken his uncle, Cadwalein. Lastly, smiling Cador's pronouncement upon the dangers of *oisdive,* i.e., "idleness," or the renouncement of warlike, chivalrous conduct, may have helped Chrétien understand better the narrative resources of the *recreantise* theme (*Brut,* vv. 10733-64). *Floire et Blancheflor* appears to have furnished a few details for the marvelous orchard in the "Joy of the Court" episode. The fashion, set by the romances of antiquity and especially by the *Eneas,* Chrétien followed with sumptuous descriptions of clothing, art objects, and horses, not, however, without caricaturing their extravagance. But the Ovidian depiction of love characteristic of the *Eneas* is not retained, nor is direct imitation of Ovid discernible in the *Erec,* though it may be possible to compare the poem of *Piramus et Tisbé,* adapted from the *Metamorphoses,* with Enide's apostrophe to death, just before her attempted suicide. The surest indication of Chrétien's clerical formation remains the mention of Macrobius, a reference that authenticates the allegorical figures representing the arts of the *quadrivium* embroidered on Erec's coronation robe. But all these borrowings are really insignificant, considering the *matière* of the romance.

For a number of reasons, it may be assumed that Chrétien found nearly all this "matter" in his principal source. His prologue (vv. 13-22) shows that he did not equate with his inspiring "tale of adventure" the formless rhapsodies of professional storytellers, for what the *jongleurs* usually "mutilate and spoil" must have been a story already somewhat coherent, one from which Chrétien could "derive" *(tret)* his "pleasing argument" *(molt bele conjointure)*. Since he has a sense of propriety in his use of words, if he *derives* from the "tale" an arrangement superior in his view, it follows that the tale must have subsumed all or nearly all the elements of this arrangement—like a program in outline. This perspective will clarify the debated relationship between the *Erec* and the pseudo-Mabinogion *Gereint*. Detailed comparison, by episodes, of the two works would lend support to the most widely held hypothesis that the Welsh narrative is not dependent on Chrétien's romance, and that both the *Erec* and the *Gereint* rely upon a common source which, in all probability, is no other than the "tale of adventure" mentioned by Chrétien. The Welsh author does not seem to deviate from his model, for his romance presents a series of episodes roughly analogous to that in the *Erec,* though without the flourish of Chrétien's *conjointure,* that "pleasing argument" which our poet could have "derived" in fact either from the *Gereint* itself *or* from the "tale of adventure." But it is quite implausible that the *Gereint* author diligently imitated the *Erec* yet deliberately chose to eliminate its *conjointure.* By contrast with the *Gereint,* Chrétien's romance is organized into three phases (a main feature of the *conjointure*), an arrangement at times stilted and oversuccinct. Nevertheless, Chrétien's "argument" is more "pleasing" and more original because it introduces a psychological development and a *sen* within a series of superficially treated adventures or anecdotes.

There has been much discussion of the motivation behind Erec's impetuous resolution undertaken at his awakening caused by Enide's tearful lament. Obviously, Chrétien the allusive poet-romancer never unveils everything for his audience. But if we read him attentively, the conduct of his characters is not really obscure, and it appears that the conflict, or discord, or misunderstanding which separates the couple is masterfully developed by means of logical, harmonious, and moral nuances. In this drama of delicate technique, all is well-ordered. Exaggerating her own responsibility for her husband's supposed fall, Enide is modest and fearful; she allows herself to harbor, under the pressure of public opinion, doubts which would probably have vanished had she believed possible an open discussion with Erec. Her unenterprising, naive attitude is already apparent in the *premier vers,* an example of the psychological *conjointure* between the beginning and the middle phase of the romance.

Determining Erec's quick decision are quite simple, diverse, yet interrelated reasons. The hero's pride, his knightly honor, is deeply wounded; and his self-esteem is assuaged by means of an impersonal manner and imperious curtness, for he is all the more incensed as he realizes how appropriate in fact are the reproaches: "'Lady, you were in the right, and those who blame me do so with reason'" (Roques, ed., vv. 2572-73). Nothing intensifies more our dissatisfaction with ourselves and our desire for rehabilitation (even at the expense of others) than legitimate criticism when we least expect it. Thus Erec also doubted Enide's love, not because of jealousy or suspicions of infidelity (as in the *Gereint*). Rather, based on Enide's vexing words perceived while he was half-asleep, on her troubled reticence, and on the forced explanation, he concludes that she too has underestimated his valor, that she has let herself be influenced by others, and that she has failed to love him enough. The possibility of a flaw in their price-less love is inconceivable to him. To abolish this refined torment, whether it be justified or in vain, he resolves immediately, obeying the exigencies of his heart and of his mind, to "try" Enide, i.e., to test her. Over and above these transparent motives there is a tacit medieval subtlety, namely, the notion that it is the husband who dominates in marriage. Enide has echoed the reproach of *recreantise,* she has complained of being wronged herself, she has in a way set herself up as a victim by prescribing (instead of advising) the rehabili-tation which, in her eyes, her spouse should undertake at once. In so doing, she not only made a blunder (which she might have remedied with a more astute use of words), but, more seriously, she has committed an error, an act of overweening pride. Therefore, from one point of view, not necessarily ours, Erec has the prerogative to decide that his conjugal "sovereignty" has been placed in question, thus justifying Enide's purgatory of obedience.

It may be wondered whether there is a contradiction between such an act of "sovereignty" and Erec's remark to Enide in the reconciliation scene: "'From this time on evermore, I offer myself to do your will just as I used to do before'" (Roques, ed., vv. 4888-90). Such words as these clearly reveal that Chrétien intended to add a courtly element to his conception of conjugal love; and however subtle an intention, we should not be misled into suspicions of inconsistency with regard to his thinking or to his hero's behavior. In no way does Erec abdicate his supremacy as a spouse or as a knight by promising to obey Enide. Now thoroughly convinced of Enide's devotion, he expresses to her anew his absolute confidence in her and in her love, knowing her, as he does, unable to give any advice that conflicts with his dignity, honor, and prowess, knowing her, moreover, capable of any sacrifice. It is through an act of free will ("'I offer myself to do your will'" [v. 4890]) that he pardons her and allows himself finally to consider Enide not only his spouse, but also his courtly lover and "lady." If he is thus profoundly moved to tenderness, he also exercises his privilege of "sovereignty," for evermore secure that he will be *perfectly* loved.

The departure for adventure is, then, at once a test and a quest for proof. Apparently paradoxical, Erec's harshness in fact attests to the depth and quality of his love. Had he simply thought to punish Enide, would he have asked King Lac to protect and watch tenderly over her, should she return a widow from the perilous voyage? Had he intended only to humiliate her, would he have ordered her, with a bit of elegance and boldness, even somewhat quixotically, to wear her most beautiful dress?[10] Enide considers herself guilty and obeys in docility. But, posting on ahead, she repeatedly sees threats of danger and expresses her anguish in deliberative monologues (the only type in the romance); and in every instance her love overcomes her dread of displeasing Erec, in every instance she breaks the silence imposed by him. Erec is not vexed by her obedience, but is in fact much happier when she disobeys, for her disobedience proves her love, a love that grows greater the more she sees the hero's extraordinary prowess: "'I knew indeed,'" she says to herself, "'that my lord was a most valiant knight, but now I know it better'" (Roques, ed., vv. 3104–3107). Some slight doubt had indeed arisen in her mind, but from one adventure to the next, her loyalty is so perfectly attested, her devotion so absolute, that Erec is reassured of her perfect love. And when the four dramatic and exemplary days are over, joy and prowess are prefigured harmoniously in the couple's reconciliation.

With *Erec and Enide,* Chrétien learned to depict delicate sentiments; yet such a remark cannot fully rate his talent, for even his secondary characters are sketched with bold, realistic, and vivid strokes. The numerous figures surrounding Erec and Enide comprise a lively spectrum, a human comedy in miniature. Arthur is a jovial, spirited king who decides, Gawain notwithstanding, to hunt the white hart, yet his benevolent character has another side: prodigal but showy, courteous but affected, he still remains the majestic sovereign, aware that he reflects an ideal civilization; Queen Guenevere, elegant, playful, alert, and very inquisitive, entertains graciously; Gawain is the noble, sensible, well-mannered, and tactful liege; the seneschal Kay, punctilious, pretentious, yet relaxed, a zealot who is punished disdainfully by Erec; Yder the haughty keeps his word though sobered by defeat; Enide's father, the poor, unfortunate vavasor, glories in his daughter's consoling love; Guivret is the unwavering friend and warrior; Mabonagrain is candid and scrupulous in his chains of love. There are, moreover, the two somehow similar yet different counts, set aglow by Enide's beauty; or those marauding knights who, at the sight of Enide and Erec, boldly divide the booty beforehand. Many other characters, sometimes just walk-ons, are all quickly and confidently delineated.

By themselves, the human drama and the double misunderstanding, filled with nuance and violence, by which the couple's bliss is threatened, then confirmed, cannot fully sum up the *sen* of the romance: *Erec* also offers illustrations of practical morality and ideal models of life. If he is to be a king, a distinguished knight must not languish in the delights of *recreantise,* even during his honeymoon; rather he must become more and more conscious of his mission, still guarding against sterile prowess. The woman's formation is no less important. As helpmate but especially as the beloved who inspires valor,[11] she must dispose of all pride, all egotism, must be self-effacing and self-sacrificing. It can also be asserted that in his first Arthurian romance Chrétien offered an apology for the marriage of love, something quite original in view of the many courtly notions in vogue. The tender, reciprocal confidence of the couple is treated poetically, yet Chrétien teaches here a lesson of equilibrium between love and the active life: love embellishes life, but it must not encompass all of life like a destructive passion. The marriage of Erec and Enide differs as much from Mabonagrain's romantic and antisocial involvement with the girl in the enchanted orchard as it does from the fatal obsession and deceit of Tristan and

Iseut. Chrétien holds out finally that the true hero even after he has surpassed others, must surpass himself.

These various meanings are not contradictory but complementary;
Chrétien did not formulate a precise thesis but was content to solicit
the concurrence of the reader's imagination—an original conception in
the art of romance.

But the charm of *Erec and Enide* has even further merits, like the
alert, high-toned style, which is sublimely balanced most often by an
easy restraint, animated with zest, and guided by the pulse of a supple,
expressive versification. To accompany the spirited narrative, there is a
brilliant variety of scenes and decors. Tonal changes sustain our interest,
renew or attune an emotion, then, without intervals, lead naturally
from a pathetic situation to a happy ending, though counterpointed
with comic relief. For example, there is the series of incidents in which
Erec, whom everyone thought deceased, awakens at the appropriate
moment from his swoon and tears Enide from the clutches of Count
Limors; with a single blow he decapitates the villien, takes advantage of
the mass confusion and exits into the courtyard of the castle, seizes a
horse being led to a trough by a boy, leaps into the saddle, pulls Enide
up to the withers and flees with her, just before their moonlight reconciliation. All this is mindful of a performance à la Alexandre Dumas,
followed by a delicious hush as the two hearts appease their torment
and consent to happiness. A thread of colorful humor and tender irony
runs through the romance but does not alter our admiration for the
hero or for the heroine.

By mixing the imaginary and the real, the Arthurian fiction is also
favorable to the tonal diversity, while, at the same time, granting access,
nearly imperceptibly, from fantasy to ideal model. The legendary world
of Britain, which Chrétien did not invent but to which he could allude,
was sufficiently known then to allow such playfulness; Chrétien himself
was doubtless incredulous enough of its mysteries to disport himself,
at the beginning of the *premier vers,* at the expense of King Arthur, by
ingeniously entrusting to Gawain the witty criticism of the theme
Chrétien himself was using: the custom of the white hart and the kiss
for the most beautiful woman. However much he may toy with it,
Chrétien's attitude toward the *matière de Bretagne*, more lighthearted

than Wace's rude skepticism, neither challenges its existence nor breaks its inviting trance. Beguiled by the unusual, Chrétien still artfully attenuates the marvelous and tempers the specious logic of myth by means of a narrative gratuitousness natural in all Arthurian subjects. In this way a poetic universe emerges, liberated in part from space and time, open to fantasy without denying human truths, a world of tradition, fixed or unstable, which thus takes on a subtle freshness, a newness surely easier to feel than to encompass exactly. Perhaps something of the Celtic enchantment abides even in Chrétien's literary craft, in the surprises, or in his faintly enigmatic narrative. Perhaps the rare atmosphere of tamed magic was interiorized, plunging to the heart of the characters, and infused either Erec's amorous wonder as he brings his fiancée to the court, or imbued that joyful metamorphosis experienced by Enide upon removing her white linen garment and putting on the magnificent tunic and mantle presented by Guenevere. All this suggests that the legendary far-off days, the splendid utopia of King Arthur hold forth an appealing perspective, capable of reflecting the *sen*—an ideal image of chivalrous and courtly civilization—capable too of setting Arthurian fiction in the direction of the philosophical novel.

At his coronation, Erec wore a lustrous robe on which four fairy princesses had embroidered in gold the symbols of the *quadrivium:* geometry, arithmetic, music, and astronomy. This implies that his royalty, like that of Arthur himself who presided at the coronation, will embrace culture and the disciplines of the mind. Among the elite of courtly society there was a deep-lying tendency to envisage and yearn for the union of learning and chivalry, a dream potentially attainable in Arthur's court where flourished polite conventions, elegant conduct, and generous prowess.

Although this intellectual vista is only glimpsed, it represents the highest form of that aristocratic civilization whose glorious image Chrétien has caught with a rare match of decorative effects—glistening gems and armor, gleaming gold, sumptuous materials, priceless furs, chairs of ivory, court ceremonies, feasts and tournaments—all luxuriously enjoyed not so much for their price as for their artifice. Like the often-repeated detail of the high castle galleries, whose windows open onto the exterior, they correspond to a world view embellished by widened horizons. The excitement of a period of renewal adds a sparkle to Chrétien's romance; reading it rather than abstract, theoretical debates will help us understand that there truly was a renaissance in the twelfth century.

One word and one theme, in harmony with renaissances and the works they inspire, capture the youthfulness of *Erec et Enide: joy*. The frequency of the word, the thematic variations, add a second *conjointure* to the disposition of episodes. Joys of love, balmy courtship, ecstasies of marriage, lost joy, joy regained, familial joy in the vavasor's home, crowds rejoicing, savage joy of falcons, collective joy, and Erec's mysterious joy at the castle of Brandigan: "Nothing could keep me from going on a quest for joy" (Roques, ed., vv. 5556-57). Arising at once from magical otherworld myths and from troubadour lyrics, the word here resounds powerfully, signifying man's conquest of his own happiness. Chrétien boasted legitimately that his story would not be forgotten as long as Christendom endured: *Erec et Enide* orchestrated a totally new tonality.

Chapter 4

Cligés

By contrast with *Erec and Enide, Cligés*—persuasively dated to 1176 by A. Fourrier—represents a significant change in Chrétien's spirit and manner: it is his most concerted, most cerebral and theoretical work, and in a way most amusing, in spite of or perhaps because of its deliberate artifice.

For the moment, Chrétien leaves the *matière de Bretagne,* or, more exactly, it is fused with a tale of Graeco-oriental character, whose action moves from Constantinople to England ("which was called Britain in those days," v. 17), then from England to Greece, not to mention the events taking place in Germany. The Arthurian coloring is thus tinged with hues of Byzantium.

Cligés is also more realistic, less like a fairy tale, although it still contains a number of implausibilities, such as unusual, magical philtres which, while not specifically marvelous, keep the plot from lapsing. On the other hand, without quite being a *roman à clefs,* there is some correlation between the narrative and several incidents associated with the courts of Byzantium, Germany, France, and Champagne. The names of Greek characters, for example, approach Hellenistic ones, and, replacing the unspecific, poetic Arthurian kingdom of Logres, there are authentic topographical indications, like England itself and its well known cities of Southampton, Winchester, Dover, Canterbury, and Windsor.

Unlike *Erec et Enide,* in which sentiments are hardly examined, *Cligés* illustrates Chrétien's interest in the psychology of love, especially nascent love. His characters examine themselves and their conflicting motives; they struggle, surrender, suffer, aspire, check their aims, and rationalize their passions—meticulous analyses that are nevertheless tedious and pedantic, dallying in the precious—a manner refurbished by Chrétien to vie with the courtly love lyric, with Ovid, with the *Eneas* author, with Benoît of Sainte-Maure, and even with Thomas of England's *Tristan.*

Indeed, *Cligés* is most unusual insofar as it offers an intrinsic reply to the *Tristan*, the famous story transformed to accommodate new courtly values, but toward which Chrétien took a critical, if not hostile attitude, apparent as early as *Erec and Enide,* and (though indeterminate in the lost tale about *King Mark and Iseut the Blond*)perhaps even in the love poem (of uncertain date). In these works, *fine amor* is conceived of as voluntary and freely chosen, in conflict with fatal passion— symbolized by the philtre. These references and allusions were directed ostensibly at the earliest *Tristan,* i.e., the archetype, or some other form of the so-called *version commune.* But it appears that it was Thomas's version, probably dating from 1170-75, that prompted the protest of *Cligés.* (There is another view, unfounded, speculating that *Cligés* and even the *Lancelot* were composed before Thomas's poem.) For a web of reasons, Chrétien, the concerned moralist, the psychologist, the romancer, faintly annoyed by another's success, probably felt at this point the need for a total rebuttal to stow Tristan and Iseut once and for all, a circumstance that *may* explain the very special character of *Cligés,* the slightly parodoxical counterpoint in its elaboration, and, at the same time, its gratuitous complexion. An "anti-*Tristan,*" affirm some critics, no, a "hyper-*Tristan,*" reply others. Why be reticent? *Cligés* is an "anti-*Tristan*" by reason of its apparently polemical intent, a "hyper-*Tristan*" by its striving, but it is best considered as a revised and corrected version, a "neo-*Tristan.*"

Doubtless mirroring the redaction by Thomas, Chrétien's romance is bipartite, presenting first the heroic love story of the father, then that of the son. The first part, a little more than a third of the work in length (2,382 lines), relates how Alexander, the eldest son of the emperor of Constantinople, comes to Britain and to Arthur's court, falls in love with Gawain's sister, Soredamors (i.e., "blond from love"), wins her affections, and marries her. While traveling across the sea together on the royal ship, with the king, to Brittany, their love is born, although they keep their feelings to themselves, revealed only in long monologues, for she is proud and modest, he too timid. But now Arthur must return to his kingdom and punish the traitor to whom he had entrusted the throne, Count Angrès of Guinesores (Windsor). Armed as a knight, Alexander wins laurels at the siege of Windsor castle, refuge of the traitor whom the brilliant Alexander imprisons. Between encounters he goes to the queen's tent to pay mute court to Soredamors; there he learns in ecstasy that woven with the golden threads in his shirt is one of the girl's hairs, but neither this revelation nor his own prowess rally him to a declaration of love. However, the wise and good Guenevere, guessing their secret, expedites matters, assists in the exchange of vows, and the wedding is finally celebrated in great merriment. Fourteen months later, Soredamors gives birth to Cligés, a product of Greek and British strains.

In the second part of the romance, we are at first transported to Constantinople. Upon the death of the Greek emperor, his youngest son Alis (a diminutive of Alexis), heeding the false reports of Alexander's death, seizes the throne. Returning to Greece with his wife and son, Alexander consents to relinquish the crown, provided his brother, Alis, swears never to marry and accepts Cligés as his heir. Shortly thereafter, Alexander falls sick and dies, soon followed by his faithful spouse, Soredamors, thus setting the stage for the story of Cligés.

Yielding to evil counsel, the emperor Alis asks and receives the hand of Fenice, daughter of the German emperor, though she is betrothed to the duke of Saxony. The wedding is celebrated at Cologne. But when Fenice and Cligés see each other and exchange glances—she a paragon of beauty, he a strapping youth of fifteen—love unites them. Fenice finds the forced marriage hateful and confides in her nurse, Thessala, skilled in necromancy: "'. . . I grieve and am sorrowful; for he who has won my heart is the nephew of him whom I must take'" (vv. 3139-41). But she has no intention of behaving like Iseut and is revolted by the very thought of belonging to two men: "'*Ja n'i avra deus parceniers./ Qui a le cuer, si ait le cors.*'" ("'Never will my body be portioned out between two shareholders. Who has the heart has the body, too'"—vv. 3162-63).

Thessala seizes the occasion to prepare a philtre of lasting strength, by which Fenice will avoid Iseut's fate: the emperor, who drinks it at the nuptial feast, will only possess Fenice in his dreams; he will believe himself awake while plunged in a deep sleep, and he will never have his sport with anything but an illusion, a fiction.

The Greeks, with their new empress, en route to Constantinople, near Regensburg on the Danube, grapple with the Saxons. Cligés scores a success, bravely delivering Fenice, abducted by twelve enemy knights, and then, in single combat, subdues the duke of Saxony himself. But, fearing to offend his diffident beloved—of whose true feelings he is ignorant—and morally scrupulous, Cligés dares not declare his love; rather, filled with melancholy, he makes his way to King Arthur's court for a final test of his chivalrous valor. Taking his leave of the empress, he utters a polite formula (or a disguised vow?), saying he is "altogether hers" (v. 4327), a *word* to nourish Fenice's amorous torment and hope during his long absence. Cligés carries the day in every joust at the tournament in Oxford, then pursues success in England, in France, and in Normandy, still bearing a memory of Fenice. Overcome by an invincible nostalgia, he returns to Greece, sees again his beloved, and speaks to her each day, yet still concealing his thought until the right moment when, metaphorically, each of them finds out the truth about the other.

Learning of the emperor's dreamlike illusions, Cligés suggests to Fenice that they flee to Britain. But she protests, refusing to imitate Tristan and Iseut and become a worthless example of scandal. Rather she would feign death and be entombed, so that Cligés could steal her away by night; then they would retreat together and live joyfully in secret. The plan is carried out; Thessala gives her mistress a potion that produces for a day and a night all the appearance of death, so much so that she is impervious to the torture of three skeptical doctors from Salerno. From the tomb Cligés rescues her and they escape to the comfort and luxury of a marvelously constructed vault beneath a tower. Although Fenice is slow to recover, causing Cligés great anxiety, the lovers finally enjoy a guiltless, scandal-free bliss.

Some fifteen months go by when, one spring day, Fenice hears a nightingale sing and wishes to see the sunlight and moonlight, to breathe again the fresh air. Then, a secret door opens, revealing a delightful, splendid, enclosed orchard, in the midst of which appears a beautiful spreading grafted tree, in the shape of a cradle, a sanctuary that will preserve the lovers until the day they are detected—by a hunter whose sparrowhawk lights in the orchard. Thus the emperor learns the truth. Cligés and Fenice manage to break away and, protected once more by Thessala's enchantments, flee to Britain. Fenice, of course, has come to resemble Iseut, but Chrétien has taken care of that: Emperor Alis is taken off by rage. Cligés and Fenice finally return in glory to Constantinople where they are joined forever in a never-ending love, Fenice thus becoming at once the beloved, lady, and spouse of Cligés.

Of the various sources assembled for this complex plot, the kernel, if only for the second part, is the theme of feigned death, which Shakespeare used in *Romeo and Juliet.* Derived from the Orient, it was best known in the medieval West as an incident in the history of Solomon's wife (cf. Chrétien's allusion, vv. 5876-78). The particular version Chrétien used and claimed to have found in a book, doubtless some Latin chronicle, in the cathedral library of Saint Peter of Beauvais, must have closely resembled the vapid account found in a thirteenth-century episodic romance called the *Marques de Rome* (cf. vv. 18-23). While later than and independent of Chrétien's *Cligés,* this brief story tells of a nephew of the Greek emperor named Cligés, lover of the anonymous empress, and of their adultery (but without the recourse to love philtres or to the ruse of feigned death). In this story, then, Chrétien would have been struck by the similarity in situation to the *Tristan*—a nephew in love with his uncle's wife. From this triangular affair, from this essentially *fabliau*-like situation, paradoxically Chrétien constructed his courtly "neo-*Tristan*."

To flesh out the scenario of the first part, Chrétien seems to have recalled, for the treason of Count Angrès, that of Mordred in Wace's account (*Brut,* Arnold, ed., vv. 13010-274). Beyond this broad parallel, the two texts betray resemblances of detail, even though, after close comparison, Chrétien emerges as a skilled adaptor, especially in his original handling of Guenevere's role. Chrétien probably found the suggestion for the betrothal of a Greek emperor with a German princess in certain historical events, like the gainless plans Frederick Barbarossa set forth between 1170 and 1174 to negotiate a matrimonial and political alliance with the Greek emperor, Manuel Comnenus. Such ingenious allusions by Chrétien to quite current affairs would not be missed by the well-informed audience gathered at the enlightened court of Champagne.

Other influences affected not so much the plot arrangement as the treatment of love. From Ovid may be derived the playful but formal description of the surprises of the heart, the metaphors of the tyrant-god, his arrows, his flame, and his stratagems, and the enumeration of the physical and moral symptoms of nascent love. These Ovidian themes had already been exploited and codified by French courtly romancers, like the *Eneas* author, whose influence on Chrétien is in fact unmistakable, especially the way he used monologues as a means of psychological analysis; likewise Fenice's precursor is Lavine, in that they both refuse to belong to two men (*Eneas*, Salverda de Grave, ed., *CFMA*, vv. 8301-4: "There must be no other partner but he alone."). In *Cligés,* however, Chrétien surpasses the *Eneas* through his use of a highly romantic psychology, a kind of love casuistry, carrying yet farther the play of metaphors toward preciosity, thus displaying a personal inclination for virtuosity—perhaps under the influence of Provençal lyric. Moreover, *Cligés* also reveals a debt to Benoît de Sainte-Maure's *Roman de Troie,* more advanced in its conceptions of *fine amor* than is the *Eneas.*[1]

Chrétien's imitation of the *Tristan* (both the "common version" and Thomas's romance) is manifest in the psychological configurations of *Cligés.* For example, there are numerous echos, whether subtle or insistent, clever or awkward, like the golden hair motif, the word play on *l' amer* and *la mer* (vv. 545-63), Thessala's fateful philtres, the subterranean palace, the orchard, and the beautiful tree with cradle-shaped foliage. Other similarities of detail can be noted, even if some passages seem polemic in nature, aimed at Thomas in particular. Certain little dissertations on the nature of love, somewhat artificial, are interesting as efforts to develop a vocabulary of psychological analysis. Thus, for instance, Chrétien contradicts those who speak figuratively of the hearts of two lovers joined in one body; for him the exchange of hearts is explained in fact by the union of two wills, better illustrated by his ingenious musical metaphor of two voices singing in unison (vv. 2817-54).

Although *Cligés* is essentially courtly in spirit, these various borrowings Chrétien combined to expound a *sen* obviously hostile to the *Tristan* and to certain notions of courtly love. Cligés and Fenice do not drink from the same cup as Tristan and Iseut, for Chrétien makes of the philtre not a *lovedrinc*, but only something to impede or give the illusion of love, something drunk, it should be remembered, without any fatal error *and* by the intended person, Emperor Alis. This is a spirited change, less moving than witty. But then, must love depend on a magic potion against the lovers' wills? In contrast to Iseut, Fenice preserves a purely feminine claim for free choice in love. Menaced by the same destiny, she refuses to behave like Iseut, who, thinks Fenice, set a bad example in not protecting her good name (cf. vv. 3145-49, 5251-52, 5309-16). But Fenice is more scandalized by Tristan's lover than by King Mark's wife. Iseut's duty was to remain faithful to Tristan and reject her shameful lot, repudiating any division between her body and her heart.

"I could never bring myself to lead the life that Iseut led. Such love as hers was far too base; for her body belonged to two whereas her heart was possessed by one. Thus all her life was spent, refusing her favours to neither one. But mine is fixed on one object, under no circumstances will there be any sharing of my body and heart. Never will my body be portioned out between two shareholders. Who has the heart has the body, too, and may bid all others stand aside."[2]

Iseut was enslaved to fatality; Fenice will struggle to remain free of exterior impediments and in full control of her destiny, thus creating the conditions for happiness through her autonomous love and will— behavior which lies outside of social and religious norms and is, there- fore, akin to the courtly ethic. This spiritual daughter of Chrétien re- sembles a stout defender of such an ethos: perfectionist in love, ready to forsake the splendor of the emperor's court, bold enough to face a humble existence or the terrors of entombment, if only she can remain with the man she loves (and who loves her, vv. 5346-60). Fenice appears as a heroine of inner freedom. In her dwells a consciousness of love, of its rights and its duties. By means of her sham death, she is delivered from a life of sham, for she dies to the world and is reborn to her true life, like the phoenix adumbrated by her name. Chrétien's intent thus reveals an abundant optimism.

However ideal or theoretical, Chrétien's solution to the problem raised by the romance of *Tristan* could only be found through perfect love as imagined in his poetic universe, realized in such a way that the discovery of the lovers' secret and the widespread repercussions of scandal cause Fenice no loss of good name. For, in the end, Emperor Alis, the court of Constantinople, and the entire world learn that in reality she belonged only to her lover and that, unlike Iseut, free from the taint of *partage,* Fenice keeps her love pure (cf. vv. 6606-21, 6631-38). No doubt Chrétien knew that his arrangement was arbitrary, that Fenice and Cligés offered improbable models of behavior, and that to use the feigned death theme itself implicitly involved an unreal example. But let us try to understand the role of playful irony in his utopic "neo-*Tristan*" (even if he did find Fenice appealing). Chrétien the moralist held in reserve another solution, already exalted in *Erec and Enide,* the marriage of love which was indeed available to Fenice, if she only dared disobey her father (v. 3169). More at ease, Alexander and Soredamors were wed by overcoming only the obstacles of their own agitation, modesty and timidity; yet their idyllic tale may also help explain indirectly the *sen* of the whole work. Early on Chrétien praises the total harmony between their hearts and bodies, and Queen Guenevere illustrates the thought when she advocates, before the engaged couple, the marriage of love (vv. 2279-310, 2340-49), an apology which, in point of fact, is not controverted at the conclusion of the romance, because, once Emperor Alis dies, Cligés and Fenice are married and "day by day their love increases" (Micha ed., v. 6639).

It may seem that Chrétien has not much altered his ideas on love and marriage set forth in *Erec and Enide,* but, characteristically, he innovates with *Cligés* by reinforcing the lovers' courtly scruples, their respectful devotion, and their sense of love service. Erec asks for Enide's hand though completely ignorant of her feelings; Alexander and Cligés dare to ask for nothing until assured of having won the beloved's heart. This moral delicacy is accompanied by an art of analysis just as delicate, another revelation of Chrétien's talent, for now the interior life of his characters is described and explained. However tormented by passion, Alexander and Soredamors, Cligés and Fenice question and deliberate within themselves, oscillating between passive states and active meditations, an ebb and flow which Chrétien deftly handles, though not without a nuance of witty (yet still sympathetic) detachment.

In this regard, the monologues deserve special attention. The method, a recent development in courtly romance, may be traced to Ovid and perhaps to the influence of lyric poetry. In the earliest romance of antiquity, the *Thebes,* monologues are rare and brief, but the *Eneas* and *Troy* romances, and Thomas's *Tristan,* offer longer, more interesting ones. In Chrétien's works, the use of monologues is found only in embryo in the *Philomena,* but his *Erec* contains a number of vigorous, dramatic ones, all uttered by Enide. At one point she accuses herself of causing her husband's *recreantise* and laments her indiscretion; in another place she wonders during the voyage for adventure whether she must remain silent each time Erec is threatened by danger; elsewhere she mourns over her unconscious, apparently dead hero. These monologues are partly lyrical, partly deliberative, not without psychological interest, but they are neither analytic nor soliloquies on love.

By contrast, the monologues of *Cligés* reveal Chrétien's interest in probing the nature of love, analysis no doubt borrowed—but practiced more skillfully—from the *Tristan* of Thomas and the *Eneas.* Sailing toward Armorica with Alexander, Soredamors, up to now "scornful of love," feels her pride yielding to the impingements of tender feelings; she first apostrophizes in a subtle manner her anxious surprise; then, after addressing her eyes, obviously in the high style, she yearns to dominate the contradictions of her heart, as may be judged from what follows, faithful to the alternating inner confusion: "'My eyes, you have betrayed me now! My heart, usually so faithful, now bears me ill will because of you. Now what I see distresses me. Distresses?'" (Such repetition by interrogation is one of Chrétien's frequent procedures, recurring several times in this monologue alone.)

"Nay, verily, rather do I like it well. . . . Can I not control my eyes? My strength must indeed have failed, and little should I esteem myself, if I cannot control my eyes and make them turn their glance elsewhere. Thus, I shall be able to baffle Love in his efforts to get control of me. . . . He addresses me no request or prayer, as he would do were he in love with me. And since he neither loves nor esteems me, shall I love him without return? What crime, then, have my eyes committed if their glance but follows my desire? . . . Ought I to blame them, then? Nay, verily. Who, then, should be blamed? Surely myself, who have them in control. . . . My heart ought not to have any desire which would give me

87

pain....If I can, I ought to banish any wish that distresses me. If I can? Mad one, what have I said? I must, indeed, have little power if I have no control over myself. Does Love think to set me in the same path which is wont to lead others astray? Others he may lead astray, but not me who care not for him. Never shall I be his, nor ever was, and I shall never seek his friendship."[3]

Soredamors, startled thus by her own confusion in this first phase, endeavors to understand herself and to safeguard her moral freedom.

Her second monologue is longer, delivered while suffering insomnia during the same sea voyage, presumably a few hours after the first (vv. 897-1046). (Intentional or not, this compression of action is mindful of that in classical drama.) Both analytical and deliberative, this new soliloquy has three parts, concluded by a choice made in complete lucidity. In the first movement (vv. 897-945), the oscillations of the one preceding seem prolonged: injuries from love, attempts to resist, arguments pro and con, and finally an unequivocal admission of love's victory ("'...and now I must follow his pleasure!'"). The second movement (vv. 946-91) constitutes a kind of vindication of free choice by the courtly lover. "'Now I am ready to love,'" asserts Soredamors, stressing the first verb: "'*I am ready* to love.'" (Emphasis added.) This freedom must be first predicated upon a desire for perfection in the art of love: "'I have a master,'" i.e., an overlord, or better, a regent, in the didactic sense of the word. Love will teach the heroine who must in a way give up her common, worldly qualities—good manners, polite attentions, accessibility—for she can be "a true friend" now only to the one she loves: love's lesson in good conduct. Then, by understanding her essence, she also earns her freedom, demonstrating to herself that her destiny is to love. Does not Soredamors mean "one gilded over with Love"? "'It is not without significance that I am called by the name of Soredamors'" (v. 962). There is little doubt of Chrétien's amusement at such gallant meanderings whereby Soredamors etymologizes her name in order to become more conscious of her destiny. It is true, of course, that her reasoning was more meaningful to a twelfth-century audience; magical beliefs still commonly recognized that a name could have an influence over an individual's character and life, for it veiled a symbolic meaning, a *senefiance*. Soredamors nevertheless concludes that she is bound to honor her name: "'Now I love and ever more shall love. Whom? Truly, that is a fine question! Him whom Love bids me love, for no other shall ever have my love.'" In the third movement (vv. 992–1046), she asks how she will find happiness, how she will inform Alexander of her love, and how she will know if she is loved in her turn. She is repelled by the shameful idea of making the first step, an action in conflict with her self-esteem and with *fine amor.* (Chrétien's emphasis here seems directed at the heroines of other romances.) Resigning herself, then, she will wait until Alexander shows his feelings, though perhaps she will be able to "lead him on by hints and covered words," by discreet allusions. (This recourse to a language of "covered words" confers a psychological support to the preciosity in *Cligés.*) But, she decides, the important thing is to love, even unrequitedly. "'If he loves me not, yet I will love him'" (v. 1046). Such is the cadence of this remarkable monologue which, for its time and form, comprises a masterpiece in miniature.

On board the same ship, during the same sleepless night, Alexander soliloquizes in his turn, much longer than both of Soredamors's monologues, yet probably the most artificial piece in the romance (vv. 625–872). Often Chrétien will speak rhetorically (or preciously) in his character's stead. It even happens that he forgets about it, as Gaston Paris noted, and addresses the audience directly: "Now I will speak to you of the arrow." From line 690, Alexander holds forth, with an uninterrupted series of metaphors, on the topic of the arrow which penetrated his heart through his eye! But, still and all, it is quite possible that these lines afforded at this time a certain pleasure not unlike ours when reading the subtleties of Proust or Giraudoux. Repeated in the beginning of the monologue is the theme of love's torment and incertitude; the obvious conclusion is that Alexander must submit to love, or rather recognize his own freedom of submission. He also avers: "'I wish it, and so it pleases me'" (v. 867). Courtly lovers will thus remain in control over their passion while ratifying love's commands and accepting its voluntary servitude.

Fenice's monologue (vv. 4410–4574) is an interior debate introduced like an exercise: "...she finds no bottom or bound to the reflections which occupy her, so abundantly are her cares multiplied." Fenice argues with herself, following the scholastic method of objections and

Chrétien de Troyes

responses to objections. While all this is somewhat ponderous, it so happens that, under the circumstances, this dialectical reasoning approximates the dialectic of the heart, causing the heroine to oscillate from doubt to hope, and vice versa. Fenice queries herself to find out if her love is really reciprocal. Her thoughts are on the sweet words that Cligés had spoken at departure for King Arthur's court—"altogether hers," *je sui toz vostre*—an equivocal revelation, offering alternatives that Chrétien easily exploited, prefacing each of them with a "but" (a logical framework). Does the farewell betray a deep passion? Is it just a polite formula, a "trite word"? Fenice weighs all the compelling evidence for Cligés' love or lack thereof. Unfortunately, the progression is broken by some precious word play on the theft of the heart by her beloved (vv. 4459-66), and especially by a fastidious sequel on hypocritical servants who flatter their masters.

Dialogue is also handled well by Chrétien, revealing his gift for the dramatic. Two scenes above all are notable for their natural, delicate continuity. One, describing the separation of Cligés and Fenice (vv. 4290-334), has yet to be written, as the author allows ("But I must have passed over something which it is not proper to omit"); the other depicts their confession of love (vv. 5157-280). Both scenes probably appealed to the aristocratic society of the time as models of worldly conversation about love. Though less felicitous, the dialogues of Fenice with her nurse at least introduce Chrétien's dramatic creation, Thessala, the confidant, missing in *Erec,* but brought to perfection in medieval romance with the character Lunete in *Yvain.*

In the final analysis, Chrétien here lays the basis for the French classical tradition even while meandering with mere preciosities which— and this is a feature so far mostly ignored—are treated humorously. Chrétien's ease with dazzling metaphors, his efforts to develop a psychological vocabulary, his fondness for variety and flexibility in his forms of analysis, though revealing some slight strain, nevertheless distinguish him as a master of brisk narration and brilliant description.[4]

Cligés must be considered particularly as an exercise in literary virtuosity. Let us at least credit Chrétien for imagining a heroine morally superior to Iseut. But he did miss the human and tragic truth of the *Tristan,* of which, in this sense, his modification implies a distortion. It is comparable to the grafted pear tree in the orchard, the shelter for

Cligés and Fenice, with its branches skillfully pruned downward by a gardener in the shape of a screen. This elegant image of courtly artifice contrasts significantly with the *bel arbre,* the bower in the forest of Morois, spreading forth naturally, and which, in Thomas's version, shaded Tristan and Iseut. By means of Chrétien's "neo-*Tristan,*" the forest is transformed into a garden of delights.

Chapter 5

Lancelot or Le Chevalier de la Charrette

So far as we know, Chrétien chose in complete freedom the subjects of *Erec* and *Cligés,* but in the prologue of his next romance (begun perhaps after starting to work on *Yvain*), he stated explicitly that he obeyed the "command" of countess Marie de Champagne and that she alone decided upon its "subject matter" and "controlling purpose" *(matière et sen).* One might say that, even though adroitly complimenting his patroness, he seems to be carefully excusing himself for both. It is surprising also that he entrusted to Godefroi de Lagny the composition of the last 1,000 lines. The current view (since G. Paris and Foerster) is that Chrétien lacked enthusiasm or that he followed the countess's instructions (however capricious) with reluctance. Thus certain weaknesses in his composition and lapses in his style may be justified by constraint and prescription. But received opinion has especially attempted to explain the contradiction between Lancelot's courtly behavior insofar as it glorifies adultery and the character of Chrétien's other romances; after all, the *Lancelot* is a sort of palinode, a recantation of *Tristan* and *Cligés.*

However favorable an interpretation, let us not imagine that the task imposed upon Chrétien produced a great struggle of conscience, for, when he abandoned it (line 7125), the essential purpose was already accomplished, even if some of his personal ideas were not expressed.[1]

But for at least part of the work, Chrétien proudly declared (vv. 27–29) that he had devoted his intellectual and artistic ability *(peine, entencion)* to the performance (in which *his* input was limited, but we should not be misled by a conventional compliment to a countess). Doubtless his alert poetic efforts would involve both a superior rendering of language and verse, as well as the disposition of the narrative and of the psychology of his characters—in a word, everything implied in his work by the term *conjointure.* Possibly Chrétien was even challenged or enticed by the difficulties of the subject—a splendid one—presented to him by the countess. It would not be necessary then to resort to sentimental reasons and speculate that Marie de Champagne was truly his "lady" in the courtly sense. Clearly, a concern for his reputation served as a stimulant: the internal contradictions alone presented a nearly insurmountable obstacle.

How, indeed, could he render credible a hero who was at the same time the model of physical prowess and energy and a lover ecstatically submissive to an all-powerful divinity? How to transfer with delicacy, from lyric to narrative, the troubadour concept of extramarital, or rather, contramarital love? Any elements that had profited the troubadour poets, of the emotional state, the allusive, the thematic, had to be amplified and harmonized to accòrd with the requirements of the narrative. Yet another difficulty lies in the essential clash between the author's moralistic tendencies, his penchant for characters who are free agents and dominate their fate, and an immoral *sen,* immoral not so much because it approves adultery, but especially because it idealizes the mystical enslavement of the lover.

Whatever his motives, it would appear that Chrétien sought to unify and ennoble the materials provided, although perhaps he permitted himself some occasional compensation for the hyperfeminism in the very thesis provided by his protectress. In this category, one may suspect certain ironic, even caricatural exaggerations. But *The Knight of the Cart* is an enchanting poem, and Chrétien no doubt accepted the proposed task without reservation. Esthetic restraints have their reward. The "command" of the countess obviously dictated conditions analogous to the disciplines of art. Yielding to it meant diminished originality but greater depth of subject. Chrétien apparently found tempting a method that would force him to exteriorize, to put aside personal feelings and capture, as a perspicacious and relatively disinterested observer, the hindsight necessary for a more objective depiction of feelings and characters. By this effort he achieved brilliant success in establishing the hero-type who for centuries endured in popular favor and who rivaled the romantic fortunes of Tristan. However objective a creation, Lancelot is still Chrétien's most subjective character. As if monolithic, guided by one inner image, he is acted upon and he acts in a mysterious universe inhabited by certain conceptions of the Celtic otherworld, themselves strangely mingled with elements of realism which in fact increase, rather than diminish, the poetic distance needed above all to span the author's personal morality.

On Ascension Day Arthur is holding court in Camelot. Suddenly, a stranger knight arrives with a challenge for the king: if he will risk Guenevere under escort of some bold champion who may win her in single combat, he (i.e., Meleagant) will release many of Arthur's subjects now held as captives. No one dares accept his challenge, except Kay. Because of a rash boon granted by Arthur, the presumptuous seneschal obtains the custody of the queen for the fearful mission—much to the consternation of the court. Guenevere is filled with anxiety, but, while mounting her palfrey, whispers allusively about someone who would not, if he knew, allow her be treated in this way. Only a certain Count Guinable overhears her, but his overwhelming discretion drives him henceforth from the plot of the story. Inevitably, Kay is vanquished and both he and the queen are taken away as prisoners. Rushing off in pursuit of the abductor, Gawain—along with two squires who each lead an extra charger—soon overtakes Lancelot, incognito, who rides faltering on a broken-down mount. At his request, Gawain lends him a fresh horse, and Lancelot returns to the fray at a gallop. When Gawain overtakes him again, he first finds the horse dead as a result of a heated struggle, then Lancelot himself, following on foot, behind a cart driven by a dwarf. Thus begins the quest for the queen.

Lancelot du Lac, the knight on foot, whose identity is later revealed, asks the dwarf if he saw the queen pass by. The dwarf answers: "'If thou wilt get up into the cart I am driving thou shalt hear tomorrow what has happened to the queen'" (Roques, ed., vv. 356–59). Now in those days, explains Chrétien, such carts served the same purpose as does a pillory today, that is, to convey malefactors to execution. In Lancelot's mind arises a choice between love and reason, between passion and prowess. The hero hesitates while he takes two steps before love conquers, and he leaps into the cart, symbol of dishonor. Gawain, startled, will follow but refuses the grinning dwarf's offer to ride with Lancelot.

In the evening, the "Knight of the Cart" is greeted with jeers upon arrival at a castle; but during the night, he passes successfully the test of the perilous bed and flaming lance. The next morning, lost in reverie, from a high tower window he witnesses a procession passing slowly below. It consists of a wounded knight on a litter, three mournful maidens, then, followed by a group of people, a huge knight, escorting his very beautiful captive. It is the queen. Lancelot falls into a love trance over this image (which moves off, then disappears). Without noticing the danger, he leans more and more out the window, unconsciously wishing to fall (vv. 569–71). Gawain saves him in time and drags him back in. To the insulting remark by the damsel of the tower (should not any knight who rides in a cart wish to kill himself?), Lancelot, because of his love, is impervious. However, the hostess consents to grant him a horse and a lance, and he sets out with Gawain in pursuit of the queen.

At a crossing, they meet a maiden, at whose request the two knights promise their service. She informs them that the abductor is Meleagant, son of Baudemagus, king of Gorre, the land "from whence no stranger ever returns" (v. 645). It is impossible to enter there without the king's permission, unless one chooses from three ways: by fording the black and deep rapids; by crossing the water-bridge, submerged equidistant from the surface and the bed of the river; or by traversing the narrow and sharp sword-bridge. Gawain chooses the water-bridge; to Lancelot is left a more perilous path.

The two friends separate. Lancelot rides in solitude toward the sword-bridge, completely lost in thought, unaware of his own existence, even of his name. Although he moves along quickly on the straight road (vv. 729–31), he knows not where he goes or whence he comes; he remembers no other creature in the world but her, her alone. Deaf to the challenge of a knight, the guardian of the ford, the somnambulist lets his thirsting horse enter the water. Suddenly hurled from his saddle, he is brought back to reality by the cold water, and in single combat defeats the insolent opponent, even forcing him to beg for mercy.

Lancelot, a perfect and completely faithful lover, resists the temptations of the flesh by dint of his love. Thus in the castle of a seductive and unbiased hostess, his gallant character and bravery are tested. Then, he nearly swoons as he beholds some golden tresses caught in the teeth of a comb Guenevere had left beside a fountain, relics he keeps fervidly with him, "between his shirt and his flesh" (v. 1469). The adventure of the cemetery (vv. 1841-966), where he raises up the heavy stone lid to the tomb destined for him, reveals his messianic role, designating him as the liberator of the captives "in the kingdom whence none escape." As he approaches, cries of hope go up; as he advances toward the sword-bridge, shouts of revolt. Here is an intermediary region inhabited by those exiled from the kingdom of Logres. These "prisoners" seem to lead normal lives, living in families, hunting, etc., but cannot return to their native land. With their help, Lancelot triumphs over the obstacles sown on his path to the otherworld, though he does manage to reprove several affronts to the "Knight of the Cart."

Finally the hero crosses the awful, vertiginous sword-bridge. This exploit is described in a superb passage, epic in its marvelous revelation of bravura, lyric in its exaltation of love, realistic in material detail and in the treatment of subconscious states (vv. 3021-149). On the opposite shore he does not encounter the lions—spectres of the imagination—he had thought to find there, but sees instead a mighty tower from which are leaning King Baudemagus, paragon of loyalty, and his son, the wicked Meleagant. They are further contrasted by the juxtaposition of their feelings toward Lancelot: Baudemagus admires his extraordinary prowess, Meleagant is enraged.

To no purpose the king counsels his son to surrender Guenevere, a prisoner treated honorably in spite of her abductor's lust. A single combat between Lancelot and Meleagant, the stakes of which are the liberation of the queen and of all the exiled, is joined the next day. From a window, Guenevere watches the match without the hero's knowledge. Lancelot is in a weakened state, not yet recovered from the wounds suffered on the bridge. An attendant, guessing the secret reason for his superhuman effort, asks the queen the name of her champion. "'The name of the knight, I know, is Lancelot of the Lake'" is her answer. Thus Chrétien subtly caused the name of the hero to be spoken for the first time in line 3676, through the lips of the divinity (whose lover until now has been ingeniously designated by periphrase). The happy maiden calls his attention to the queen watching from a window: "'Lancelot, turn about and see who is here taking note of thee.'" Ecstatic, he fights with his back turned to his adversary so as not to lose sight of his idol. A desperate warning from the maiden helps him to force Meleagant into a position between himself and the tower. From then on, sparked by his love, with renewed vigor, he presses him not up to the wall but exactly up to a line this side of it, from where he can still see his lady. In great ardor (the text suggests that the image of love's fire has become an inner reality), still along the ideal radius, he pushes back the crippled Meleagant, who, only through the queen's intervention (urged by Baudemagus), escapes total defeat. Chrétien has artfully disposed here a rare blend of action, description, and psychological truth.

The villainous Meleagant refuses to concede defeat, and, while obliged to surrender the queen, he hopes to force her to return to Gorre. For this reason, Lancelot consents to meet him again in combat, at Arthur's court, one year to the day after Meleagant has issued a challenge. While the exiled pay tribute to their liberator, Lancelot himself, led to the castle hall, is received by Guenevere. Unexpectedly, she treats her deliverer with coldness and scorn. Forlorn, Lancelot sets out toward the water-bridge, in quest of Gawain, but is arrested by the people of the country. At the false report of his death, the queen finally relents and reproaches herself bitterly. In a monologue, she repents for her cruelty, laments her lover, thinks of suicide, then gives way to life so to better expiate her sin (vv. 4215–62). Her sadness causes her to go without drink or food for two days. And at the word that *she* is dead, Lancelot's companions must prevent him from hanging himself.

Finally the lovers are reunited at the court of Baudemagus; Lancelot boldly requests from the queen an explanation for her reception after his victory over Meleagant. With feigned surprise she quips a teasing response, at once playfully ironic and dogmatically serious. His fault had been to hesitate two steps before mounting the cart. To his would-be confessor, the penitent lover pleads guilty, and the lady grants him total absolution, and a tête-à-tête that night, pointing to a certain window, "not with her finger but with her eye" (Roques, ed., v. 4507).

Later, Lancelot stands in the orchard below the window of the queen's chamber (which is also that of the seneschal Kay, not yet recovered from his wounds). Guenevere had promised nothing but the sweet nothings possible between the bars of the window. In amorous desire Lancelot breaks the strong, sharp iron bars that separate them, heedless of his cut hands. He enters the chamber where the seneschal is sleeping, then kneels before her as if she were a saint, "holding her more dear than the relic of any saint" (v. 4671). In the queen's bed, he receives her favors to the full, the supreme reward, the marvelous "joy...that will not be revealed by me, for in a story it has no place" (Roques ed., vv. 4677-81). At dawn he departs, straightens the iron bars, then repeats his bowing adoration at the chamber door, and returns to his lodgings.

In the morning Meleagant finds her bed stained with Lancelot's blood, but he charges her with misconduct with the wounded Kay. At this, Lancelot, carefully taking an oath, offers to defend Kay's (and the queen's!) innocence in a trial by combat. Once more he fights Meleagant, and once more he spares his life only at the intercession of Baudemagus and the queen.

He sets out to rescue Gawain, but is ambushed and imprisoned by Meleagant. Absent now from Baudemagus's court, it devolves upon Gawain, rueful survivor of the water-bridge adventure, to escort the queen and all the exiles to Logres. Lancelot will now attend the tournament of Noauz, for his jailor has permitted him to take part, once he swears to return to prison without delay (vv. 5379-6078). She even lends him vermilion arms and her absent husband's horse. At first, incognito, he eclipses all the other jousters. But Guenevere, more to reassure herself (vv. 5720-23, 5888-95) than to test gratuitously the perfect lover's obedience, conveys to him through a damsel that he must play the coward and do his "worst." Lancelot complies at this point: "he would never do anything unless he saw in it his shame, disgrace, and dishonor" (vv. 5690-91). He is thus turned to ridicule. The next day, Lancelot's response is so completely submissive that Guenevere is now certain that he belongs to her "altogether." Again at her behest, before the jousting begins, he must do his "best." Lancelot carries off the honors of the second day's contest, but, to keep his word, he returns to Gorre in secret.

This time, Meleagant has him imprisoned not far from Gorre, near a channel, in a specially devised tower. (Godefroi de Lagny's conclusion now begins, thus ending Chrétien's account here.) The doors are walled up; there is no exit but a small window through which passes each day a small allowance of food. Meleagant visits King Arthur's court and demands that the battle (decided upon earlier) take place in one year. But the swaggering scoundrel is finally reduced to a melodramatic traitor. In fact, his sister frees Lancelot, the "Knight of the Cart," who, in the final combat, happily ends the life of the villain.

The poem may be divided into two contrasting parts; the first, ending with the passage of the sword-bridge, has been severely criticized as illogically constructed and filled with improbability. The second part, on the other hand, is more coherently centered about the dramatic relations of Lancelot and Guenevere in the kingdom of Gorre, the machinations of Meleagant, and his final punishment. Filled with a plethora of reversals, mindful of *Cligés*, the plot, at times insipid yet cogent, appears to have been constructed by Chrétien himself. It is generally admitted that some debris of Celtic mythical elements, perhaps an unwieldy "tale of adventure" about a voyage to the otherworld, formed the basis for the story. However plausible a view, can anyone profess that Chrétien was so hypnotized by his imposed model that he never tried to touch up its content? On the contrary, we can count on his conscious consent to its inherent intrigue, a mysteriousness fatal neither to his art nor to his poetry. We sense also that Chrétien could control at will any diffuseness natural to such material.

The story is enhanced poetically through its seemingly fragmentary character—the adventure is selected from a legendary biography that opens with the fabled childhood of the hero (as alluded to briefly in verses 2354-62)—and its elliptical succession of darkness and light encourages the reader's complicity. Absent from *Erec* and *Cligés,* the quest motif is here gossamerlike, for it artfully suspends interpretation, offering instead an enigmatic narrative liable to provoke and retain our curiosity. The double arrangement—Lancelot at the sword-bridge, Gawain on the water-bridge—introduces not only a significant narrative antithesis, but also one of psychological import. And the prodigious adventures, however absurd at times, are in a way not incongruous with the soul of our strange, magnificent hero. In harmony with his inner thoughts, the many signs, trials, and confirmations only reveal his inimitable nature.

Thus Chrétien's case is reconstructed from within, in a manner considerably suggestive of the "pleasing argument," or "well-organized narrative," implied by *conjointure*. Whether it be a description of Lancelot's thoughts about his lady, or of his firm resolution to meet perils and prove to himself his fitness to undertake the most fearful exploit of all (vv. 874–81, 1108–116), or be it even a comment on his vigilance, while in ecstacy, over keeping to the shortest path (vv. 1373–95, 2154–69, 2278–91), the adventure is never narrated gratuitously, but, by some expedient, is nearly always inseparable from the exemplary portrait of Lancelot. Thus the quest, which risks being filled with digressions, revolves around the hero's character. The gradual effect of the episodes leading up to the sword-bridge converge upon an imposing image, a blameless knight—in a way a saint of courtly love. From this perspective, the idea of discontinuity between matter and meaning may be laid to rest, even though the unity of the romance may also gain from the queen's character or from the deft handling of her heart's passion.

Be that as it may, the plot preserves the contours of Celtic myth. A schema, closely related to the conception of the otherworld and well attested in Irish and Welsh, would present with variant forms the following pattern: A mysterious stranger claims as his own a married woman, often a fairy princess, and, either by force or by obtaining a rash promise from her husband, takes her away to his otherworld realm. The husband pursues the abductor, triumphs over obstacles, enters the impenetrable region, and wins back his wife. In Arthurian tradition before Chrétien's time, Guenevere had already been cast as the heroine of an abduction story of this type (*aithed,* "elopement" in Irish). Such appears to be the theme depicted on the bas-relief, dating probably from the first half of the twelfth century, on an archivolt at Modena cathedral (cf. ut sup., chap. 1, pp. [34–35]). If this iconographic testimony is rejected, there is the *Vita sancti Gildae (Life of Saint Gildas)* by the Welsh cleric Caradoc of Llancarvan, dated before 1136 (or around 1160, at the latest). Here we read that Melvas, king of the Summer Country, carried off Guennuvar, the wife of Arthur, to his dwelling in Glastonbury, i.e., the town of Glass *(Urbs Vitrea),* an inviolate refuge protected by swampy stretches of reeds. Then, with the intervention of the abbot of Glastonbury, Melvas returned her to Arthur without a struggle. This edifying Glastonbury version was adapted from a Welsh form of the otherworld abduction. Melvas, or rather Maelwas is a compound from the Welsh *mael*, "prince" and *gwas*, "youth"; the character is analogous to Maheloas, lord of the "Isle de Voirre," mentioned in the *Erec*.[2] And despite corruption it is recognizable in the form Meleagant (from the *Lancelot*).

The Celtic theme of the abduction and otherworld adventure subsists beneath the characteristics of twelfth-century civilization, beneath the chivalrous and courtly coloring that Chrétien, in his own right, conferred upon the tale. Yet sprinkled here and there in the *Lancelot* are expressions like "the kingdom whence no stranger returns," or "many are those caught in the trap of the realm whence no one escapes." Such motifs seem less related to Celtic matters than to conventional legends about death, whether they be popular beliefs or illustrious myths of Graeco-Roman antiquity. (Guenevere has been often compared to Persephone, Eurydice, or Alcestis.) To one of these traditions has been related the primitive meaning of the cart, which, in Chrétien's poem, symbolizes a love stronger than shame or public reproach; presumably before becoming the infamous cart, with an ethical connotation, it is supposed to have been the ancient, mythical cart of death, surviving to the present, for example in Breton folklore. (There have also been very dubious analogies suggested between the cart and the chariots in which several Irish saga heroes travel to the otherworld.) But our hypothesis remains, substantiated by the fact that Chrétien, not always concerned with coherence, maintains certain details of a traditional nature. The driver of the cart is the dwarf, a character in many legends who often has chthonian associations. At the end of the first day's quest, dwarf and cart both disappear mysteriously (v. 448); finally, there is an important adage which claims that it is an evil omen to encounter the cart: "When thou dost see and meet a cart, cross thyself and call upon God, that no evil may befall thee" (vv. 343–46). This saying egregiously conflicts with the context and with the sense of the motif manifest in Chrétien's romance.

It is possible, then, that in his mind, or even in his source, two different conceptions were somehow fused. But generally the fundamental idea of the narrative and most of the episodes prove clearly that the kingdom of Gorre is neither the kingdom of the dead nor a mere mythical region reduced to human or feudal scale. At the very least, the abduction and liberation of Queen Guenevere derive manifestly from a tale of the Celtic otherworld and preserve the broad outline of the *aitheda* (pl., abduction or elopement-type tales).

By what bridge did Irish and Welsh themes reach Chrétien? Such a query is justified if we assume that, apart from his own creative talents, he had at his disposal only a few banal, euhemerized lines from the *Vita Gildae*. It has been implausibly claimed that the principal matter of the *Charrette* was furnished by this *Vita* alone, yet it features neither the *aithed* (sing.) theme nor its benchmark, the capture by means of a "rash boon," a motif which, in the primitive forms is laid to the abductor, but which Chrétien here shifts to the seneschal Kay.[3] Moreover, the *Vita sancti Gildae* lacks the following themes: the heroine's honor pledged for a certain period; the progression of the quest; and the role of the hospitable host, who knows presumably which itinerary to follow and what perilous paths to take in order to reach the realm of the abductor. Finally, would it not be a curious aberration if a hagiographic production inspired the countess Marie and Chrétien with the idea of a narrative which redounds to the glorification of courtly adultery?

Lancelot du Lac is no newcomer. In the *Erec*, Chrétien ranks him third in the list of Knights of the Round Table. He reappears sporadically in *Cligés* at the tourney of Oxford. But Chrétien did not invent the character: even prior to the *Erec*, Lancelot belonged to the *matière de Bretagne*. His name implies some existing legend or highlights his most significant trait, namely, his childhood and formation under the care of a water-fay. In the *Lanzelet* of Ulrich von Zatzikhoven subsists a form of this legend. Loosely constructed, closer to a "tale of adventure" than to the romance, the German poem preserves Guenevere as victim of the *aithed*. But although Lanzelet on one occasion wards off danger on her behalf, he is definitely not her liberator, and no guilty relationship exists between them. We cannot reject the hypothesis that Lancelot had already become the queen's lover before Chrétien so depicted him, yet this transmutation accords so well with the *sen* of Chrétien's romance that it may be plausibly attributed either to Marie de Champagne's initiative, or to a collaboration that the author obviously did not refuse in spite of himself. While recognizing the role of tradition in the

Charrette, we must not consider Chrétien as a slave to it, or as a poet unwilling to introduce independent materials within his arrangement. For example, one new, spontaneous feature that carries certain Ovidian reminiscences is his rather awkward imitation of Thomas's *Tristan*—in the episode of the nocturnal tryst and bloodstained bed.

But his most original achievement is evidenced by his control over the psychology of his characters. A comparison of Lanzelet and Lancelot would demonstrate that a fairly vague figure has been transformed into a well-defined, clearly individualized character. Chrétien here created a stunning fictional type that survived with few changes even beyond the Middle Ages. In Lancelot courtesy and chivalry are flavored with ecstasy. Of this type, Lancelot possesses the cogent contours due to the faintly reportorial repetition of his dominant trait—absorption in the thought of the queen—symbolized concretely by such images as the knight on the cart, in such acts as swooning before the comb and hairs of his lady. This trait is exaggerated in such feats of heroism as crossing the sword-bridge, and even to the verge of caricature in the episide at the ford, or the struggle with his back to the adversary. Don Quixote is adumbrated in a way in Lancelot. Like all literary types, he is in some measure drawn from life, yet still he exalts the fancies or real feminism of the precious courtiers of Champagne; and, in a wider and more lasting sense, Lancelot idealizes the boldest refinements of the whole courtly world.

A representative hero, then, at least in an imaginary sense, Lancelot is original yet typical, if not archetypical—with a metaphysical side. Nonetheless he is quite individualized, and, in avoiding excessive stylization, Chrétien devised with him perhaps his most accomplished invention. One has the impression that Lancelot's deep, paradoxical reveries and trances, even depicted graphically like cataleptic phenomena, had their counterparts in Chrétien's own time, in subconscious or pathological states, in the actual experiences of religious mystics. Chrétien has modeled, in accord with the *sen* of the work, the lover's ecstacies on those of the contemplative engulfed in meditation. Still another innovation is the association within one being of two startling, contradictory tendencies: Lancelot the perfect lover typically abdicates his self, his personality, but in the intervals between trances he is the most lucid, the most reflective, the most practical of Chrétien's characters. He consults with men of prudence, debates within himself, and keeps his composure in the face of the gravest dangers; he is equally capable of irony or of disdainful callousness. By a sort of inversion his most rational act is to use the magic ring given him by the fairy princess who nurtured him, not to work a spell, but to break one, to eliminate his belief in charms, to verify reality (a good example of Chrétien's resistance to the marvelous, vv. 2347-67, 3138-43). Lancelot's psychological dimension is not the result of chance or indifference. If in fact Chrétien undertook the *Lancelot* only reluctantly, the possibilities of the theme became soon seductive enough to interest him in his hero, the queen's lover.

For Lancelot's lady is the queen, who must—more than any woman—remain the very image of inaccessibility, falling under no suspicion. Her rigorous, tyrannical attitude does not arise alone from pride or from a calculating application of dogmatic maxims; her feminine honor and queenly dignity are also at stake. One must recognize that her precautions are doubled by cruel coquetry and that she takes pleasure in lording it over the most valiant of knights. Analogous to Laudine (in *Yvain*), what Chrétien apparently at this period had in mind was a dominant female, more haughty than amiable, a grand feudal lady of great esteem who takes more than she gives. But she is more than that; just as Lancelot cannot be dismissed as the "martyred lover," Guenevere differs too from the sexual martinet, *la belle dame sans merci*. For even when she commanded Lancelot to fight his worst at the tournament of Noauz, it was not with the whimsical, selfish intent to render him contemptible or to debase the chivalric ideal. If she ceased to inspire prowess, she would be a traitor to herself.

Yet is not this same Guenevere—whom some have considered only as the haughty and willful mistress—extremely degraded when, at the beginning of the romance, she is turned over to Kay and made captive by Meleagant? Is she not also faithful to her love? Before the pursuit for the queen, Lancelot's love existed, as she herself knew (vv. 208-16); she had perhaps already shared in it, though chastely (vv. 4242-47) up until the nocturnal tryst in the kingdom of Gorre. This encounter is prepared by inner stages indicated no doubt with more subtlety than emotion, yet not without a tragic tone, blended with a concern for propriety, something like sentimental comedy. Doubtless too, the apparently surprising coolness toward Lancelot, the victor over Meleagant, observed by the queen in public can be explained by an impulse of pride, or of spite, or of imprudent coquetry, or again by her constant concern for her reputation, especially in the presence of Baudemagus, who is after all the guarantor of her honor. But perhaps also with this conduct Chrétien endeavored to have her deceived by her own deep feelings. In any case, a dramatic circumstance—the false report of Lancelot's death—is necessary before she repents of her "sin," that foolish cruelty which she manifested only, she says, "for a joke" (*a gas*, v. 4223). This situation also causes the admission of love to spring to her lips—in a monologue. Was this simply a skillful and delicate plea (in other words), as has been supposed, for the attenuating circumstances in favor of the queen's future behavior? She does, after all, seem clearly conscious of her passion or surrenders to it only when she cannot be unfaithful to King Arthur—except in thought. This tact, this veiled excuse is at least realistic. Yet, it is even more obvious that she chastises her own pride. To the bitter sadness over not loving her loyal lover as he deserved (vv. 4244–45: "'if only once before he died I had held him in my arms!'") is linked *her* sincere desire to expiate and die, even though at the end of her monologue she changes her mind and resigns herself to live as if by a more refined penance: "'I would rather be beaten alive than die and be at rest'" (vv. 4261–62). Chrétien allows himself here perhaps some further irony. Yet with or without the countess Marie of Champagne's consent he does not hesitate to paint in Guenevere a despairing woman who judged herself guilty of grievous wrong to her lover.

The queen's torment and love's triumph establish or hint at an equality of sentiments, always favored by our author, as he avows: Lancelot "...is he to whom she altogether belongs, and he is hers in like manner" (vv. 5893–95). Such equality of love does not really contradict the maxims which assert the supremacy of the mistress: "The man who is a perfect lover is always obedient" (v. 3816); "...everything that one can do for his lady-love is to be regarded as a token of his love and courtesy" (vv. 4377–78; cf. vv. 3979–80 and 5913). These sentiments doubtless express the *sen* desired by the countess, corresponding to certain of the *Regulae* in the *De amore* of Andreas Capellanus, and reflect the spirit that reigned at the court of Champagne, rather than the personal values of the author. Chrétien was too wise a moralist to misconstrue the intrinsic dangers in a doctrine of mystical submission of will and conscience to the whims of a lady. But Lancelot's love service is not represented as a cause of failure; as the text shows explicitly, the hero's superhuman exploits would be impossible without his perfect love, his absorption in thoughts of the queen (cf. vv. 3126–29 and 3739). As in *Cligés,* Chrétien accepted the substance of courtly love which proclaims love as an indispensable, autonomous virtue with claims overriding those of social law. Thus, Lancelot's voluntary humiliation (when he mounts the cart or does "his worst in battle") cannot really cause him inner shame, for the true courtly lover does not consider the nature of his conduct in light of public opinion.[4]

Thus indeed the *sen* and its prime doctrine, the worship of woman, sufficed to solicit Chrétien's creative, psychological bent. Such a profane religion went far beyond the more or less sacrilegious gestures of devotion paid to the queen as a *cors saint* ("holy body"); it penetrated to the depths of the hero's soul, in the form of scruples of conscience and mystical privileges. Like the Christian before God, the lover must never cease being worthy of his lady, must live in dread of sinning, in a spirit of contrition; he suffers patiently every affliction, as humble as a believer, ready to endure all for his faith. His offerings must be completely free of hesitation or regret. Lancelot's sin was to hesitate a single moment before climbing into the cart. In this way, the new religion of love, exacting, heart-probing, judges actions on the basis of their motivations, their secret intentions. Yet it will exalt with graces, like the ecstasies of contemplation, or the quiet power to pass serenely through every trial. When to no avail the comely maiden of the castle attempts to seduce Lancelot, no struggle takes place within his soul, for his gratuitous emblem of selection is impassibility (vv. 1234–54). In the domain of the absolute, such love, born mysteriously, seems immortal.

Lancelot does not obey a code but the law of his heart. In this way, he is indeed an authentic hero of Chrétien. But this does not mean that he represents the author's ideals. Within the limits of matter and meaning, perhaps even because of these restraints, Chrétien the observer placed himself in the presence of his personage. Thus conceived and elaborated by the poet, more or less against the grain, the cult established itself in the secular realm even more firmly. Along with Perceval, the startling Knight of the Cart is Chrétien's most artistic creation. Long endures romantic interest in the queen's deliverer, the misunderstood, magnificent knight, lost in his rapturous dream. This is the hero whom the adventure of the tomb endowed with the aspect of a messiah—a seedling for a future flourishing in an immense *Prose Lancelot.*

Chapter 6

Yvain or
Le Chevalier au Lion

After *Cligés*, Chrétien de Troyes, in both *Yvain* and the *Lancelot*, returns to the *Erec* narrative type, there to stay even with his *Perceval*. More than just a framework, Arthurian story will now again inform his poetry with fabulous themes, however attenuated or humanized. Conducive to heroic idealization, adventures again abound in an unspecific Britain; strange events and profound legends swarm, yet are circumscribed by neat psychological situations. The reader's share is a double pleasure of mystification and ethical truth, for never did Chrétien realize a happier blend of the two. While he does exploit more than previously the affluence of the marvelous, he also daubs the affections with greater variety, passing effortlessly from the tragic to the comic. This versatile equilibrium explains and justifies the prevailing opinion that *Yvain* is Chrétien's masterpiece.

Chrétien had probably undertaken the *Yvain* before commencing the *Lancelot*, and perhaps the two romances occupied his attention simultaneously between 1176 and 1181. A. Fourrier has produced arguments for this chronology, and it is curious that, in the *Yvain,* the plot of the *Lancelot* is interpolated. Gawain is prominent up to the episode of Yvain's folly (vv. 2804-3340), then disappears from the story, reentering at the *dénouement* (vv. 4737-5106; 5810-6509). His eclipse is not a sign of inaction, but, in fact, of preoccupation with the rescue of Queen Guenevere and the pursuit of Meleagant in the kingdom of Gorre. Chrétien has timed it well so that Gawain is unavailable for the *Lancelot,* and thus free to participate in a rather complex episodic arrangement in the *Yvain.*

However interwoven, these two works are not in the same key. *Yvain* is faintly mocking, or sentimental, or occasionally satirical toward *la dame.* As with *Erec,* the work suggests greater originality, its subject doubtless selected spontaneously and without coercion, not at the behest of a patron. There is no attempt, as in *Cligés,* to match the morality of the *Tristan;* no endeavor, as in the *Lancelot,* to glorify the rigorous doctrines of *fine amor.* With great artistry, Chrétien has sketched here the conflict between marital obligations and the chivalric ideal of adventure. He does so as an impartial moralist, in complete probity, though not without irony. The moral of the story remains haunting, discreet, and allusive—not bombastic.

Either Chrétien's enthusiasm or his artistic autonomy seems to have kept him from mentioning any of his sources. All we have is a vague allusion to a lay, either lost or unreal, *"Laudunet"* (Laudine's father, vv. 2152-53). We have good reason to believe, however, that some lost tale provided his canvas, one he artfully imbued with vivacious brilliance and wit. Even the prologue (vv. 1-41) has a new ring. In the days of King Arthur, the poet asserts, there reigned prowess and courtesy: bold knights were faithful to their love, which might be merited only by striving after worth. Now everything has changed: love is much abased even by those who boast of it. If we force the meaning, this contrast sounds bitter and pessimistic. But, in fact, Chrétien transposes the regret of the "good old days" by introducing a nostalgic view of Arthurian legend. For a lament on the bygone era of true love is really a guise for banter, more graceful and serene than spiteful or sad. Like an overture, the prologue harmonizes this banter with an incontestably noble accent—*maestoso*—indicating the key in which the whole romance is developed.

Indeed, running the gamut yet in counterpoint, *Yvain* is a tragicomedy of adventure and love, in which fantasy and reality, tenderness and irony, idealism and scepticism are opposed. Even tears and laughter are there; sometimes there is even a bit of buffoonery, which the author curtails forthwith, unwilling to deride his subject, for he loves his characters even while smiling at them. These diverse tones are orchestrated in the score with virtuosity. Chrétien once again anticipates, at

times prefiguring the art of Boiardo and Ariosto. Yet another innovation
is the poem's resemblance to a play: numerous spectacular dialogues;
surprises in the plot resolved by a comic device; and, especially, the role
of Lunete, the confidante who skillfully leads the game and, with a
malicious brio, stars in the avowal scene—all suggest a dramatic mode.
Clearly, Chrétien has here encountered a script in tune with his temper-
ament.

Erec and *Yvain* are Chrétien's best-designed works; there is, in fact, a
striking parallelism in the structures of the two poems. Each of the
narratives falls into three parts. At first a long exposition, taking up
nearly a third of the whole (up to line 2475 in *Yvain*), tells how a marvelous adventure leads the hero to marry a beautiful and worthy bride
(in *Yvain*, the widow of the man whom he had just killed). The wedding
is celebrated with glorious feasts attended by Arthur's court. Then a
crisis causes the action to rebound: their wedded happiness is seemingly
lost forever. In the end, the hero achieves the reconquest of happiness
and increases his own worth by becoming clearly conscious of his
chivalric duty. On the way, his adventures illustrate a continuous will
to surpass himself; of these the most mysterious apparently takes place
in a castle of the otherworld. After this period of trial, knight and lady
are reconciled and left to enjoy deep, reciprocal love.

On the feast of Pentecost, at Carduel (Carlisle) in Wales where Arthur
held court, a knight named Calogrenant tells how, seven years before,
he had been hospitably entertained by a vavasor in the forest of Broceliande, where he met a monstrous churl watching a herd of wild bulls
in a clearing. The villein directed him to a fountain. After producing a
violent storm by pouring water from the fountain on a hollow block of
emerald, Calogrenant had been attacked at the return of calm. A knight
unhorsed him and he was thus obliged to return ignominiously on foot.

Moved by this narrative, Yvain swears he will avenge the shame of
his cousin, Calogrenant. Yvain is goaded on by Kay's sarcasm and hopes
to precede, in the adventure, King Arthur who will soon visit the marvelous spring. This knight is also fascinated by the unknown danger of
it all·and yields to his desire for glory and his natural curiosity. Therefore, he secretly sets forth alone; crosses the untamed expanse; is received by the vavasor and fair daughter; meets the ugly guardian of the

bulls; finds the spring in the shade of a pine tree; without hesitation pours water on the block; and in combat with the defender of the fountain, wounds him fatally. Pursuing him to his castle, Yvain is suddenly trapped in the gateway between two portcullises.

But he is saved by the damsel Lunete out of gratitude for a service he had rendered her at the court of Arthur, where she once came as a messenger. His reward is a marvelous ring: the bearer has only to turn the stone within the palm to become invisible. Now his enemies, the people of the castle, invade the small room, looking for him in vain. Then Yvain witnesses the funeral procession of his late antagonist and the grief of his most beautiful young widow, Laudine: mad from despair, she cries aloud, swoons, awakens, and begins anew to tear her clothes and pull her hair. Suddenly the wounds of the dead man open again, the warm blood flowing, clear evidence that the killer is present, for according to a well-known belief, a dead man's wounds bleed anew in the presence of the murderer. Again angered searches are made, again without results. The lady curses this bedevilment, and the missing murderous coward is accused of having taken away her "good lord's life," "the best of the good." At a small window, the "treacherous one" cannot stop staring at the grieving widow. The accidental prisoner has fallen violently in love with his enemy and now would be her voluntary captive.

With Lunete skillfully favoring Yvain's cause, three days later Laudine marries him—the slayer of Esclados the Red (her first husband). This solution, though surprising, arises naturally from the situation; widened by neat observations and deftly phased nuances, the gyre-like turnabout makes for classic scenes, a masterpiece of virtuosity and fine comedy. But there is more to the romance than this distinguished *fabliau*-like theme of feminine mobility.

Soon after the wedding feast, Arthur and his knights arrive to attempt the adventure. The king pours a full basin of water on the block, and the storm is unleashed. Yvain in his new capacity of defending the spring hurls Kay from the saddle, thus chastising the overzealous boaster. Yvain is recognized and welcomes the party at his castle. All is joy and gaiety. Tender bonds there unite Gawain, sun of chivalry, with Lunete, as unique as the moon by her wisdom and courtesy.

However, Gawain becomes his friend Yvain's instigator. In a brief, well-turned discourse, constituting a pivotal sequence, he cautions him to maintain his reputation for prowess and against the dangers of idleness (vv. 2484–538). "'What? Will you be one of those . . . who degenerate after marriage? Cursed be he by Saint Mary who marries and then degenerates!'" He who has a beautiful wife or mistress must strive after worthiness, or else she may withdraw her love. "'Slip off the bridle and halter and come to the tournament with me, that no one may say that you are jealous.'" Furthermore, adds Gawain the elegant, pleasures are lost by habit; happiness must be achieved by anticipation and delays. Yvain ends up persuaded, fearing the censure of recreancy. Laudine reluctantly consents, but warns her husband that if he does not return within a year her "love will change to hate" (v. 2564). In a touching farewell, Laudine gives Yvain a magic ring, symbol of fidelity and pledge of protection for the loyal lover.

Absorbed in feats of arms, the hero allows the year to slip by, and when a messenger from Laudine denounces him as a traitor and a liar and takes back the ring, Yvain is traumatized from shame and grief to the point of stark madness; he flees the court and resorts to the woods, aided only by a hermit's charity. Then, one day, the lady of Noroison cures him with a marvelous ointment, and he saves his benefactress from the attack of the hostile Count Alier. Journeying on across the forest, he rescues a lion from a fiery serpent, and the grateful beast does homage to him, henceforth becoming his companion and protector. Now, the "Knight with the Lion," still loyal to his lady though pardon is hopeless, will defend women in distress. He delivers Gawain's niece from the horrible giant Harpin, then hurries to save Lunete, condemned to the stake as a traitress by Laudine. At the castle of *Pesme Aventure* ("Evil Adventure") he liberates three hundred victims forced to work at weaving by an avaricious master. He defends the younger daughter of the lord of *La Noire Espine* ("The Black Thorn") against the partisan of her elder sister who is bent on appropriating an inheritance. The adversary turns out to be Gawain. When, after exchanging terrible blows, the incognito antagonists discover their identity, each wishes to concede the victory to the other, but Arthur intervenes and settles the case between the rival sisters.

Yvain feels that he will soon die from the lack of Laudine's forgiveness. But he decides to give up his sterile laments and carve out his own happiness: his lady must choose between reconciliation and per-

113

3. Yvain Succors the Lion.
(Princeton University Library, Garrett MS 125, fol. 37r.)

petual hurricane. Accompanied by his lion, he returns to the fountain and unleashes a terrible storm. Lunete tricks her mistress into the promise of reconciliation with the "Knight of the Lion." Bound by solemn oath, Laudine is at first furious when she discovers that the knight is her husband, then relents and pardons Yvain who begs forgiveness. This is the beginning of an "enduring peace" between the loving couple.

While the first part of the romance forms a unified whole, the rest is somewhat diffuse, less rigorous in arrangement, though with his *conjointure* Chrétien has still accomplished a fine gradation of adventures. After the year of purposeless and selfish tourneying with Gawain, there follows a period of disgrace and folly—a psychological and moral watershed. Yet from this low ebb in his fortunes, Yvain rises through a series of generous and selfless acts, becoming a hero of useful prowess in the service of the weak and oppressed. Accompanied by his regal ally, the model of loyalty must also perform his penance and undergo a supreme test (in combat with Gawain) to demonstrate his prowess and magnanimity. Once he is rehabilitated in his own eyes and judges himself worthy of pardon, he willfully precipitates the conclusion. Moreover, the roads to adventure sometimes crisscross by design. At the center is Arthur's court and especially the marvelous fountain, which, both in the beginning and later, is the focus of action: Yvain returns there by chance to save Lunete from the stake, and later comes back again to release the storm. The fountain thus creates a sort of unity of place in that the principal events are centered there, however diverse the decor elsewhere. Finally, the dramatic interest of some episodes— Lunete threatened and saved from the stake, the dispute between the rival sisters—is maintained by their occasional entwinement with other episodes (Harpin, the castle of *Pesme Aventure*). Here begins the method of interlacement which will be fully developed later, for example, in the thirteenth-century *Prose Lancelot.*

This careful program may be best appreciated by comparing it with the Welsh text, *The Lady of the Fountain,* or *Owein.* In their general lines the two stories run parallel up to the deliverance of Lunete from punishment; then the Welsh author simply adds three lines, saying that Owein and Lunete "went to the dominions of the Lady of the Fountain. And when he came away thence he brought the lady with him to

Arthur's court, and she was his wife so long as she lived."[1] Another adventure, in which Owein conquers the black oppressor (corresponding to the *Pesme Aventure* episode) and delivers the captives, is simply tacked on to the main plot. From the comparison emerges also Chrétien's restraint in elaboration, while, at the same time, he demonstrably transforms a dry and irrelevant narrative into a lively and dramatic scenario. It is in fact extremely improbable that Chrétien's *Yvain* furnished the model for the Welsh story. Like *Gereint, Owein* probably reproduced a "tale of adventure" that Chrétien used as a framework, but the Welsh text still sheds light on his creativity and craftsmanship.

Doubtless already crystallized within the "tale of adventure," patently the common source of *Yvain* and of *Owein*, were the mythical elements of the subject. The magical background is indeed difficult to explore, especially if we look only in one direction. The marvelous fountain theme amalgamates ancient rites of sympathetic magic, of sacred marriage and violent substitution, survivals of which are found in mythology and folklore the world over; however, the conjunction of the spring with the release of the storm, with the reception of the hospitable host, and with the meeting with a monstrous herdsman all argues in favor of a Celtic origin. So too does the love of the hero for a lady who was formerly a fairy princess of the fountain and who had as confidante and intermediary a second fairy princess.[2] Likewise, the conception of the otherworld is transparent in the castle of the *Pesme Aventure* episode. But, on the other hand, the theme of the grateful lion undoubtedly derives, with some embellishment, from the famous anecdote of Androcles.

Into this fabulous web Chrétien has spun an array of details drawn from daily life. This tendency toward realism in *Yvain* is represented both in material civilization—costume, furniture, arms, combats—and in socio-economic concerns, such as the remarkably open complaint of the poor weavers in the castle of *Pesme Aventure* (vv. 5185–346). Chrétien there sympathetically echoes the misery of workers he may very well have observed in certain ateliers of Champagne. The precise figures in which their earnings and the profits of the two devil masters are given must reflect a contemporary, unfanciful reality. Nevertheless, Chrétien still manages in a compelling way to fuse the fabulous and the real.

Classical antiquity is revived especially through Ovidian imagery, subtlely adapted, like the "sweets of a love which develops late are like a fire in a green bush," slow to burn but of a longer and more enduring heat (vv. 2519-23). Minimal metaphorical depiction (even less frequent than in *Cligés*) of amorous sentiments, of nascent love and its pangs, and a few notes relating to the changeability of women sum up Ovid's support. But this influence is quite limited by comparison with Chrétien's immediate source, which already told of the dead man and of his widow unfaithful to his memory. Such a tale, with many misogynistic variations, was probably quite popular, so that there is no need to go back as far as the widow of Ephesus, about which too much has been said; there is nothing except a broad resemblance to suggest that she was the model for Laudine. Of course, Chrétien could have been reminded by a passage on Dido from the *Eneas* romance (vv. 1600-1610), and perhaps more by Jocasta's conduct at the beginning of the *Thebes* romance (vv. 223-62). Yet even this episode is only a sketch next to the incomparable scenes of Laudine's turnabout in *Yvain*, sprinkled with artful gradations.[3]

Clearly, the *fabliau*-like scenes with Laudine and Lunete are fortuitous, offering Chrétien a difficult, tempting gamble, an apparently uncommon problem that he did in fact resolve: presented with a widow whose husband has just died tragically, how, *without serious improbability,* to depict her marrying her husband's slayer three days later. He accomplished it because he had the conspicuous good fortune to wager on a set of plausible circumstances for the sudden turnabout. First, the land will soon be threatened, for Arthur will come "next week" with his host to attempt the adventure of the fountain (line 1617). How is Lunete so well informed? Quite simply because a certain *Demeisele Sauvage* (no doubt a "forest-damsel") wrote a letter about it to Laudine (vv. 1619-22)—an obviously humorous invention. Second, if Arthur and his knights arrive, will not someone respond, one servant in the huge castle, one vassal of the household? Unfortunately, they are all cowards; almost by design, not a single one is worth a chambermaid! (vv. 1628-37). Third, another stroke of luck occurs: it so happens that Yvain is the son of Urien—a fine match! This gives Laudine an additional yet invincible reason to marry him (vv. 1811-19). Lastly, the trump card is Lunete, the active, guileful, disinterested confidante and *maistre*

117

(v. 1593), full of candor in her discussions with Laudine. But why does she plead Yvain's cause so anxiously? Obviously she is bound by ties of gratitude. And she will soon bring about his happiness by isolating him just long enough so that the impatient, intimidated lover, when beckoned, will leave his retreat with perfect timing. This combination proves faultless, and the serious motives soon become quite apparent in a most effective way.

Laudine's decision, then, is fully motivated by external circumstances. Essentially, the one rationale on which all the others hinge is the necessity of defending the fountain as if it were a frontier. The *enor,* "honor," means both the possession of and responsibility for property, implying material and human care and pride of ownership. The "honor" imposes obligations and forbids weeping, as Lunete reminds Laudine: "'You ought to be considering how you will defend your spring, and yet you cease not to weep!'...'It is not fitting that so great a lady should keep up her grief so long. Remember your honourable estate and your very gentle birth'" (vv. 1623-25; 1670-73). Still and all, for a twelfth-century audience the sudden remarriage of a great heiress needed no explanation and hardly a justification: relative to feudal duty, the fountain could not remain undefended. Equally credible and even more natural is the curiosity, at first intellectual, then emotional, that leads Laudine to the same idea: remarriage to another man, superior insofar as he defeated the first. This movement is revealed by the monologue (vv. 1760-72) through which Laudine imagines that the unnamed slayer appears before her as if at a tribunal and, at the end of an interrogation in which she herself cross examines and answers the questions, he is acquitted. That same curiosity of hers is finally convulsed in impatience, to the point that the illusion vanishes. No longer can the young widow deceive herself or her clever confidante. She acts out a pretty comedy when she treats her wooer, the naive, repentant pretender, with hauteur, even after she has decided on marriage. In the same way, she consults her vassals *pro forma* (vv. 2038-2149) even though sure of their assent. What is comical here arises from the juxtaposition of factual reality and the quite natural deception of a woman bent on protecting her honor.

It was also Chrétien's good fortune to gamble on an accelerated narrative. Even though we may cite him for his excessively dry observation, however penetrating and quizzical, or for his overrefined use of scholastic reasoning, as when Lunete proves to Laudine "irrefutably" (v. 1704) or by categorical deduction that she must marry the victor, is not this very dryness of style apt and morally compelling? After all, the lady did not necessarily cherish her first husband (or else the whole episode would become intolerable). The widow's loud keening is consonant with the funeral ceremony; there is no specific mention of a personal attachment to the dead man, and she grieves over the "good" defender of the fountain, deploring his loss with outcries. But the dead man remains nothing more than an abstract image. For all that, Laudine's turnabout does not occur for personal reasons either, for she has resolved to remarry even before setting eyes on her future husband. She yields at once to a certain sense of duty, to curiosity, to impatience, and perhaps because of some imponderable reasons, like the charm of novelty or the vigor of youth. A marriage of reason was paramount in so exceptional a situation, if only to avoid indecency. In the second stage, the segment is enhanced by the shift to a marriage of inclination, not incongruous with the rest of the romance. For, during the nuptial ceremony, Laudine is very much in love with Yvain, now no longer invisible to her. This interior truth, which she herself keeps back, is elicited by the distinct revelation of the heroine's concurrent vanity *and* inner feelings of ardor.

> [Her people] ... beseech her so insistently that she consents to do what she would have done in any case. For Love bids her do that for which she asks counsel and advice; but there is more honour for him in being accepted with the approval of her men. To her their prayers are not unwelcome; rather do they stir and incite her heart to have its way. The horse, already under speed, goes faster yet when it is spurred.   (vv. 2137–47)

Chrétien relates his faintly coarse or grating *fabliau* in a somewhat abrupt manner, yet his style is so supple as to intensify the matter, the narrative so neatly scored as to take on a musical quality, passing from adagio to andante, then, more precipitously, to allegretto and allegro.

A glance at a passage of this type will help us to appreciate better Chrétien's light touch in shading his characters. After the night when Laudine, in her own mind, adjudicated the murderer's acquittal, she longs to know his name, his *estre* ("appearance and character"), and his lineage (v. 1793). Lunete has just taken "the subject up where she had let it drop" the day before. The lady bows her head, sorry for her anger toward her servant. She is now prepared to humble herself more as a simple tactic than because of genuine repentance, and, in fact, apologizes: "'I wish to beg your pardon for the insulting words of pride which in my rage I spoke to you without reason: I will follow your advice'" (vv. 1795-98). In the preceding conversations Laudine used the informal *tu* with Lunete; now she uses *vous,* a diplomatic move. Then she asks in a somewhat distant and indifferent tone: "'So tell me now, if possible, about the knight of whom you have spoken so much to me: what sort of man is he, and of what parentage?'" (vv. 1799-1802). Here indeed is what she is dying to know, yet she will only advance in prudence, with many precautions, dreaming up various obstacles: "'If he is suited to become my mate, and provided he be so disposed [This is pure coquetry, for she has guessed by now that the knight would not reject her.], I promise you to make him my husband and lord of my domain'" (vv. 1803-6). Now the irreparable is out, it is yes, whereupon Laudine shudders with thoughts of her noble reputation, and is understandably curbed by them: "'But he will have to act in such a way that no one can reproach me by saying: 'This is she who took him who killed her lord''" (vv. 1807-10).

Lunete has won the match, but savors her victory with a discreet malice. Instead of disclosing immediately the knight's name, she extols him, thus pleasantly exacerbating Laudine's patience: "'In God's name, lady, so shall it be. You will have the gentlest, noblest, and fairest lord who ever belonged to Abel's line'" (vv. 1811-14).

Laudine becomes angry: "'What is his name?'" This time Lunete comes through with "'my lord Yvain.'" Chrétien has heightened the vitality of the whole dialogue by deleting interpolated clauses like "she says" and "she affirms"; as might be done in a theatrical script, one could write next to each reply either "Laudine" or "Lunete."

Hearing the name "Yvain," Laudine expresses her satisfaction: "'Upon my word, if he is king Urien's son he is of no mean birth, but very noble, as I well know'" (vv. 1868-18). She certainly knows her Arthurian genealogy. Now all trace of scruples disappears and she would like the marriage to take place forthwith: "'And when shall we be able to see him?'" (v. 182). This decorous "we" returns to center stage feudal concerns about the defense of the spring and of the land.

"'In five days' time,'" replies Lunete. She has no intention of divulging Yvain's presence in the castle nor her own efficacious assistance to him; and her credibility depends on a reasonable delay to give him time to come from Arthur's court. Lunete is also hoping that the five-day interval will indeed seem too long for Laudine; she cannot deny herself the appeal of acting out a pretty comedy on her own. Therefore, the lady grows impatient: "'That would be too long; for I wish he were already come. Let him come tonight, or tomorrow, at the latest'" (vv. 1821-23). "'My lady, I think no one could fly so far in one day. But I shall send one of my squires who can run fast, and who will reach King Arthur's court at least by tomorrow night, I think; that is the place we must seek for him'" (vv. 1824-31). Obviously, "him" means Yvain. In the following lines, a nice comic effect accrues from the ambiguity of the pronoun which appears to stand for the messenger but refers to Yvain as well, whose name, in fact, is avoided by both Laudine and Lunete. The two images, one of the messenger "who can run fast," the other of the knight who should already be there, seem confused in her restless mind: "'That is a very long time. The days are long. But tell him that tomorrow night he must be back here, and that he must make greater haste than usual. If he will only do his best, he can do two days' journey in one. Moreover, tonight the moon will shine; so let him turn night into day. And when he returns I will give him whatever he wishes me to give." (vv. 1832-41). From such generosity it might be inferred that by "him" Laudine means her Yvain and not the messenger. Lunete's rejoinder shows she was not fooled: "'Leave all care of that to me; for you shall have him in your hands the day after tomorrow at the very latest'" (vv. 1842-44). But who, if not Yvain himself? He will be there not tomorrow but the day after, his arrival thus coinciding with the messenger's return. Lunete agrees to shorten the delay from five days to two, but to ask any more would be impossible!

Here, then, is an example of Chrétien's best manner in *Le Chevalier au lion.* The incisive originality and the quality of the dialogue make for a situation indistinguishable from a veritable comedy of character.

Nature here holds forth: it is the characters themselves and the inflection of their voices that reveal inner thoughts and mysteries of the heart. A similarly witty and alert circumspection, along with the ease and clarity of style, informs the whole romance. Though touched sometimes by a preciosity mindful of *Cligés,* it is yet one purified and less stilted, for the theoretical dissertations have been more or less preempted by fortuitous and true-to-life metaphors, such as the lady as the lover's "enemy." The painter of love has loaded his palette with new and special tones. A raw lyricism invigorates Yvain's monologue (vv. 1462-506), as he falls more and more in love with the young widow, whom he watches longingly from his little window, while she, right after the burial of Esclados the Red, interrupts her grieving despair only to read "her psalms in her gilt-lettered psalter." Lyrical likewise is the hero's declaration to Laudine: "'Love? And whom?' 'You, my lady dear.' 'I?' 'Yes, truly.' 'Really? And how is that?'" Thus she queries him at the end of an interrogation, supercilious yet gracious, guiding him toward the desired goal—and he avows: "'To such an extent that my heart will not stir from you, nor is it elsewhere to be found; to such an extent that I cannot think of anything else, and I surrender myself altogether to you, whom I love more than I love myself, and for whom, if you will, I am equally ready to die or live'" (vv. 2025-32). Later on Yvain's love folly adds a tragic element to the picture of passion and sets the character of the "mad lover," a literary type with a long future.

Less obvious, here and there in the romance falls a penetrating elegiac accent, such as when Chrétien furtively allows himself to confide to us his nostalgia for the "good old days" of true love (vv. 18-30, 5394-95); or when we hear the lover pining, for instance, at Yvain's inadvertent return with his lion to the magic spring, as he laments over his loss of love's joy and invokes death (vv. 3531-62); or when he bids a melancholic farewell to Laudine: "My lord Yvain weeps and sighs so bitterly that he can hardly find words to say: 'My lady, this date [the limit of a year] is indeed a long way off. If I could be a dove, whenever the fancy came to me, I should often rejoin you here'" (vv. 2579-84). But, alas, Yvain will forget to return to his love at the right time. The faintly refined lines of *Yvain* nevertheless possess an elegiac purity that calls to mind La Fontaine's "Two Doves," a comparison suggested by Yvain's desired metamorphosis. Is there not in that exquisitely pol-

4. Yvain Battles the Giant.
   (Princeton University Library, Garrett MS 125, fol. 56v.)

ished fable a similar conflict between love and adventure? One might well imagine Chrétien adding a gloss to his poem, a bit of advice, mindful of La Fontaine's two birds of peace:

> O lovers, happy lovers, must you fly the nest?
> Fly, then, but never far away.
> Fly to a world of beauty fixed between you two,
> Forever different and new.[4]

Such colorful variety can in no way conceal the psychological cogency of the work. The principal characters are well drawn: Laudine, high lady of the domain of Broceliande, is alert and proud, reputable and willful, noble but ungenerous, a conceited but loving soul. In spite of appearances she is not inconsistent, whether she moves from hate to love or, inversely, from love to hate. She is as affected as her husband at the moment of parting, and later returns to him the magic ring doubly powerful in that it protects while testing his loyalty. After Yvain's departure, she remains faithful, counting the days, perhaps watching daily a painted calendar in her chamber. But the date set for his return passes with no sign of him. Laudine has good reason to think herself betrayed by an unfaithful man; and just as her hate had once changed to love, she reverts now to hate, for, as she had knowingly warned Yvain: "'...but be sure that my love will change to hate if you stay beyond the term that I shall fix'" (vv. 2564–67). Both obstinate and impulsive, Laudine cannot bury her resentment.[5] But if, deep in her heart, her love has been crushed by *amour-propre,* it is not dead. This is why the conclusion hangs together so well from a psychological point of view. Clearly, since Laudine would herself never consent to a reconciliation with the traitor, it falls to the inimitable Lunete to preserve her vanity, so that henceforth her love may be reinvigorated but not revealed. Logical and subtle, Chrétien's Laudine represents perhaps his deepest probe of the affective life.

Lunete is clever and guileful, yet essentially loyal. We perceive her courage in the opening *fabliau,* and, again, when she is condemned to the stake, her role is easily elevated to pathos. Yvain, the knight-errant, is the third character in the group who evolves. From the beginning, he has enduring qualities: he is brave, impulsive, magnanimous, and direct, but he is also a hero who makes himself and surpasses himself through trials. Even the secondary to episodic characters are all individualized at least with simple sketches. They form a profuse gallery of unequalled original, human types—however much they may display a new, sometimes exaggerated, tendency toward humorous fantasy. As in his earlier romances, Chrétien was not content to tell a story merely for its own sake, and in *Yvain* he offered a lesson in wisdom and nobility; but it would be rash to formulate its complex and subtle *sen* in perfunctory terms. Essentially, it *is,* more or less, the conflict between love and adventure, yet this discord is not sustained. In the final analysis, the solution is a compromise; if only the hero had not forgotten the time fixed for his return. This explains how Yvain sinned against Laudine and against love. Chrétien thought, like Laudine, that Yvain was required to expiate his fault, but he deemed also that her righteous anger could not last without end. Thus Yvain's prowess, his remorse, his penitence, and his fidelity atone for his guilt, and, in the end, the author, sympathetic toward such compromise, reconciles the couple. This accommodation is, in fact, both for the knight and the lady, a victory over themselves, for *he* surely increased in merit through atonement and *she* finally renounced her deep pride. In the shadow of the lady's sovereignty follows marital equality, integral and reciprocal: "... for love, which is neither false nor feigned, is a precious and a holy thing" (vv. 6051-52).

Chrétien's great genius here interrelates the themes of love and of chivalry, thus achieving a unified *sen* in the romance: the lover's guilt was indeed atoned for by knightly feats. Yvain's chivalric ascension accords then with the courtly ethic, which meant that love's dignity was based on the worth of the beloved: Laudine had the right to condemn Yvain; it was her duty to pardon "The Knight with the Lion." Love's torments thus rehabilitated Yvain by advancing him from egoistic prowess to a higher chivalric notion, to the consciousness of a mission. He becomes the perfect knight of law, of pity, and of charity, as the companionship of the lion attests.

By stressing the realization of earthly happiness "in this mortal life" (v. 6797), Chrétien's moral is more one of conciliation than of opposition. The peculiar quality of *Yvain* is also one of plenitude and harmony (corresponding to an apogee in the rise of romance and of the secular, courtly ethos), a harmony composed of various voices and different tonalities. Chrétien was not unaware of polyphonic chant which was making notable progress in his day and which he himself in a way defined by evoking the concert of birds assembled in the pine tree above the marvelous fountain: "...for all the birds sang in harmony, yet the note of each was different, so that I never heard one singing another's note" (vv. 465-69).

Likewise, in the romance, the individual voices, even the dissonances, are organized into a superior harmony. It is just possible that this harmony is the result of good fortune in a privileged world—the aristocratic elite of the heart. Let us ever be mindful, however, that Chrétien did not initially confer upon his characters such preeminence. Rather, the most pregnant *sen* suggested by the most noble "Knight with the Lion" is that perfect happiness may be attained only by trials.

Chapter 7

Perceval or
Le Conte du Graal

Chrétien's last romance, left unfinished, was dedicated to Philippe of Alsace, count of Flanders, who died at Acre on the Third Crusade, in June 1191. The poet was doubtless truthful in his assertion that he followed his great patron's "command" and that he had received from him (around 1179-82) a *livre,* containing some version of the Grail story.

Whether the gift itself was splendid or not matters little, for from Philippe's gracious hand came an admirable subject whereby Chrétien "acquits himself" well, as he says, so that without realizing it he created a myth: with Chrétien's last work, born of a fusion, coalesces the inspiring story of the Grail.

Many have wondered what the "book" contained.[1] The answers to this question tend to be influenced by theories concerning the origin of the Grail legend. Some have surmised that it was written in Latin, that it set forth some type of ritual about the Grail as a Christian relic or liturgical vessel; others have plausibly argued that it was a "tale of adventure" filled with Celtic marvels. Yet further disagreement exists as to whether the story of Perceval was already linked to the legend of the Grail. The two stories could have existed independent of each other: in *Erec,* Perceval le Gallois is listed among the knights of Arthur's court and he reappears in *Cligés* where he is dubbed a "man of great fame"–a rather nondescript hint of the hero-to-be (Micha ed., *Cligés,* vv. 4773-74). The Middle English romance (ca. 1370), *Sir Perceval of Galles (Sir Percyvelle)* has not a word of the Grail or the Fisher King. Even though the question has been much disputed, it seems most

127

probable that *Sir Perceval* derives from a "tale of adventure" relating stories of Perceval's childhood *(enfances)*, independent of the Grail. These indications suggest that Chrétien's *Conte du Graal* is the result of a synthesis, although it still remains undetermined whether there existed an earlier amalgamation in the "book," or whether it may be attributed to Chrétien's own initiative.

But the dedication to the count of Flanders stands firm. The praise Chrétien bestows on his Maecenas, however grandiloquent, reaches a higher level than mere flattery. Filling nearly the whole prologue, its accent is such that it may very well accord with the *sen* of the romance: it celebrates the chivalric ideal by which worldly glory gives way to Christian humility and divine love. The panegyric is made up mainly of paraphrases and quotations from the gospels and contrasts the ostentatious largess of Alexander the Great with another largess, i.e., inner piety and spirituality, "charity" in the strictly religious sense of the word. In point of fact, there is a correspondence between this prelude and the Good Friday and hermitage episodes, which appear late in the romance, because the religious ideal predominates at the consummation of Perceval's ascent. Chrétien's goal seems to have been this: to direct, across a series of initiatory experiences, through naive bravery and half-understood lessons, a noble adolescent, ignorant of everything and most of all of himself, yet essentially generous and good, to comprehension of his duties and the discovery of the divine.

As in the proem of *Lancelot*, Chrétien again indicates discreetly his own efforts to assure the literary quality of the work: "Chrétien...strives to put into rhyme the best tale which may be told in a royal court" (vv. 62–64). We sense here his confidence, the felicitous probity of a maestro in full array. We may infer that his thoughts were turned not only to the beauty of the style but also to the structure of the narrative, for his conception of the genre included improvisation, however controlled by the sources.

The *Story of the Grail* is not a well-organized narrative since Chrétien did not finish the work. But enough of the redaction survives (9234 lines) to suggest that certain internal inconsistencies were unplanned. Most striking is Gawain's considerable role: at l. 4747 he moves to center stage, and the rest of the poem, utterly unrelated to the central theme, is given over to his adventures, with the single exception of a critical episode of some 300 lines, when Perceval reaches his uncle's hermitage. This duality of interest has seemed to certain critics so gross a flaw in composition as to justify exculpating Chrétien entirely for it. Becker would reduce his authentic work to the first 3427 lines (up to Perceval's departure from the Grail castle); Hofer more generously would assign to him all Perceval's adventures, but those of Gawain to an awkward continuator—even though Gawain's "romance" is written in Chrétien's most brilliant and inimitable manner. Hoepffner adjudged that two independent works, both unfinished, were unscrupulously stitched together after Chrétien's death.

Be that as it may, there are good reasons to believe that it was the poet's own intention to give Gawain a minor but still significant role. Nowhere is it written that Chrétien could not change his artistic style. With *Perceval* his conception of the romance form could have broadened to permit greater allusion. This dual interest was not a novelty: already in *Lancelot*, Chrétien maintained a sort of parallelism between the roles of Gawain and the hero. In *Perceval*, he causes Gawain to undertake a secondary quest for the bleeding lance (vv. 6158–98), thus paralleling Perceval's search for the castle of the Fisher King.

The direction of the narrative is not always clear, for the marvelous tale included some strangeness and mystery, wisely retained by Chrétien. These amusing, seductive qualities are enduring in his work: already in *Lancelot*, the extraordinary is deftly bound to his narrative manner—suspenseful, enigmatic—and now the *chiaroscuro* will truly whet our curiosity. The *Conte du Graal* is also characterized by a more subtle and original method of composition: by progressions, Chrétien relates almost everything through Perceval's eyes. This mode of presenting facts as they happen and as they are gradually explained in part for the hero results logically in a psychological *and* artistic impressionism. Here is another reason for the uncertainty and obscurity in the romance, yet neither its impressionistic style nor the author's smiles, nor even his apparent inattention, should lead to a misunderstanding of its concerted structure.

Perceval's silence at the Fisher King's is closely related to his naivety, or simplicity, a trait especially nurtured by his loving and fearful mother. His initiations unfold gradually: once again Chrétien traces in story the evolution of the hero's personality, but never before was his program so extensive, for the young Perceval is at first a quasi-primitive creature, "the young fool." Nothing reveals more the existence of an elaborate structure than Chrétien's two explanations of Perceval's silence: the first says it arises from excessive docility, a too-strict obedience to warnings against loquacity (vv. 3202-12, 3243-53, 3290-303); but, according to the hermit, if Perceval did not ask the question—an error—it was because of a "sin against his mother," his heartless desertion of her when she swooned and died in sorrow (vv. 3591-606 and 6392-414). These two explanations are complementary, rising in stages, each valid on its own plane. The second offers a spiritual perspective, changing the Grail adventure to a drama of conscience. The lack of judgment which, in psychological and more worldly terms, kept him from asking the liberating question, corresponds to the absence of grace in the religious order. Only let the hero feel the weight of his sin, let his heart be moved by charity, and grace will do its work, leading him to a third, yet higher, plane. We may suppose that if Chrétien had completed his poem, his hero would have returned to the Grail castle to accomplish the miracle. Thus, Perceval's adventures would harmonize with the spirit of the prologue.

These different levels and this progressive development suggest already the great depth and breadth of *The Story of the Grail*. But surely Chrétien was aware that, in order to embellish his subject with charm, there must remain tantalizing concealments, in a way unfocused mysteries, unlike the interpretations found in so many later romances of the Grail and of the Holy Grail. Rather, Chrétien was to hint at merely probable or possible meanings. If so, the refusal to explain clearly, the narrative ambiguity (notably in the procession scene at the Grail castle), implies a deliberate symbolism: he has freely allowed ancient myth to subsist, yet around it he creates an atmosphere of Christian spirituality.

One received opinion makes of the *Conte du Graal* a *Bildungsroman*— a kind of twelfth-century *Telemachus*—presenting models of behavior; it would be grouped then in the category of simple didactic literature. This view is not altogether false, only incomplete, for at a certain point Perceval rises above the didactic stage to seek his personal path through inner suffering. It is then that he truly begins to be himself.

Thus one may judge better the sense of Gawain's adventures in relation to Perceval's. For those who see the "Grail Story" solely in terms of its didacticism, the explanation is simple: Chrétien presented Gawain as a noble and elegant model which Perceval must ever strive to match. But this interpretation takes no account of artistic lengthening in the romance. In the first part the uncouth manners and laughable blunders of the youthful "fool" brought up in the Welsh forest contrast with the refined savoir vivre of Gawain. Yet the two personages are almost equal, even in courtesy, in the poetic episode of the blood drops on the snow. But then their adventures and destinies diverge: Perceval, the only Perceval at the Round Table, chooses to undertake the difficult quest for the Grail, while the chivalrous Gawain lets himself be carried along in a whirlwind of frivolous, worldly adventures or misadventures. Henceforth, they are no longer on the same level of excellence, and within the organic spatiality of the *Conte du Graal,* Gawain is presented as a counterpoint—not antithesis—to Perceval. Clearly, it cannot be maintained that Chrétien intended to oppose the two, like a clumsy sketch next to a consummate model. The one, after protracted confusion and despair, arrives at the hermitage, enters the path of repentance, and becomes a new man before leaving again for parts unknown (since the romance is unfinished); yet we suspect that he somehow found the Fisher King's castle again. But Arthur's nephew remains unchanged: ever courteous, tactful, preoccupied with mundane glories and chivalric honor, Gawain's grandeur is not diminished, although, upon closer examination, he comes through as a static character, one whose prestige is indeed tarnished, someone destined for some kind of debasement. But let us now give a brief sketch of the poem.

Perceval's mother, in perpetual mourning over the death of her two older sons and her husband, raises her youngest in a remote forest dwelling, ignorant of chivalry and its perils.[2] But one spring morning (stunningly described), the Welsh youth, so far unnamed, meets five knights, and his inner destiny is awakened. He decides immediately to go to Carduel, where Arthur dwells, "the king who makes knights."

The poor mother obtains from her stubborn son only a three-day delay. Consenting reluctantly, she makes him a cumbersome outfit

5. Yvain Rescues Lunete.
(Princeton University Library, Garrett MS 125, fol. 58v.)

"à la mode de Galles," and gives him some parting advice, in haste, about his behavior with damsels, about seeking the companionship of gentlemen *(prodomes),* and about entering churches to pray to the Lord (though Perceval has never yet seen a church!). She also reminds him of Christ's passion, of the mysteries of the Eucharist and of the Redemption (vv. 567-98).

As Perceval goes off, he turns for a moment only to see his mother fallen at the end of the bridge, "as if she had dropped dead." But he whips his mount and gallops forth "through the great dark forest" (vv. 622-30). That is his sin.

Mistaking a splendid tent for a church, he enters and, recalling his mother's counsel, kisses exuberantly a damsel lying within. After the youth leaves, her jealous lover returns and, convinced of her infidelity, forces her to ride forth in sad array. In the meantime, at Arthur's court Perceval makes a heroicomic entrance, is insulted by the sarcastic Kay, but is greeted as the best knight in the world by a laughing maiden. Then, by throwing a javelin in the eye, he kills the Red Knight who had insulted King Arthur and Guenevere, and with help strips him of his arms and charger. In the castle of the friendly and benevolent Gornemant de Gohort, the "young fool" learns the correct way to hold a lance and shield, how to manage the charger and handle a sword. He receives the order of knighthood, and Gornemant instructs him in the moral principles of chivalry, also warning him about courteous discretion, for loquacity is a sin.

But Perceval cannot put aside thoughts of his mother who had fallen from the end of the bridge. Is she dead or alive? At least he does know that she swooned because of his departure (vv. 1580-92). Thus he refuses to tarry with Gornemant de Gohort, whose niece, Blancheflor, will detain Perceval a little longer. This beautiful maiden is beseiged in her castle of Beaurepaire, threatened by famine, because of a cruel enemy, Anguingueron, seneschal of a knight, Clamadeu des Iles, who covets her land and her person. Perceval's arrival saves her. He vanquishes the enemies and sends them as prisoners to Arthur. The hero now has a mistress and begins to be courteous, stirred by love, by its emotions, mixed with forthright sensuality and tender pity for the defenseless woman. Heretofore purely instinctual, the hero now acquires a sense of moral autonomy and inner freedom. At Beaurepaire, he continues to enjoy the embraces of Blancheflor, and though she seeks to keep him, and though he promises to return, he leaves her, being haunted by the image of his swooning mother. Moving to another level, Perceval will go to experience the Grail adventure. All day, lance at the ready, he has ridden in solitude, continually hoping in God to find his mother alive. In prayer he comes to a deep river of the Fisher King, "the wounded one." Directed to his castle nearby, Perceval is received in the hall by his magnificent and sickly host, already arrived, and he obtains from the "blond maiden" a sword "destined" for him (v. 3168). Then he witnesses the enigmatic procession of the bleeding lance, candelabra, the gold-encrusted vessel called a *graal,* and the silver carving platter *(tailloir).*

Through the octosyllables flows the charming scene—noble, graceful, and mysterious—of visual artistry. However extraordinary, nothing mars the impression of harmony. There is beauty and youth, and especially beautiful is the one carrying the *graal* in the center of the procession; there is an unpeculiar indication of distinctive gestures: the lance grasped in the middle, the *graal* held between the two hands; there is a painstaking progression of the effects of light, with the prodigious luster of the *graal* twice told: first the strange brightness emanating from it, then the splendor of its gold and jewels, before and after the passage of the platter. Hardly less brilliant are the contrasting colors of the precious metals, the red blood and white lance—all expressive of a startling visualization elegantly accomplished.

Though fascinated by this cortege as it passes again to enter another chamber, and though amazed, for he would like to know why the lance bleeds and whom one serves with the *graal,* Perceval controls himself, recalling Gornemant's injunction against too many words, and asks no question. Then an exquisite meal is served, and, with his host, Perceval partakes of the abundant food. With each course, he sees the *graal* in all its splendor, again crossing the room, but still he masters his curiosity. When he wakes in the hall the next morning, he finds the castle deserted. Perceval accoutres himself unaided, finds his horse already saddled and the castle bridge lowered; he rides off on his steed, just crossing the drawbridge as it is raised up rapidly. He is nearly upended.

Riding on across the forest without a hint of his recent humiliation, he sees a young woman lamenting and grasping her dead friend. He greets her, and, when she learns that he spent the night with the rich Fisher King, she submits him to a detailed interrogation.[3] She upbraids him violently for his silence about the bleeding lance and about the *graal*. The maiden then asks his name and the hero "guesses," by a kind of divination, that he is Perceval of Wales (vv. 3573–77). Rather, Perceval "the wretched," she answers, and she informs him in detail that if he had spoken he would have healed his infirm host, causing great rejoicing. She says that his silence is the consequence of his sin in leaving his mother. (She knows all this since she is no other than his first cousin.) At the news of his mother's death Perceval is saddened, but he controls himself, putting aside sterile regret and refusing filial anguish: "'I must now take another road . . . The dead to the dead, the living to the living'" (Roach ed., v. 3625). His other way will be one of action, the easiest form of illusory freedom. Perceval's conduct will remain chivalrous and generous, but will neither open his eyes to repentance nor lead him to the spiritual life.

He next meets the maiden of the tent, mounted on a wretched palfrey, her face worn by tears, and followed by her jealous lover, the Proud Knight of the Glade. In reparation, the hero forces him in combat to admit the girl's innocence. Some days later, after a fall of snow, Perceval sees a flock of wild geese, pursued by a falcon. One is wounded and blood falls on the white field. Perceval hastens, his hunting instinct awakened, but the wild goose has flown off again: there remain only three drops of blood on the snow. The bright red contrasts with the white, and Perceval, leaning on his lance, falls into a prolonged reverie on the fresh color of his love Blancheflor.[4] This amorous ecstasy, almost involuntary, is his first sign of introspection.

Now Arthur's court, in quest of the hero, was camping nearby. The strange attitude of the contemplative invites Sagremor to interrupt and lead the dreamer to the king, but in his brashness he is unseated. The seneschal Kay goes to threaten him, but he too is knocked out of his saddle, breaking his arm in the fall. But Gawain, the model knight, alone understands that worthy thoughts preoccupy the unknown youth. He alone succeeds, through courtesy, in bringing the love-smitten hero to Arthur's camp. Thus the two noble knights become companions. Because of the report of Perceval's deeds, the widow's son is deemed worthy to sit at the Round Table. Queen Guenevere speaks for the whole court when she greets him: "'You are most welcome, as a knight whose high and noble prowess has been well proved'" (Roach ed., vv. 4593-95). Thus closes, seemingly, a cycle. Were it Perceval's fate only to match Gawain, the story could end here. But such is not the case. After the court returns to Carleon for a two-day celebration, a damsel of fantastic ugliness rides in on a mule and accuses Perceval for his muteness at the Grail castle. The devastating consequences for the Fisher King and his land are irremediable. The infirm king will continue to suffer, unable to govern, and in his wasted kingdom women will become widows, damsels will remain orphans, scores of knights will die. Before going off she mentions two high adventures to tempt the valiant: that of Castle Orgulous and the more difficult liberation of the Maid of Montesclaire. These are at once undertaken by Gawain and other knights. But Perceval alone vows that he will not sleep two nights in the same spot, that he will in fact not rest until he repairs his error by finding the *graal* and bleeding lance and by comprehending their mystery.

The episode (vv. 4603-746) is brief but crucial if we would grasp the general structure of the romance, such as Chrétien seems to envisage it. The narrative pivots at this point and dilates unexpectedly; as in the *Erec* and *Yvain,* a crisis causes the action to rebound. Perceval's role is enriched with new meaning as he is directed away from the involvements of the other Knights of the Round Table.

The Loathly Damsel continues to pour out curses and scorn on the unworthy hero, implacably proclaiming his responsibility for all to hear: "'All these calamities will befall because of you.'" Most disastrous of all—something his cousin had not mentioned in the forest—is that his error is unforgivable, that once missed, the opportunity will never knock again. Perceval is at a crossroads: one way will be the easier, more orderly path, gaily embellished with worldly glory; the other seems to lead nowhere. Perceval chooses to undertake the impossible adventure, the conquest of the Grail. In this sublime moment, the hero's liberty is proven, for Perceval refuses fate, refuses to despair over the irreversible. Indeed, the revelation by the loathsome messenger that the Fisher King would never be healed was a most cunning trap. Neither Gawain nor the others have a mind to replace Perceval on the quest for the Grail and lance. The Loathly Damsel offers adventures within their reach, dangerous, bestowing "supreme glory" (line 4708), but merely chivalrous. She even seems to snigger a bit as she sees false hopes glimmer in their eyes.

Thus an antithesis between Gawain and Perceval is established in this episode, although Chrétien shuns the obvious and direct, expressing it discreetly with a very simple, pregnant line to underscore the contrast: *"Et Percevaus redit tot el,"* "But Perceval spoke otherwise" (v. 4727).

This autonomous, willful decision, made by a hero of inner freedom, distinguishes Perceval from the brilliant court to which he belongs. Yet he still has in view no other battles or trials but chivalric adventures, no other concerns of a spiritual nature. And he manifests no repentance. There has been no mention of his mother, and Perceval is unmindful of God.

For five years he performs magnificent acts of chivalry, but has not yet found the way to the Grail. Morally confused, he has never entered a church and has forgotten God (vv. 6217-37). He has not grasped the religious significance of the adventure, for his soul remains unrepentant.

A graphic and remarkable event causes him great agitation and awakens his conscience: the sight of penitent knights and ladies in a deserted forest on Good Friday. At their direction, he reaches a hermitage where he falls to his knees weeping at the chapel door. The good hermit hears his confession and Perceval acknowledges his fall in the Fisher King's castle, reproaching himself for his failure in the Grail adventure, for he has forgotten God. Hearing his name, the hermit sadly explains to him that his tongue had been tied at the Grail castle because he had left his mother in a swoon. Perceval here learns, moreover, of his whole ancestry: the Fisher King is his cousin; the Fisher King's father (Perceval's maternal uncle) has been an invalid for fifteen years and has not left the chamber where the glorious procession passes. But he is of so pure a spirit that a single Mass wafer brought to him in the *graal,* "so sacred a thing" (line 6425), suffices to keep him alive. Thus the ascetic and mystical background is revealed, something Perceval has not fully understood since his visit to the Fisher King's castle.

For his penance, the hermit (another maternal uncle) gives Perceval counsels of piety and charity which the nephew sincerely promises to follow. For two days Perceval must share the hermit's frugal food;

137

Chrétien de Troyes

he attends Good Friday services, adores the cross, and feels peace arising within his soul. He receives Communion on Easter Sunday. The narrative then returns to Gawain, telling nothing more, ending abruptly. Never before had Chrétien set forth a structure of such complexity. According to our summary, at least three "well-organized narratives" *(conjointures)* and three meanings are superimposed. In the first stage of Perceval's growth he serves an apprenticeship as the "young fool." The treatment is racy and supple, though its natural acceleration cannot conceal the gradually concerted tableaux bundled in narrative segments, to mark turning points in the life of the hero. These episodes are filled with human truth both for Perceval and for us, each of them representing the different phases of human existence. The first level, then, is psychological, during which Perceval's "naivety" explains his error of judgment in failing to ask the fateful question at the castle of the Fisher King.

A second stage, a moral drama, is revealed when the progressive development of the adventures reaches a climax. It is characterized by a problem of continual interest to Chrétien, that of the hero's awareness of his duties and inner freedom. In Perceval's case, these are asserted, even though the Loathly Damsel predicts failure, when he sets out to undo the wrong he has done.

The third is a spiritual experience, depicted as a slowly dawning consciousness of his mother's suffering and death. This is the cause of Perceval's muteness. Previously uncommitted to grace or repentance, he is redeemed spiritually on Good Friday.

Understood as a symbol, the Grail corresponds to each of these stages. The passing of the cortege illustrated Perceval's amusing but tragic naivety *(niceté)* as well as his fervor, completely spent on the enjoyment of prestigious marvels found in chivalry. Then he undergoes a glimmering awareness of his own inner freedom roused by the vision of the Grail. And finally, the image of the eucharistic Grail brings a full illumination and purification of the hero.

Thus interpreted, the romance must be confronted with the complex legend, to which the Grail is integral, in that it furnished the title of the work. But this is only half of the story. For the legend also comprises the Fisher King, his castle, and his pathetic kingdom; it includes the fateful questions which, if asked during the procession (Why is the lance bleeding? Whom does one serve with the *graal*?), would heal the king and bring joy to his land. But whence comes the strange tale? Is there a connection between it and the rest of Perceval's adventures? For this complicated problem, the most diverse opinions have been held. It is most difficult of all because, to examine it properly, one should consider all medieval traditions of the Grail and compare the various versions. One single fact is unquestionable in the *Conte du Graal,* one guiding truth, namely, the heterogenous character of a highly elaborated legend. Christian notions mingle with magical marvels of paganism, grafted in such a way as nearly to compromise the narrative coherence.

According to the theory of Christian origins, the bleeding lance is no other than the Holy Lance of Longinus, and the grail, containing the Mass wafer (perhaps a consecrated host), supposedly designates a liturgical vessel, or ciborium, or chalice, or ciborium-chalice, or perhaps even a pyx, thus somehow related to eucharistic ritual. Whatever its variants, this religious interpretation is in harmony with the spiritual cast of Perceval's experience on Good Friday and is in essential conformity with the late and partial revelations by the hermit (although he says only that for fifteen years the repeated service of the *graal* is a host borne like food to the Fisher King's father, but gives no explanation for the bleeding lance). Yet the most knotty problem of all is to determine whether the liturgical, Christian theory—which nearly coincides with what might be called a revelation of the *sen* in the hermitage episode—suffices to explain the *whole* legend. For the fact is that it does not agree in many details with the text.

To designate a liturgical vessel as a *graal* is surprising in itself, and certainly no more appropriate for a ciborium or chalice. As evidenced by a number of citations, a *graal* (similar to the carving platter or *tailloir* carried by the second damsel in the cortege), is a part of a vessel unattested except in the service of a profane meal of delicacies. In his Latin chronicle dating from the beginning of the thirteenth century, Helinandus of Froidmont has significantly defined the contemporary meaning of a *graal: "Gradalis autem sive gradale gallice dicitur scutella lata et aliquantulum profunda, in qua pretiosae dapes cum suo jure divitibus solent apponi gradatim,... et dicitur vulgari nomine* 'graalz.'" ("The Grail is the French name for a broad and somewhat deep dish in which delicacies are often set before the rich in different rows....It is also called in the vernacular, '*graalz*.'")

One must then imagine the Grail as a dish *(scutella)* in the medieval sense of the word: a plate or dish, with no hint of vulgarity, of a particular form notable for its width, not for its depth: *lata et aliquantulum profunda,* "broad and somewhat deep," but most likely much wider than deep *(aliquantulum* is not *aliquantum).* Helinandus specifies also that a *graal* was used to bring exquisite food to the table of the wealthy and that it was silver or of some other precious material. Thus the presence of a *graal* in the Fisher King's castle at first would normally call to people's minds an aristocratic usage, with the exception of the fact that the golden object which fascinates Perceval is exceedingly bright and splendid. Other occurrences of the word—both earlier and later than Chrétien's romance—do not controvert Helinandus's definition. Within a brief description of a knightly meal in the epic poem *Girart de Roussillon* (ca. 1136-80) are cited grails with gold spangles—*greaus ab aur batuz*—beside goblets, basins, and vases *(orçols)* both large and small; "goblets, grails, candelabra" is found in the same poem, in an enumeration of precious objects (W.M. Hackett, ed., vv. 1622, 6370). A more interesting example, suggesting clearly that a *graal* is to be distinguished from a small cup or bowl, occurs in the decasyllabic version of the *Roman d'Alexandre* (ca. 1170): when a pilgrim sat down as a guest at a seneschal's table, two passages specify that he "drank from his bowl of pure gold" and that he "ate with him from his *graal.*"[5] Finally a passage in the *First Continuation of Perceval* relates that a *graal* is wide enough to allow a boar's head to be brazed *upon* it, a characterization in agreement with the epithets used by Helinandus, *lata et aliquantulum profunda.*[6]

Nothing authorizes us to believe that Chrétien imagined the *graal,* carried across the "hall" in the Fisher King's castle, in any other way except as a wide and hollow dish.[7] Even if it were not so for authors who followed in his wake, Chrétien gave the word a precise, technical meaning, one it perhaps had among the twelfth-century nobility. Moreover, one passage, paramount for the understanding of the story, implies that the enigmatic and sumptuous *graal* was large enough to hold good-sized fish. Thus Chrétien, through the hermit, explains to Perceval whom one serves with the *graal:* "'And believe me that the rich Fisher

is the son of the king who causes himself to be served with the grail
[del graal]. But do not think that he takes from it *[qu'il ait]* a pike, a
lamprey, or a salmon. The holy man sustains and refreshes his life with
a single Mass wafer'" (vv. 6417-24). This allusion to fish by which the
father of the Fisher King is perhaps nourished must be associated with
the origins of the legend. So too, when the fish are replaced by a host
with no apparent correlation to the new and startling revelation in
meaning, the significance is obscure. A dropped stitch, an awkward
change is noticeable here. Does the mention of the pike, lamprey, and
salmon, as has been claimed, have anything to do with the Grail service?
The immediate context and manner of the passage imposes the view
that the *graal* could be used to carry large fish to the "holy man." The
expressions used by Chrétien ("And believe me," "do not think")
would be absurd if the eventuality mentioned was altogether improbable
or contradictory to the form and size of the Grail. It is the better part
of wisdom, then, to keep to Helinandus's definition when considering
the *graal* in Chrétien's romance. Critics have attempted, more or less ingeniously and laboriously—always without success—to transform this
wide and hollow dish into a bowl similar to a ciborium or chalice.
Does this suggestion mean that the Grail borne ceremoniously—yet
without a single pious gesture—to the Fisher King's father carries no
religious value? Obviously not, for each time it holds a wafer and is
qualified by the hermit as "so sacred a thing." In Christian tradition
there is in fact a supremely sacred vessel that easily conforms to the
"broad and somewhat deep dish," a single one, the dish used at the
Last Supper. However odd it may seem, we must recognize the equi-
valence, even if purely symbolic, between this holy *paropsis* ("small
dish") and the Grail of the mysterious castle, although the evangelical simplicity of the one cannot match the obviously amazing allusive-
ness of the Grail, which itself turns our eyes always to other horizons.

Before he saw the *graal*, Perceval watched a young squire carry,
"grasping by the middle," a bright white lance. There is no accompany-
ing light. Its special feature is that from its white point of iron a drop of
blood oozes down to the hand of the squire. This is the "lance which
bleeds," as Chrétien calls it, and the expressions he uses in this regard
imply that a drop of blood continually reappears at the tip before dripping down the length of the handle: "the lance of which the point

141

bleeds, though there is no flesh or vein there" (vv. 3549-50); "Sin cut off your tongue when you saw before you the bleeding point which never has been staunched..." (vv. 4656-58); "...the lance of which the point continually bleeds; and never can it be wiped enough to keep a new drop of blood from forming again at the tip" (vv. 6113-15); "the lance of which the point cries tears of bright blood."[8] This last usage seems altogether conclusive: the dripping or oozing of the lance is continuous, tear after tear, drop after drop, intermittently, or perhaps rapidly or slowly, whereupon each drop, once formed at the point, oozes down the shaft. No medieval author ever conceived of the "lance which bleeds" as not bleeding. It even happens that in certain Grail romances the effusion of blood is almost a violent hemmorhage. Though Chrétien is more tasteful and discreet in his poem, nothing in the text justifies the supposition that he limited the marvel of the lance to an indelible trace of a single drop. Now is this "lance which bleeds" simply the Holy Lance? One detail suggests Chrétien's intention to connect the two lances: at the Fisher King's the blood flows down to the squire's hand; and, according to the legend of Longinus, from the wound in the crucified Christ's side, blood and water flowed the length of the lance down to the blind centurion's hand, who then regained his sight by rubbing his bloody hand over his eyes. But this faintly recondite analogy does not dispose of the whole mystery. Explore as one may the complex history of the origin of the Holy Lance or of the relic's peregrinations, nowhere is any miracle chronicled about blood flowing from its point. As far as we can determine, it is only after Chrétien de Troyes and his narrative tradition that the Holy Lance emerges as the lance which bleeds. Here again is an apparent mutation in the *Conte du Graal*, and, if so, it must be taken either as a personal religious meditation that compelled the poet to invent alone this splendid ornament of ever-flowing blood, or else his lance which bleeds derives from a source other than religious literature on the Holy Lance; thus, somehow considering the latter, he naturally associated two different concepts.

One motif seems to substantiate the second of these hypotheses, the devastation of the kingdom of Logres by the lance which bleeds: "It is written that the day will come when the whole kingdom of Logres...will be destroyed by this lance" (vv. 6168-71). It is quite

142

6. Yvain Vanquishes the Two Demons.
(Princeton University Library, Garrett MS 125, fol. 26v.)

doubtful that this destructive role can be reconciled with the Holy Lance, instrument of the Passion and the Redemption. And for what reason would the usually indulgent author of *The Story of the Grail* decide that the Saviour's vengeance must now strike down Arthur's realm through the Holy Lance? The kingdom of Logres is already Christianized, as the Good Friday episode demonstrates. If its prestige and enchantment endure side by side with religion as in most Arthurian romance, there is no justification for a divine chastisement as harsh as the *destruction* of an entire country. Thus, it is all the more likely that in this motif survive some mythical features relative to the marvels of Britain. The lance which bleeds is apparently a compound of pagan and Christian elements.

There is no question of attributing a religious significance to the cortege of the lance and *graal,* yet we cannot determine the amount of significance in relation to other elements. Does the procession represent Holy Communion given to one dying? In this view, it is in an emergency that the holy viaticum, contrary to the liturgy, is administered by a woman. But the Fisher King's father is not sick as such, only an ascetic who, for fifteen years has sustained his life solely by being served with the Grail. Other critics have suggested further the Great Entrance Rite of the Greek church, a Byzantine interpretation even less substantiated than the preceeding, for with each of these opinions we are forced to admit that Chrétien somehow ingeniously travestied the liturgy.

More preferable are the nonliturgical definitions advanced by Roques:[9] it is the lance of Longinus that bleeds, reminiscent of the eternal and ever-renewed sacrifice of the Redemptor. The *graal* is the eucharistic vessel "in which the Church visibly and symbolically gathers the blood of Christ." The procession viewed by Perceval would be "like an animated, living tableau of the immobile symbols of the crucifixion," and thus closely related to a frequent iconographic theme in late twelfth- and thirteenth-century religious art. For example, a miniature from the *Hortus deliciarum (Garden of Delights)* represents, on the right and left below the cross, two contrasting allegorical female figures, *Ecclesia* and *Synagoga* (the "church" and the "synagogue"). The latter is blindfolded, but *Ecclesia,* wearing a crown, gathers in a chalice the blood flowing from the wound in Christ's body, made by the lance of Longinus, who, in fact, stands next to *Ecclesia,* and holds his weapon slightly tilted, while extending his other hand toward Christ's face. There is no good reason to doubt that this scene influenced the elaboration of the cortege, and the notion that a summary image of Christian dogma was observed by Perceval is easily assimilable to the spiritual character of his adventure.[10] This theory is persuasive also because, according to it, *Ecclesia* can be the "legitimate bearer of a sacred vessel," thus solving with elegant simplicity the insoluble problem which the role of the Grail damsel presented to liturgical theorists. Nevertheless, certain curious anomalies subsist if we assume that Chrétien used no other source but this allegory.

But we must go on to point out the striking differences between textual evidence and the miniature in the *Hortus deliciarum: Ecclesia* at the foot of the cross gathers the divine blood in a chalice held up with a single hand. The damsel in the procession grasps the *graal* "in her hands"; blood from the lance cannot flow into it (the Grail) because it bears the single Mass wafer which sustains the Fisher King's father. All other Grail romances that represent the mystic and graphic vision of the redeeming blood gathered in the eucharistic vessel post-date Chrétien. If, on the other hand, the dogmatic meaning connected with the succession *both* of the lance *and* of the *graal,* taken solely as Christian symbols, were inherent and indispensable to Chrétien's elaboration of the cortege, is it not odd that the *graal* alone crosses the room with each course-change of the meal (vv. 3291, 3299-301), but without any mention of the lance? Nor must we forget that Perceval was a visitor there for only a single night, while one has served with the *graal* for some fifteen years. But is it a service that includes *Ecclesia* or not? Are we really certain that *Ecclesia* is to be unquestionably identified with the "beautiful, gracious, splendidly-garbed" damsel? Appeals to personifications or allegorical readings are not usually Chrétien's style.[11] But let us concede (putting aside for the moment the second damsel of the procession) that the poet made an exception in favor of *Ecclesia.* Then we must also allow that he took great pains to disguise her, for indeed, why is her crown gone, why is there no cross, no "cross-shaped standard," which is held in her left hand in the *Hortus* miniature? And especially why not leave her the title of *dame,* "lady," suitable to the spouse of Christ, rather than designate her with the merely honorific *demoiselle* ("damsel"), *pucelle* ("maiden"), and finally with *on* ("one"). This indefinite pronoun is only used by the hermit as he relates that with the *graal* the Fisher King's father is served: "...the Mass wafer which comes [literally that one brings to him] in the grail."[12] It seems that Chrétien did not consider this feminine character as *Ecclesia,* or else he has in no way hesitated to alter her form. Another important fact shows that no medieval author after Chrétien considered the damsel of the *graal* as an allegory of *Ecclesia.* For instance, in the *Didot-Perceval,* she is replaced by a "squire"; in the *Prose Lancelot* she falls in love with Lancelot and becomes Galahad's mother. It will be noted that her latter-day development in Grail literature did not exactly inspire thoughts similar to the scene in the *Hortus deliciarum.*

Certainly Chrétien's refined style might confuse us enough to miss his hidden intentions. But would he allow himself to use an unwieldy mystification to distort a religious allegory, if *indeed* it produced his vision of the cortege? And would this effort then be art or illusion? In matters of artistic creation the opposite seems more poetic and more natural, if, that is, we consider the whole narrative and its tone within the whole legend. Rather than depicting a travesty of religious mystery, our author raised, it would seem, a magical and primitive tale to the level of inviting Christian phenomena.

The culminating interpretation of the *Conte du Graal* must include a religious meaning, but one that should not conceal the text, which, in fact, clearly reflects the original theme: service from the Grail involves food. The wafer brought to the Fisher King's father is defined as a food that nourished because of the supernatural power of the dish in which it comes: he "sustains and refreshes his life" (line 6424); it is "sustenance" for "twelve years" (vv. 6427, 6429) for the old man. Service from the *graal* is first of all a miracle of food, a fundamental legendary feature that survives in all, even the most Christian, versions.

The impression one has when considering the cortege and *graal* scenes is not so much one of dogmatic symbolism but rather of its romantic religious character, in harmony with the legendary atmosphere with which Chrétien imbued his romance of adventure and chivalry—in spite of certain rationalizations or a few hidden winks about the marvelous. Chrétien's supposed remembrance of some precise liturgical tableau or of some allegorized theological conceptions cannot explain fully the easily seductive ambiguity floating around the lance and *graal*. A magic is there, fitting for the free play of imagination and subtle compromise, favoring more poetic symbolism than matters of orthodoxy. The two realms—the nimbus of Christianity that seems to illuminate the damsel of the Grail, and the marvels of Britain, with a surfeit of damsels of Arthurian fiction—are not necessarily mutually exclusive.

Moreover, it is audacious and arbitrary under any circumstances to isolate either lance or *graal* from the other formants of the legend. But whence derive the rich Fisher King and his castle? Whence comes the Loathly Damsel? Certainly she does not appear in Christian tradition. To what beliefs are related the power of the question which would cure the infirm king, restore his sovereignty, establish happiness and prosperity in his kingdom? The function of this theme is essential, for it creates a psychological and dramatic link between the passing of the two objects and the destiny of both the Fisher King and Perceval. If suppressed, all is mutilated. And if the theme can indeed be reconciled with a Christian interpretation of the romance (we note that it has been eliminated from the narration in the *Quest of the Holy Grail—Queste del Saint Graal*), who would venture to affirm that its origin is neither primitive nor magical? One must ask then what would have been the primordial meaning of the question in relation to the eucharistic mystery.

This does not mean that to search for a non-Christian origin of the legend will solve all the problems. For the legend, or variants of it, is known in folklore and mythology the world over. It has been connected with vegetation cults; with ancient oriental mysteries, such as the cults of Attis, Osiris, and Adonis; and even with various myths whose common feature is the seasonal alternation of death and resurrection. The "waste land" (which is more latent in Chrétien's romance than in other versions of the Grail story) conjoins the sterility of the land to the infirm king's wound and to the return of fertility when he is healed. Perceval's visit to the castle of the Fisher King (the "maimed") has been seen perhaps provisionally as broadly analogous to an unsuccessful initiation to a fertility rite.

But the most interesting parallels have been drawn with Celtic traditions—not surprising, generally speaking, in an Arthurian context. From this angle, the *graal* would go back to one of the marvelous containers mentioned in many Irish and Welsh tales–caldrons, baskets, drinking horns, bowls, dishes, plates of plenty—all of which emanate some degree of magic insofar as they freely dispense drink and food. These objects, symbols of wealth and fertility, most often belong to otherworld treasures and talismans of kingship; sometimes they were won on journeys or raids by heroes. Now the food-producing function of the *graal* is not as evident in Chrétien's work as in the later romances. For Wolfram von Eschenbach it grants to each guest his fill of food and drink; in the *First Continuation of Perceval* and the *Quest of the Holy Grail,* circulating without support from table to table, it distributes one's choice of food automatically. But in Chrétien's work the nutritive feature of the *graal* is not suppressed, only attenuated or oriented toward a religious meaning. The reiterated passings of the *graal* in the hall, at each course-change during the knightly feast, may possibly have some sort of relationship with the unending profusion of delicacies. With discretion, Chrétien specifies merely a simultaneity of the two events, though he customarily diminishes the marvelous without completely effacing it. He seems to be performing with both the real *and* the supernatural in the two scenes, so that the strange goings and comings of the *graal* perhaps represent a survival of its magical powers.

A "lance which bleeds" (or at least a bleeding lance) also exists in Celtic mythology and literature. An otherworld talisman like the dishes and bowls of plenty, it is a divine, royal weapon, alternately a lance of fire and a lance of blood red, a terrible instrument of vengeance and destruction. For example, the intense heat of Celtchar's burning warrior lance may be cooled only by plunging it into a caldron of poisoned blood, whereupon blood flows profusely from it, then drips, then the lance turns back slowly to flames. Obviously, the image of the lance in Chrétien's harmonious, imposing description does not correspond to such mythical primitivism. But Chrétien was an artist, and as such was doubtless capable of reworking and refining any raw material impinging upon him, and could, for the flowing blood, substitute a single, recurrent drop. In this way, he might effect a mystical protraction toward the notion of *the* Holy Lance and the eternal Redemption. Nevertheless, the lance which bleeds will bring the fall of the kingdom of Logres; thus it retains some kinship with the mythical Celtic lance, though Chrétien's intention was clearly not to designate two different lances in an identical way, as has been conjectured.

The only plausible origin so far advanced for the mysterious, wealthy, and infirm Fisher King also brings us to Irish and Welsh legends. It remains quite problematic to trace out the whole apparent pedigree, so that we hesitate to single out one mythological ancestor for this character. Among various possible progenitors—all somewhat interchangeable— the hero Bran, Bran the Blessed, seems the least unconvincing since part of his legend suggests parallels with the story of the Fisher King. Bran, a marine divinity or one associated with the sea, or, in certain adventures, an otherworld king, possesses a marvelous caldron and a horn of plenty. Renowned for his luxuriant hospitality, he suffers from a battle wound made by a lance in his foot, so that he must give up his throne. By comparison, Robert de Boron calls the Fisher King both Hebron and Bron, the latter name considered by several scholars as related to Bran. Granted that these are thematic, not identical, analogies between the two characters, yet, as is known, the transmission of Celtic mythology to Arthurian romance involved a certain rupture or mutilation of the mythical schemata. Just as the legendary Irish oceanic circumnavigations *(immrama)* were reduced, as Philipot noticed, to the crossing of a river or of a castle moat, a marine deity might be transformed into a fisherman. Thus, the Fisher King's castle in Chrétien's romance emanates the marvelous aura of an otherworld palace: at first invisible to Perceval, it suddenly arises, near a river of deep rapids, from nowhere (vv. 3466–82), and its inhabitants mysteriously disappear. It has also been observed that the disposition of the hall in which the Fisher King receives Perceval is mindful less of a medieval castle than of the royal palace of Tara in Ireland, with its banquet hall *(bruiden)* presided over by an otherworld deity. There we find the hearth in the middle of the room, the warriors seated around it on couches, with the king's place situated in front of the fire. The exact form of *the* tale known to Chrétien, or more probably that of the *tales* he synthesized, is lost, but nevertheless certain correspondences between various Celtic myths and the character of the *wealthy* Fisher King must be recognized. For, in fact, the epithet *wealthy* is apt for a master of a marvelous castle in which circulates, at each meal, a golden *graal* encrusted with precious stones, the most beautiful gems "that exist in the sea and in the earth." Nor does it seem inappropriate to associate the epithet with the theme of abundance and perhaps with the enigmatic name Fisher King. Chrétien's explanation of the name, by the way, that he fishes because he can no longer hunt, typically does not reflect a primitive notion, but does demonstrate a kind of secondary rationalization often associated with the processes of mythology.

Other parallels have been drawn concerning the cortege, the waste land theme, Perceval's silence which presumably was the result of an ancient *geis* ("taboo," "injunction"). Further parallels deal with the meaning of the questions (apparently related to the surrender or restoration of kingship), with the Loathly Damsel (conversant with Perceval's error), and with the damsel of the Grail. The latter two perhaps have an affinity with a mythical figure, the "Sovereignty of Ireland," whose two-fold aspect was manifested either as a radiant maiden or a monstrous witch. In each case it is possible to note both the analogies and the dissimilarities. In a word, the major themes of the Grail romances may be found within the body of Celtic mythology, but nowhere in the extant medieval narratives are these themes organized or disposed in any way, except in the form of a scattered, disjointed puzzle.

It is possible, however, that a general schema, or a kind of mythical Celtic archetype formed a nadir for disparate tales. In his study, *La Légende arthurienne et le Graal,* Jean Marx has endeavored in particular to reconstruct its fundamental schematic coherence, basing his ideas on both Irish and Welsh materials and on the corpus of Grail literature. The pattern, then, would be that the quest for the Grail departs from the terrestrial court in response to a call from the otherworld, threatened with sterility and death. The realm surrounding the magical castle of the otherworld king, or Grail castle, was once extraordinarily fertile but now has become the waste land because the king was dealt a "dolorous stroke" by some magic weapon—lance, javelin, or sword—that is, one of the marvelous, talismanic objects of the otherworld kingdom. There would thus be at the outset a close relationship between the lance which bleeds and the wound which caused the Fisher King's infirmity. The king has been killed, crippled, or maimed especially in his virile parts by the dolorous stroke, a catastrophe with repercussions or near-repercussions in the whole terrestrial court. The hero, the chosen

150

one, will then penetrate the Grail castle, overcome obstacles, vanquish the effects of the dolorous stroke, heal the infirm king, restore fertility to the earth, and, will himself then become king of the Grail and of the otherworld. All these motifs—the dolorous stroke *and* its abrogation, the maimed king, the waste land, the quest for the Grail, and the talismans of sovereignty—together form a transparent and grandiose mythical structure, a provocative reconstruction which, in fact, is not altogether fanciful, even if it has been severely criticized for injecting themes properly belonging to twelfth- and thirteenth-century Arthurian romance into Celtic mythology. Yet between the two areas certain fundamental patterns seem unquestionable, and it would only be logical to attribute precedence to the mythological conceptions. Still, the very spine of the primitive, hypothetical schema remains just that, conjectural, even though the proposed hypothesis is ingenious and at times convincing.[13]

Today *The Story of the Grail* has become an adventure especially for erudite critics anxious to explain the origins of the mysterious and intriguing legend. Their own quest is strewn with enigmas, pitfalls, and temptations, difficulties arising mostly from the far too fragmentary documentary lacunae. To research the Grail legend, Arthurian scholars have to face the ever-diminishing mythical framework, must own their ignorance of Chrétien's immediate sources, must reckon with the unfinished state of his poem, and must recognize the scintillating subtleties of his narrative, all of which deterrents aggravate our doubts and incertitudes. But it has also happened that overly systematic critical attitudes or exclusively biased views regarding a single theory have perverted or complicated the possibility of open debate.

One fact, however, is in no way subject to doubt: the *Conte du Graal* as we know it amalgamates Christian elements with those emanating the marvelous and the magical. Every attempt to interpret the romance according to only one of the two great antagonistic theories, the Christian and the Celtic (or at least the primitive), any attempt to deny the work any contact with the *matière de Bretagne* and Celtic mythology, is doomed forthwith to reveal its shortcomings because textual anomalies will always crop up in the process. But for the Grail and for the lance which bleeds, a unilateral explanation cannot suffice. The blend of pagan marvel and Christian supernatural calls forth the logical alternative that either the *Conte du Graal* paganizes the Christian input or it Christianizes pagan input. To choose one or the other can remain a matter of personal preference, but the first option runs counter to the history of literary ideas. With the second we can more easily embrace the strange and equivocal nature of narrative.

It would really not be difficult to disclose briefly how the pagan primitive tale was Christianized. Even though we still have to accept the problem of working within the probable, all the marks of a seam between the primitive myth and its Christian reorientation have not worn away. The terms *graal* and *tailloir* ("paten," "carving platter") simply do not harmonize with the word "Mass wafer," and, in my opinion, when the hermit reveals that instead of the pike, lamprey, or salmon, the *graal* serves, for his only nourishment, the Fisher King's holy father with a "host" *(oiste),* this is a most crucial passage in every sense of the word. If, on the other hand, we consider the nutritive power of the host as a consequence of the sacred nature of the *graal,* and that its presence *in* the *graal* cannot be explained by any kind of outside intervention, we may presume that the magical power of the receptacle of plenty survives in the *graal* of Chrétien's romance, just as it apparently survives in subsequent versions. In other words, Chrétien would have drawn from the mythical concept the notion of a receptacle that regenerates boundless nourishment. But, mindful also perhaps of certain hagiographic legends in which an angel or a dove brings a nourishing host to a saintly anchorite, he might have substituted a small wafer for the theme of abundance, represented, it seems, by the enumeration of large fish that the *graal,* in an earlier version, may very well have served the rich Fisher King. In this way, Chrétien would have achieved, in addition to a spiritualization of the theme, a kind of dilation—from quantity to quality; the transmutation of the fish into the wafer would parallel the change of the primitive *graal* into a Christianized one: "Do not believe" (to paraphrase the hermit's words), "in a *graal* with multiple fish; the true one is that of the single wafer." Here is uncovered the *new sen* by which the tale waxes, and the shift effects a double surprise: first the contrast between what *was* believed and what *is* learned, then the disparity between the size of the receptacle and the meagerness of the miraculous nourishment. The modification is also a modulation: the *graal,* "so sacred a thing," now a transcendent one, adumbrates *the* Holy

Grail. Even unexplained, the transfusion evokes, at a distance, the mystical image of the Last Supper dish, yet without overstepping the limits of symbolic suggestion. But the Christian interpretation of the marvelous dish remains nevertheless bolstered by the magic given.

It is also possible that the Fisher King's father was invented to enhance the Christian meaning of the tale. Rather curiously, this personage is missing in several versions; perhaps the original legend told only of the Fisher King. In any case, the invisible ascetic, chronically confined to his chamber, serves to create the enigma of the cortege. Over and above the profane and brilliant feast in the castle hall, the character represents the spiritual plane, a notion veiled until the moment when Perceval's conscience awakens to contrition.

Is there anything unusual about our author's Christianization of a pagan tale? To such a question there can be only one resounding answer: a multiplicity of examples exists that demonstrate the medieval tendency to "moralize" pagan fables, once their latent power of converging toward religious truths was understood. The kind of prevalent mental attitude and the method involved in the systematic reinterpretation of Virgil and Ovid through adumbration and symbolism should be considered as equally operative for all legendary fiction, not just for that of Graeco-Roman antiquity. Now it is true that Chrétien hardly betrays a "moralizing" tendency in his earlier romances, although he was always careful to enhance the *matière* with an original *sen*. But his *Conte du Graal* marks a change in direction: the evangelical interest of its prologue and the hermitage episode have no equivalent in *Erec and Enide, Cligés, Lancelot,* or *Yvain.* Nevertheless, a pristine "moralization" of the Grail remains comparatively diffuse and poetically buoyant.

If he raised a tale of fancy to the threshold of Christian interpretation and elicited the idea of Redemption by the passing of the lance which bleeds and of the *graal,* this may enable us to explain the ambiguous atmosphere, the *chiaroscuro* ("light-dark") of sacred and profane that bathes the scene surrounding the cortege. This very ambiguity, adhering to the narrative structure, whereby, in fact, two different levels are juxtaposed or rather superimposed, is at once indicative of a rational, prudent, and suggestive style. But it also becomes, either because of Chrétien's perfected talent or because of the splendid subject, a form of poetic invention. A symbolism of marvelous objects emerges from this ambiguity; it illuminates the miraculous sustenance in the enchanted abode of the rich and infirm Fisher King, and it throbs with thoughts of Christian mystery. Like filigree, a *conjointure* binds the texture of the narrative to successive images of the ambiguous and symbolic *graal.* The creative continuity, whereby profane manifestations are elevated to religious ones, parallels, in part, Perceval's own development from a near-savage and quasi-heathen (he has some inkling of Christian dogma, but lacks charity) to knighthood, courtesy, and spirituality.[14]

Perceval is indeed the true hero of the romance. Gawain's adventures belie the deliberate contrast indicated in the "Loathly Damsel" episode, and they reveal that he could not be the definitive model set before the "widow's son." Yet his mode of action remains patently exemplary in many circumstances. Gawain indeed possesses the merits of faultless prowess, scrupulous attachment to chivalric honor and tact, elegance and politeness, but this varnish hides a basic frivolity, a preoccupation with earthly glories, and an incurable weakness for casual amours. In spite of his sympathy, is there not a muffled irony in Chrétien's treatment of a model knight, the brilliant nephew of King Arthur, that leads Gawain to one disappointment after another?

Let us recall one episode when Gawain was about to liberate the Maid of Montesclaire and is deflected from it. A certain Guingambresil appears and, before the court, challenges Gawain, accusing him of treachery in the death of his father, the king of Cavalon. The customary single combat is to take place in forty days. Gawain departs, anxious to keep the rendezvous with Guingambresil. But on the way he does not fail to become interested in the "Maid with Little Sleeves," younger daughter of Tiebaut of Tintagel. It is a zestful situation to find the great champion and veteran lover risking his honor by delay, all for a very young, very innocent girl. But in the course of the journey, he breaks a promise made to himself, thus risking his honor and good name simply for the sake of a mischievous but interesting sweet thing with beautiful eyes. In the keep of Cavalon castle, he is trading sweet nothings and ardent kisses with a charming damsel, the king's sister, when suddenly they are interrupted by the attack of rioting townsmen. After a heroicomic battle, he only manages to escape the impasse by swearing to quest for the bleeding lance. But, in fact, Gawain does none of that and his adventures become ever more curious. Beyond the "Pale of Galloway" he steps into a heteroclite universe of reality and otherworld fantasy. Half-caught in the "evil maiden's" trap, he survives quite well a series of insults, until a new adventure, faintly analogous to that of the Grail, hints of his return to prestige. Crossing a river, he enters an impressive castle and spreads joy among its melancholic inhabitants after a successful test with the "marvelous bed." But he liberates no one. Surrounded by feminine entities, among whom he is surprised to find his grandmother, Ygerna, the hoary queen, with his mother, wife of King Lot, and his sister, Clarissant, Gawain himself is left condemned to become the prince of a courtly gynaeceum and forever a prisoner of enchantment.

Chrétien's account ends shortly after alluding to other episodes: the love between Clarissant and Gawain's enemy, Guiromelant, the proximate arrival of Arthur's court, warned by a message, and so on. We shall never know what continuation he had in mind. But he had sufficiently progressed with his narrative to give a clear feeling of contrast between the adventures of Gawain and of Perceval. It is not an accidental, witty insight. The first, yearning for no other equilibrium but his own, more a tourist than quester of worldly prowess, always led on by his love of universal praise, ends up by lowering himself. The second, dissatisfied with himself, tormented by the unfulfilled desire of a new ideal, enters the path of repentance, thus holding out a more austere, nobler, and purer message.

The right interpretation of the *Conte du Graal* will always remain at once difficult and problematic because of its symbolism and because of its unfinished state. But, in the final analysis, its incompleteness is its special beauty, its mystery, its charm. Like a splendid fragment that evokes dreams of the whole statue, we might say that, had Chrétien brought it to a final conclusion, his romance might not have stirred to the same degree the immense fires of imagination which have prolonged for centuries the effulgence of the Grail.

Chapter 8

Originality
and Influence

All the unknowns of twelfth-century literary history and the extensive
lacunae in Chrétien's biography blur with uncertainty any serious effort to measure precisely his originality. However enticing the works
may be, the shadows (to choose one major problem) surrounding the
very genesis of his Arthurian romances remain filled with unanswerables.
Even though, due to nearly complete ignorance of his immediate
sources, we are prevented from evaluating their influence, we assume
that the *matière de Bretagne* existed before him and we suspect that, in
spite of his scorn of them, he was indebted in some way to various unknown predecessors. However, the virtual borrowing of subjects or
themes is much less important than their treatment, and, in fact, in
Chrétien's case, his poetics reveal most clearly and most precisely his
innovations in romance and his creative talent. Certain indirect testimony, like the Middle High German *Lanzelet,* the three Welsh romances,
The Lady of the Fountain, Peredur Son of Efrawg, and *Gereint Son of
Erbin,* as well as Chrétien's own pithy declarations regarding *matière,
sen,* and *conjointure,* tend to prove that, until his *Erec and Enide,* Arthurian narrative had not risen beyond the level of what Chrétien himself
called the "tale of adventure"–by apparent contrast with the more
elaborate structure of his romances. Everything within his work points
to a lively sense of the craft of fiction and, for a medieval romancer,
to an unequaled degree of esthetic awareness. His distinct contribution
was to cut classical features into a form yet to be determined, bringing

it to perfection through creative imitation and sophisticated invention. Of course, there were other authors at this time who devised and applied artistic principles of composition that might be called *courtly,* but the word *classical* does not seem to suit their endeavors. These rivals, among which the most remarkable is Thomas of England, along with Chrétien, turned a page in French literary history. Yet it seems more appropriate to grant Chrétien primacy over his literary generation.

Indeed, for the second half of the twelfth century, his output is exceptionally rich by comparison with his contemporaries, whom he outproduced in sheer numbers of works. (Assuming that the lesser ones are those not extant, the five romances are preserved in a quite abundant manuscript tradition, a sign of success rather than chance.) But, better still, it is in the choice of subjects that Chrétien manifests most energetically his great artistic vision, from one romance to the next, even when he must work at the behest of a patron. Dovetailing as if fortuitously in a complementary series of alternations and compensations, the diverse themes are joined with a kind of unique dynamic approach to human truths. Thus, the amorous and heroic ardor of *Erec and Enide* contrasts with the slow and precious sentimental analyses and the bashful boldness of sincere hearts in *Cligés;* in succession, the voluntary and mystic disciplines of the courtly lover in the *Lancelot* are followed by the surprises of adventure and love and by worldly bliss lost and regained in the *Yvain.* And, finally, we have the image of chivalry imbued with divine love in the *Conte du Graal.* However concerted this interplay, Chrétien remains throughout a keen observer, one who easily combines ironic and empathetic modes: within the totality of his work, diversity provides the key to harmony. Like a true artist, Chrétien is enabled by his gift to create his own poetic world, a personal one that goes beyond mere ornamentation and pretty expression. Chrétien's deft hand is felt when he delights in viewing and depicting the spectacle of society; his style (his lifestyle, in a way) is to consider the problems of ethics and of action, to *shape* the conduct of his characters, and to make them ideal models of life.

Chrétien's prologues do not really embody what could be called edifying aims: the rhymster tells pleasant stories to divert the audience. Nevertheless, our author remains a moralist, scattering here and there proverbs and maxims, tarrying sometimes with a brief pronouncement on the vices and virtues. Or he will slip in an occasional reflection, a bit of practical advice, or he will let one of his characters speak on his behalf; indeed, certain of his lines sound like moral precepts. In this way, the real meaning and didactic value of a given tale become clearer. The *sen,* his important concept, which is evidence enough of the moralistic intentions in his works, at once recalls the finite nature of man and his world and excludes the notion of art for art's sake, a remote idea for medieval authors. Even though the proem to *Erec and Enide* (vv. 11-12) may advise unequivocally "....that one ought always to study and strive to speak well and teach the right," Chrétien's lessons usually remain more tacit, more subdued, almost inexpressible; with all possible variations in mind, the *sen* must be deduced, according as the levels differ, to include episodic development and character description. The reader's share is a double measure of ethical solace and unobtrusive food for thought. Perhaps Chrétien was thinking of himself and of the interpretation of his whole work when, in *Yvain,* he entrusts Calogrenant, who is to tell of his earlier misadventure at the marvelous fountain, with the declaration that, in order to grasp his narrative, more important than that of the *ear* is understanding by the *heart* (vv. 149-70). Thus arises already the relationship between the story itself and its moral, a notion not unlike that expressed by Voltaire's proclamation in *The White Bull:* "I choose that a story should be founded on probability, and not always resemble a dream. . . . And I desire above all, that under the appearance of fable there may appear some latent truth, obvious to the discerning eye, though it escape the observation of the vulgar."[1] This is why *Erec and Enide, Yvain, Perceval*, and even *Cligés* or *Lancelot* are moral rather than thesis romances, for in each case, a well-defined psychological problem is resolved and the situation each time is so crisply handled as to lay bare the human heart and set forth an art of living. As always, however, the solutions offered accord with the chivalric courtly ethos of Chrétien's elite audience.

The very aristocracy found a kind of social justification in the flattering Round Table fictions whose rules of good manners and noble sentiments were easily learned. The court of Arthur—the king who makes knights—helped set upper-class lifestyles, but it also appears as a privileged center, a collectivity which arbitrates in matters of prowess and which, through praise, may celebrate a hero's glory. Some of Chrétien's most brilliant episodes highlight this normative function of the Arthurian community, in which the lords and ladies of Champagne and France ideally participated. But only in error would we reduce the moral of Chrétien's works to the mere observance of dogmas pertaining to a single, refined social group. For his prominent heroes act on their own, while Arthur's court and its courteous paragon, Gawain, cannot but reflect a certain conformity. Erec, Yvain, and Perceval each respond to generous instincts or to their own conscience, autonomous in their inner freedom; Fenice endeavors to control her inner destiny; and Lancelot himself, the willing slave of love, obeys the law of his existence to the point of scorning social respect. Somehow, in every romance, Chrétien manages to set apart the true hero from all the others. When the most perilous of strange adventures, the "Joy of the Court," arises, Erec ignores the warnings of friendship and the anguished pity of the crowd: "'Nothing could restrain me from going to seek the Joy'" (vv. 5424-25). Similarly, as Yvain advances toward the castle of *Pesme Aventure,* he says: "'...my wayward heart leads me on inside, and I shall do what my heart desires'" (vv. 5176-77). As for Perceval, he alone of the Round Table resolves, against all hope, to attempt the quest for the Grail, even after the Loathly Damsel's imprecations. Across adventures and trials, by their failures and by their exploits, the exemplary heroes loom large, take on character, and become what they are. The most lofty moral of Chrétien's romances, too often forgotten, lies in fact in this very display of individual dynamism, in this simultaneously subjective and objective development of personality. It is unthinkable, of course, that Chrétien would have us admire strength or prowess for their own sakes; the gigantic and naive Mabonagrain—who would be a gem of a knight were he not so large—the victim of an extravagant love service, the valiant upholder of a barbarous custom, is undone by the hearty Erec.[2] The hero, then, must give his all yet retain a sense of moderation and justice, an equilibrium of audacity in check which corresponds to the optimistic *finales* when all the virtualities are realized and reconciled. For, in the end, heroes like Erec or Yvain persevere, determined not to sacrifice love to glory or glory to love, and attain thereby a more beautiful, more human happiness, won in plenitude.

This confidence in the hero and in his inherent resources seems to be one facet of courtly humanism. Until his *Conte du Graal,* Chrétien's ethos is almost uniformly free of religious concerns, filled with profane meditations on man and his world. God is not ignored, he just remains a distant abstraction, a kind of guarantor synonymous with the right. With one exception, we might even say that chivalry in Chrétien's Arthurian romances is nearly that of a lay civilization: Knights of the Round Table, indifferent to the Crusades, never fight enemies of the faithful. The spiritual role of the clergy is nonexistent; religious ceremonies are reduced to sheer convention, ornaments of social life. Not a single heartfelt religious emotion as such elicits prowess.

The *Conte du Graal* brings a change in spirit. As the hermit says to Perceval: "'Believe in God, love God, worship God'" (line 6459). Thus charity, human and divine, is now praised as the yeast of the interior life. The notion of sin and repentance, missing from Chrétien's earlier romances or else reserved for the psychology of love, becomes a moral reality; on Good Friday, pious knights and ladies walk shoeless, dressed as penitents, for the salvation of their souls—a significant image setting a new pace for the romance of adventure. After writing his first four poems, perhaps Chrétien's opinions on chivalry changed; perhaps the purely courtly and profane notion of knighthood was felt to be insufficient, or, possibly in line with Philippe of Alsace's views, it needed renovation. Still, the religious inspiration of the *Conte du Graal* does not go as far as asceticism or mysticism; rather it proclaims that a knight must live according to Christian charity, must repent devoutly for his sins, must hear Mass daily and not leave before the end of the service; he must also honor priests and defend widows and orphans. Such are the hermit's accessible, humanly attainable counsel, by which the eager Perceval will abide.

Between the romances of *Lancelot* and of *Yvain* and the *Conte du Graal* the change is quite marked, but is it a fundamental one? To call it an abrupt break would be inaccurate, for it is not so much dramatic as gradual. Nowhere in *The Story of the Grail* does Chrétien recant courtly values, except that for Perceval courtly love—as revealed in two episodes, one at Blancheflor's castle, the other in contemplation of the blood drops on the snow—has new meaning. With Chrétien's last romance, the ethos of his entire work is broadened significantly, though not to the extent of including a theoretical conflict between secular and religious ideals. As we have said, the ethical problems are treated alternatively, as if in a kaleidoscope. Under these circumstances, how shall we characterize his ethos in a comprehensive way? Its embodiment does not lie in abstractions, like honor, love, and God, which, though distinct, are complementary in his romances rather than mutually exclusive. The ethos of his works is manifested no less harmoniously, but much more in the arena of life and action, by analogous solutions, destined to safeguard at once the reciprocity of social relations and the spontaneity of conscious decisions. On the one hand, Chrétien stresses the art of urbanity, elegant manners, polite language, discrimination in mundane cheer, loyalty, self-control, and liberality, and, of course, disdain for the vulgar or envious—all the qualities of a twelfth-century gentleman. But he also idealizes the difficult, the heroic, the almost superhuman quest for happiness purified by trials of valor. These two aspirations confer an upward movement on Chrétien's ethos and on the structure of his romances, so that values swing from hedonism to abnegation, and always with the subtle interplay of nodal antithesis or of rationally attenuated paradox. Chrétien's conception of love and chivalry encompasses both this hierarchy of values and the blend of the real with the ideal.

In his most accessible way, Chrétien is adverse neither to joie de vivre nor to civilized dilettantism. On his list of diversions enjoyed by Arthur's court in Laudine's castle are flirting, or "amiable regards" *(accointances)* that unite lovers like Gawain and Lunete, and the "love tokens" *(donoi)*, by which is traded the small change of sentimental pleasures (*Yvain*, vv. 2441-67). Here indeed is an indulgent passage, even a little ironic, judging from this decrescendo: "... [there were ladies] of exalted birth, so the men could agreeably employ themselves in caressing and kissing them, and in talking to them and in gazing at them while they were seated by their side: that much satisfaction they had at least." This atmosphere of courtly sensuality does not put Chrétien off, yet he does not prolong it, but flavors the narrative with a brief comment for the ladies: "... such persons may properly be rated as fools for thinking that a lady is in love with them just because she is courteous and speaks to some unfortunate fellow, and makes him

7. The Battle of Yvain and Gawain.
    (Princeton University Library, Garrett MS 125, fol. 38r.)

happy and caresses him. A fool is made happy by fair words and is very easily taken in." With this brief disquisition the author sets apart courtier's trifles from true love. The amiability of the lady is a mark of noble breeding; and only deluded fools and fops misinterpret the full play of flirting in society.

Chrétien was in no way a puritan. But over and above casual affections and coquetry, beyond the charm of the simple love pledge, he conceives of love as a profound sentiment by which our destinies are engaged and by which, through a kind of reenactment in his romances, happiness is threatened, guarded, then augmented. The situations are always various, the problems are never quite the same from one work to the next (though the *Lancelot* seems to be marginal to his own ethical views). But in general Chrétien tends to rework or add nuance to courtly notions, both as adherent and heretic of *fine amor*. His personal ethos is emphasized when he refuses the fatality of love, rejecting the love philtre drunk by Tristan, and when he insists on the primacy of willful election of the beloved. For him, *fine amor* is a gift enjoyed and a religion practiced by the "members of its order" (*Yvain*, line 16). By contrast, Chrétien does not hold to the principle that love and marriage are incompatible; illegitimate or uncommitted unions of passion are condemned, so that the marriage of love is considered the ideal solution: *"Qui a le coeur, si ait le cors"* ("Who has the heart has the body, too"—*Cligés,* line 3163). Thus are reconciled the affections and the reason, love's sovereign privileges and respect for the social code. Chrétien's apology for conjugal love must in fact be seen as quite original and persuasive for a time when marriage was often no more than a feudal contract in which little account was taken of the woman's consent. Chrétien was patently capable, then, of withstanding the clannish prejudices of courtly society. His greatest merits as a moralist are doubtless his depictions of conjugal devotion and his celebrations of total marital mutuality, characterized as a marriage of minds in which rights and duties are shared, in which happiness must be won unselfishly, and in which love and chivalry must correspond.

Like that of love, the chivalric ethos is revitalized in each romance, also moving in an ascending rhythm, gradually unfolding an ever nobler ideal. Unlike the epic hero, the Arthurian hero is above all associated with individual prowess. In Chrétien's works, he fights neither for house, nor king, nor religion. (Alexander, of course, in the beginning of *Cligés,* who defends King Arthur, proves the rule.) Residing in an indeterminate and fabulous Britain, without a formal frame of reference and, in a way, prefiguring the knight-errant, he seems more a champion of civilization in opposition to barbarism.[3] But the Arthurian hero seeks *adventure* first of all to try himself, to increase his worth, and to join the virtual with the real while succumbing to the charm of the marvelous. There is in all this a certain virtuosity beguiled by fame won in tourneys, which Chrétien describes with graphic vitality, especially at the opening of *Yvain,* but which is only a prelude to a still loftier image of knighthood. Expansive because of some inner torments or because they are conscious of missions, his heroes, his knights of the right, will come to defend the weak and deliver the oppressed, an ideal remarkably exalted in Chrétien's last three romances. Erec accomplished only a single act of prowess, namely, the liberation of the pathetic prisoner from two giants. Lancelot, Yvain, and Perceval represent at once a more militant and rueful notion of chivalry, given to self-sacrifice, to a kind of sainthood. This quasi-religious concept in itself will elevate Lancelot and Perceval to the status of predestined heroes, although Chrétien's moral hierarchy abhors asperity, for he prefers multifarious psychological depiction.

Chrétien's artful depiction is not limited to primary characters: surrounding the hero, a number of varied episodic roles sustain and stir the illusion of life. From scene to scene, from one romance to the next, without contrivance and as if by the mere movement of the narrative, the tableau of a whole society is pieced together. While Chrétien's manner is quite unlike that of Balzac, it would not be inaccurate to designate his work as a twelfth-century *Human Comedy,* for, like Balzac's novels, his poems are peopled with characters inseparable from their social conditions, and they are not always condensed from the upper strata. By means of a widening perspective, noticeable especially in *Yvain* and *Perceval,* Chrétien's sights fall on townsmen and peasants and on contemporary political and economic realities. Finally, with the world of Arthurian story, in which the author's imagination seems to move naturally, Chrétien spins a vast, seamless web, a human comedy in which time meets space and whole biographies are elaborated.

And it is most curious, to say the least, that Chrétien, in his successive romances, employs well before the "frantic glutton for life" the technique of recurring characters.

His use of it, of course, involves especially the somewhat official representatives of continuity, those of the Round Table, King Arthur, Queen Guenevere, and Kay the seneschal, as well as the king's nephew and counselor, Gawain. Chrétien clearly took particular delight in the last named, whose portrait is limned to completion as each poem unfolds. Less admired in the *Lancelot* or *Perceval* (by whose disconcerting heroes he is eclipsed) than in *Erec* or *Yvain,* Gawain remains throughout the soul of courtesy, elegance, liberality, and bravura. A knight is ranked by jousting with him, for never did he suffer defeat in battle, unless, like Yvain, you could equal him. To him more than to any other belongs the honorific "my lord," a title that soon became his alone, like a mark of distinction.[4] My lord Gawain is also a worldly knight and a ladies' man who, of course, has no thoughts or time for marriage—love's butterfly cares not to alienate his liberty. His code of life, which he gladly expounds to his friend Yvain threatened by *recreantise,* is a mixture of sporty, chivalric energy and epicurean wisdom, an economy of amorous pleasures stimulated by interruptions and kept up by delays: "'Pleasures grow sweeter through postponement; and a little pleasure, when delayed, is much sweeter to the taste than a great pleasure enjoyed at once. The sweets of a love which develops late are like a fire in a green bush; for the longer one delays in lighting it the greater will be the heat it yields, and the longer will endure its force'" (*Yvain,* vv. 2515-23). The antithesis of the noble, refined, desultory, and sometimes bemocked Gawain is the seneschal Kay, uncourteous, abusive, presumptuous, but zealous and faithful. Thus Chrétien controls and contrasts stress and silence, darkness and light in his undivine comedy.

Even though his artful sense of technique seems pervasive here, and even though the multiplicity of secondary characters is easily diversified and enlivened through fantasy and humor, Chrétien's guide nevertheless at all times is the study of mankind. Perhaps like La Bruyère later at Chantilly, at the court of Champagne he could doubtless sample humanity at will. Can we not assume that he was inspired by living models for his sketches, among many others, of Baudemagus, of Gornemant de Gohort, or Calogrenant? This latter, in fact, Chrétien turns into a discreet model of urbanity, a great knightly gentleman, detached enough to joke about his own misadventures at the fountain of Broceliande; by contrast, in the Welsh story of Owein *(The Lady of the Fountain)*, the analogous character, Cynon, stands out rather because of his flashy fury. But to this same Calogrenant, amazed by such ugliness, and curious as to what kind of creature he is, the monstrous churl, busy watching wild bulls, answers in stout simplicity: "'I am a man'" (line 330). How robust and profound a statement, for immediately it links the cultivated mortal Calogrenant to the teratological oaf, a character behind whose frame lurk the shadows of man's fate. The villein's response would be a fitting epigraph to Chrétien's whole fictional output, in which he ever offers a portrayal of man.

This portrayal is clearly seconded by diverse situations and a graphic handling of attitudes and gestures, but is not limited to a sparkling parade of superficial characters. Even in a quick character sketch, his gift of catching the latent comes through. Undeniable as well is his talent as psychological analyst of love, especially versatile in laying open the mysteries of the female heart. With each, from Enide to Clarissant, the last in his lively procession of heroines, he holds up the mirror to a new facet of love.

Chrétien has been sometimes belittled for his cool, superficial manner, or for his overly witty, jejune style. In a sense, these criticisms are justified; Chrétien is less emotional than intellectual. Though more awkward, Thomas of England's probes of Tristan's amorous anguish are more forceful and penetrating; his empathy with the hero is more intimate. True, Chrétien can engage interest and sympathy for his favorite characters, but almost always, at some point, he turns or steps back, and seems faintly amused by them. Is this necessarily a shortcoming, however? Rather, this hindsight is beneficial for comical and humorous effects, as well as for the study of characters. For this loss of emotional power we are compensated by a gain in lucidity.

Contrary to certain claims, he does not altogether avoid tempestuous passions, yet he prefers to circumvent the storm rather than to cross it: he strikes sail just long enough to describe Lancelot's despair, Guenevere's remorse, or Yvain's folly. He only once represents the pangs of jealousy—in the Proud Knight of the Glade—who believes his mistress unfaithful and is haunted by a real image of betrayal (*Conte du Graal*, vv. 3855-76). Although Ovidian in inspiration (*Ars amatoria*, 1: 661-78), Chrétien retouches the theme with originality: as articulated pointedly by the jealous one, the Latin sermon, by variation, acquires dramatic force and the terseness of a watercolor.

Chrétien is at his delightful best in slow-motion scenes of lovers, startled or troubled by thoughts of love, who seek self-understanding. Shades of feeling and deep-seated contradictions Chrétien thus unravels concisely; such depictions are all part of his quest and transcription of human truths. And it is upon these that is predicated his heady penchant for somewhat theoretical debates. A similar tendency reduces psychological analysis to examinations of inner conflict and cases of conscience, although introspection by a given personage usually concludes with a rational and deliberate decision. For this reason, many critics have recognized in Chrétien a foreshadowing of classical style and expression.

In *Cligés*, for example, even though conventional mannerisms are not avoided, order and clarity temper the speed of monologues and the direction of dialogue, so that the palpable is never hidden by excessive logic or stiffness. But Chrétien's mature experience in matters of life and of technique doubtless enable him to find more buoyant procedures. And he often attains that ethereal moment when his narrative technique disappears completely, when characterization and sentiment are transposed, without artifice, by means of verbal and tonal modulation: then it is that we can not only visualize, but also hear the characters through Chrétien's living words.

Yet another innovation is achieved because of Chrétien's regard for reason and free will; he does not fail to appreciate the importance of affective states or the role of the subconscious. With his deft and pervasive psychological method, he explores or at least alludes to those half-hidden mental states in which free will falters, in which illusions seek shelter, and in which dreams suppress reality. In Alexander's monologue, for example, the excessively subtle, hypertrophic imagery is not just part of some literary game, for, through it, a cause and effect relationship is established between the lover's timidity, the avowal repressed by passion, and his obsessive delirium (*Cligés*, vv. 536-38, 602-8, 627-28, 654-57, 2282-83). Elsewhere appears the phenomenon whereby, once cued, Laudine demonstrates to herself that she does not have the right to hate her husband's slayer, that she could even love him (by a kind of auto-suggestion, ostensibly defined by the witty progression of "the bush which only smokes with the flame beneath, until someone blows it or stirs it up," *Yvain,* 1778-80). Lunete's words are the first spark; then, unknown to Laudine, an inner process causes smoke, in other words, anger, her indignant reaction, as well as the rationalizations hiding the reality of her new feelings; and the flame that dissipates the smoke is her increasingly stronger desire to remarry. With a light but positive touch, Chrétien could depict the hidden harmony between confused affections and the self-deluding intellect. Also related to the handling of subconscious states are the rapturous ecstasies of Lancelot and Perceval, or Lancelot's hallucinatory lions at the end of the sword-bridge. It was truly a stroke of genius to associate such observations with the portrayal of exemplary heroes and with their growing consciousness as part of their personality development.

Chrétien's gifts as moralist and psychologist have not always received their full due, but there is unanimity regarding his admirable imagination and talent as a writer.

He was a born artist no doubt, yet he manifestly enhanced his competence through study and reflection. The pervasive influence of education, of the arts of rhetoric, and of the humanist tradition reminds us that his work cannot be dissociated from a whole literary movement. His poetics of the romance genre are not altogether his own: other courtly authors betray analogous tendencies. With a phrase like *dire en uni* ("to keep to one account," "to collect, gather [material] "), Thomas of England, for instance, expressed in his own way a concern for logic and coherence not unlike Chrétien's *conjointure.*[5] However, by his sense of proportion and equilibrium, Chrétien stands out among contemporary narrators, none of whom combined the internal harmony of *matière, conjointure,* and *sen*—a disparity arising either from the content itself, or from individual excellence, or both. In any case, Chrétien's artful accomplishment alone may be duly compared to the cup given as a reward to Alexander by King Arthur (*Cligés,* vv. 1536-46, 2214-15). Very fine and rich first because it was of gold, it is more esteemed because of the workmanship—the artist's expertise—and, still again, in truth, of most value because of the precious decorative stones set outside it. One might say that through this praise the author wished to enfold within its graduations his conception of romance. Does not the hierarchy of three elements seem to correspond to that of *matière:* one must be able to select a potentially obliging subject; of *form,* without which there is no true creation; and, finally, of *sen,* which illuminates the entire work, like the precious gems that give the trophy its superb dazzle?

In *Erec, Yvain,* and even the *Conte du Graal,* certain parallelisms of plot indicate a deliberate preference for a specific type of structure. The schema, perfected in Chrétien's first Arthurian romance, is characterized by a tripartite composition: a first adventure concludes with the mutual bliss of hero and heroine; then a crisis emerges to link an interior, psychological drama to a moral and social conflict and causes the action to rebound. The third part of the triptych is larger, consisting of a progression of adventures, of which, one most mysterious and marvelous expands the hero's role and ends happily with the reconciliation of the lovers. This methodical pattern is pliant enough to permit variations, but from poem to poem its general features are identifiable. Moreover, in every case thematic or cognate analogies divide the schema, although their order may be altered; examples include the preponderant role of the Arthurian court in the economy of the narrative (the *locus* from which the hero departs or to which he returns, by which he is sought or met); lodging with the hospitable host; battle with a Red Knight; insults avenged; and the passion of a marvelous fairy or of a most beautiful woman. Furthermore, judging from a comparison with the Welsh romances *Gereint Son of Erbin, The Lady of the Fountain,* and *Peredur Son of Efrawg,* it seems likely that Chrétien took the initial framework of his romances from his sources. His innovation was to organize with skill and cogency a yet rough diamond, to cut from it a still latent or virtual form *(conjointure).* With restriction and depth, he augments, like classical writers, the dramatic and psychological interest of the subject; he interrelates convincingly outer behavior and inner motivation, thereby seeking to create an entity in which everything dovetails. Thus he transforms the "tale of adventure" into romance. Chrétien can also implement rhetorical doctrines with great skill. In *Cligés,* he emulates Thomas's *Tristan,* applying studiously the method of "bipartition" recommended by the *artes poeticae* (manuals of poetics and rhetoric): he gives first the story of the parents, Alexander and Soredamors, which takes up almost one-third of the narrative before the son is introduced. However, in the *Lancelot, Yvain,* and *The Story of the Grail* he ingeniously shifts the principle of dualism to the partial parallelism of the adventures by making of Gawain a "brilliant second" in relation to the main hero. It may be noted that in the manuals of rhetoric, elegant and graceful style—a quality everywhere manifest in Chrétien's works—is praised. But was such a style derived solely from poetic doctrines? Though not worthless, the influence of his pedagogical formation cannot report to us about his personal talents, about the secrets of his craft, or about his charming manner as storyteller and poet.

Chrétien is first of all a master of rapidity. He narrates effortlessly, seemingly without deliberation. From *Cligés* we select one sample among many of his incredibly buoyant methods of introducing characters. As Alexander arrives at King Arthur's court, and the king is ready to sail for Brittany, no mention has yet been made of the heroine. But lines 420-21 tell specifically of Alexander's awesome liberality, so much so "...that the king, the queen, and the nobles bear him great affection." In this way, Guenevere enters on stage. After fifteen lines, the maidens of honor appear: "...King Arthur set out the next day, accompanied by the queen and her damsels" (vv. 436-37). Eight lines later, Soredamors is presented: "Into the ship in which the king sailed there entered no youth or maiden save only Alexander and Soredamors, whom the Queen brought with her. This maiden was scornful of love ..." (vv. 441-46). Thus the story slides along with ease, moving toward the depiction of nascent love. With this skillful and agile narration Chrétien means to hold our interest through sustained enigmas and surprises. Long before authors of detective stories used the technique, Chrétien delights in delayed explanations, which entail to some extent the introduction of *suspense*—especially in the *Lancelot* and *Le Conte du Graal*—effected by mingling mystery with mystification. Along these lines, then, is another aspect of his craft, the deliberate narrative tempo, accelerated or slackened at will, like the analyses in free indirect discourse which alternate smoothly and rhythmically with direct narration. Following Calogrenant's retrospective flashback narrating details of his journey to the fountain of Broceliande, we learn of Yvain's impetuous rush to adventure, during which time the same series unfolds, but episode and image are abbreviated according to a precipitous cadence to translate the hero's impatience.

To the diversity of narrative movement must be added Chrétien's even more subtle tonal variegation. The almost imperceptible shift from the serious to the pleasant, or from the tender to the ironic, produces a kind of iridescence not unmindful of the ethereal games of nuance by La Fontaine—whose manner, in fact, in "The Bear and His Two Companions," for instance, seems foreshadowed in form and content by the fablelike scene in *Erec,* in which five thieving knights divide the coveted booty before attacking (vv. 2925-58). Chrétien's tonal changes easily lend themselves to humorous treatment; sometimes while relating high adventure or amorous drama he secretly amuses himself: the witty thought, the pointed trifle, the incisive "I think" or "it seems to me," and some verbal fantasies and puns are all characteristic stylistic signals of his intimate diversion, though the reader's share is balanced by many authorial smiles and winks of complicity. It must be understood that this detached manner and discreet freedom with humor in no way compromises the beauty of the story or the grandeur of the hero; rather, like an intellectual accompaniment, it adds to the narrative flavor and is necessary in fact for ethical distance. Sometimes also a more intense, objective humor emerges from the situations themselves or from characterization. Finally, let us note that in the *Knight with the Lion* and *Perceval*, he betrays a propensity for farce and caricature.

All combined, these diverse effects, controlled surprises, assorted tones, and the blend of tragic and ironic, leave an impression of virtuosity, of a kind of verbal acrobatics inherited perhaps from the study of dialectics. In this way Chrétien is able to perform brilliant, moving, though gratuitous variations on the related themes of feigned death and thwarted suicide. Enide, believing Erec dead and herself guilty for it, is on the verge of suicide until restrained by the count of Limors and his people. The two themes reappear with slight modification in *Cligés* (vv. 6220-84) and *Lancelot* (vv. 4175-440). Derivation from *Piramus et Tisbé* is quite apparent, but Chrétien suppresses the tragic conclusion and never lets his heroes die. This paradoxical pathos, based on error caught in the nick of time, culminates with a fourth variation in *Yvain,* when the personage ostensibly ready for suicide is none other than the lion. One might complain of parody here were it not for Chrétien's real capacity to balance off emotion and humor. Returning by chance to the fountain beneath the pine tree, Yvain swoons in sorrow, mindful of his former happiness. In falling, his sword slips out and pierces his neck. At the sight of blood, the lion "... thinks that he sees his master and companion dead." In despair he will kill himself by rushing on the sword which he has taken up in jaws and placed on a fallen log, with the point up, handle steadied against a tree trunk. At the eleventh hour, Yvain recovers and the noble beast restrains his fatal leap (*Yvain*, vv. 3485-525). It is hard to resist a smile here, and yet the lion's conduct echoes that of Enide, the most devoted and most touching of Chrétien's heroines.

As if a cross between something from the bestiaries and from the fairy world, this humanized lion alone proves how much room for articulation our author leaves himself in dealing with the marvelous. But, however aware that a legendary atmosphere fascinates, Chrétien carries off in his romances a poetic impression of spatial and temporal distancing. Doubtless reaching him in a more or less deteriorated state, the fabulous tales, the subjects of which, by adding moral and psychological interest, he created from within, on occasion lose something of their original coherence. But we must not, as others have often done, rush to charge him with absurd and uncontrolled primitive marvels, or with contradictory improbabilities in his narrative. For Chrétien's artful storytelling must include the strange and the unexplained, inasmuch as his audience expected bewilderment, intrigue, and escape. Is it really credible that, imprisoned with her lover, Mabonagrain, the damsel of the enchanted orchard, suddenly turns out to be Enide's cousin? Can we accept without hesitation the fact that Guenevere also had to cross either the sword-bridge or the water bridge—the only access to the kingdom of Gorre? But logic fails next to mysterious otherworld adventures. However Chrétien adapted the mythical to twelfth-century civilization, the inconsistencies of the narrative seem in part deliberate, suggestive again of the imaginary, the poetic, the ambiguous realm beyond. Certain blurs of *chiaroscuro* between the supernatural and some logical explanation are met particularly in *The Knight of the Cart* and *The Story of the Grail*.

As if at play Chrétien marries the extraordinary tale to observations of reality. Concrete details, small facts, or sketches relating to social and material life—castles, furniture, clothing, arms, hunting, feasting, tourneying, and feudal customs—continually inject familiar, human truths into the magical atmosphere. This unartificial union does not jeopardize, but materializes the marvelous. Notable, too, is that as an episode increases in fantasy, realistic traits accumulate proportionately— such as in *The Story of the Grail.*

Such realism is, in fact, habitually graphic and salient. Chrétien's power of description is expressive, exact, and unusually varied. For example, depiction of myriad battles is as integral to romance as to epic (although collective battles are the exception in romances of adventure). Chrétien's accomplishment in the literary order is an act of prowess indeed, so much is he capable, throughout his whole work, of diversity in wielding the ordeals of the joust and clash of arms. Wace had already broken the tradition of conventional schemata in epic descriptions, but Chrétien outdistanced him by direct observation of attitude and movement, though he did not turn altogether from doctrinal precepts regarding *the* brilliant ornament, *descriptio.* In particular, the *artes poeticae* had rhetorical principles for "descriptions of people," whereby, it was taught, one must present in descending order, detail by detail, from head to toe, the physiognomy of characters. For his portrait of Philomena, Chrétien applies these formulas, as well as for the more subtle portrayals of Enide and Cligés. But in truth, beginning with *Erec,* he seems to sense the danger, if not the absurdity, of fashionable descriptive themes, which often become awkward or tedious in narration. He refuses to describe Enide's chamber in King Evrain's dwelling (vv. 5570-79) or to enumerate the food served at Erec's coronation (vv. 6939-43). Similarly, in *Cligés,* he omits a dubbing scene: "...now that they are knights I will say no more of them..." (line 1209). He refuses to relate in detail the splendrous wedding feast of Alexander and Soredamors (vv. 2358-60) or the celebration for the betrothal of Emperor Alis and Fenice (vv. 3245-47). Elsewhere he boasts of not tarrying over useless specifics (vv. 4636-39, 5137-39). He wittily avoids a minute portrait of Fenice, which he paints by not painting it, confessing in malicious modesty that he finds himself unable to represent such beauty: "...for if I should live a thousand years, and if my skill were to double every day, yet should I waste all my time in trying to tell the truth about her" (vv. 2732-41). Such remarks are obviously directed at his rivals, and sometimes at himself—for he too is sometimes guilty of the fault, yet the barbs characterize his quite personal conception and practice in matters of style.

Part of his original manner, in fact, consists of replacing stylized and continuous description with brief, picturesque traits, matching the narrative in a functional way. These light, selective touches are felt at the proper moment by their dramatic and ethical significance. The story thus becomes a moving description, often subjective, because everything appears as if seen through the eyes of the characters. This impressionistic style is noticeable as early as *Erec* and dominates the three last romances. Instead of the usual inventory-portrait, for example, how much human life is everywhere manifest at the funeral of Esclados the Red; how much human truth is apparent in the successive tableaux, the varying attitudes in which Laudine's beauty is reflected in the ever more amorous gaze of Yvain!

During the brief moments of respite from her vehement mourning, the young widow "...reads her psalms in her gilt-lettered psalter" (vv. 1414-15). The reader has guessed that the lover is less interested in the book than in the beautiful hands holding it; yet the brilliant, illuminated letters cannot escape his attention. This small detail of light and color simultaneously communicates Yvain's visual impression and awakens the narrative. Chrétien is also a master at setting the descriptive trait, but not only as a miniaturist who reproduces tiny facets of reality or sketches a line, gesture, or movement; he can also mount a whole scene, control lighting or perspective, and give life to an entire fresco (e.g., the tournament of Noauz in *Lancelot,* vv. 5786-844, or the Grail procession, vv. 3190–343). To all this description the role of imagery is no less important. Sometimes the metaphors are a bit contrived, like the three different joys and honors won by Alexander in a single day, the town of Windsor, the best kingdom in Wales, and the hand of Soredamors, "...the greatest joy of all was the third—that his sweetheart was queen of the chess-board where he was king" (*Cligés,* vv. 2371-73). Sometimes, less ingenious, a simile may smack of simplicity, like the "nag" that is "as fat and round as an apple" (*Lancelot,* line 2299); or, when Yvain is healed from his folly by a marvelous ointment, he is quite amazed to find himself "as naked as ivory" (*Yvain,* line 3020); to defend the lion the hero attacks the serpent shooting fire from its open throat, "which was larger than a pot" (line 3368). Often a comparison is amplified to take on grandiose epic rhythms, such as in this passage drawn from the single combat between Cligés and the duke of Saxony (*Cligés*, vv. 4070-79):

> As espees notent un lai
> Sor les hiaumes qui retantissent,
> Si que lor janz s'an esbaïssent,
> Et sanble a ces qui les esgardent,
> Que li hiaume espraingnent et ardent.
> Et quant les espees resaillent,
> Estanceles ardanz an saillent
> Ausi come de fer qui fume,
> Que li fevres bat sor l'anclume
> Quant il le tret de la favarge.

("Upon their resonant helmets they play such a tune [lai] with their swords that it seems to those who are looking on that the helmets are on fire and send forth sparks. And when the swords rebound in air, gleaming sparks fly off from them as if from a smoking piece of iron which the smith beats upon his anvil after drawing it from the forge," trans. by W.W. Comfort, p. 144).

In all battle descriptions, there was nothing original in the banal evocation of lance shocks upon arms or the clicking of swords. The image of sparks around the helmet is found as early as the *Chanson de Roland* (line 3586; *"Des helmes clers li fous en escarbunet,"* "And fiery sparks come flashing from their helms," trans. by P. Terry). Chrétien artfully rejuvenates these conventions, but first we observe the affectation of assimilating to the tumultuous cadence of swords a *lai*—a word which must be taken here in the sense of "musical composition" executed on the Celtic harp—an excessively subtle metaphor that nevertheless seems to imbue the battle with a lyrical and humorous quality. On the other hand, the comparison between sparks shooting from helmets and red iron struck on the anvil introduces a forceful and familiar realism; and the powerful sonority of the lines emphasizes the descriptive brilliance. No northern poet before Chrétien could match such style.

His literary generation understood the importance of art; more and more consciously they would interrelate poetic creation with language and expression, the instruments of poetry. Cultivated courtly society, more so than the audience of the *chansons de geste,* appreciates now variety and purity in vocabulary, brilliance and clarity in syntax—in a word, elegant style. It is at this time that the idea of "good French" begins to emerge, a formula implying esthetic awareness, doubtless predicated upon the existence of a literary language based, for the most part, on the Ile-de-France dialect (i.e., Parisian). However that may be, Huon de Méri, in the thirteenth century, credited our author with spreading abroad "good French by the handful." Chrétien is without peer for his manipulation of the French language at this period: he exploited to the full its resources of precision, logic, harmony, and plasticity.

Chrétien was a craftsman with words. He displays an extensive vocabulary, filled with the right words and carefully chosen images, chancing sometimes the felicitous but daring expression. Even in syntactic innovations he excels: he was apparently the first to use temporally the conjunction *que que,* "during"—usually "although." One may sympathize with the need he felt to forge new syntactic tools: the octosyllable line carried with difficulty the many temporal locutions of the language (e.g., *dementres que, endementres que, endementiers que, parmi tot ce que,* "while"), quite suited to the epic decasyllable, but cumbersome in the lighter verse of romance and contrary to its vivid style.[6] Similarly, Chrétien expeditiously introduced the usage of *lors que* "while" to bend grammar to artistic needs, and at a time when an able writer could do so without blame. The respective tense values, hardly differentiated in the twelfth century, are particularized in his works, in accord with the various narrative levels and ethical nuances.[7] Chrétien also understood the use of full periods, while marking off subordinate relationships clearly.

His originality is no less manifest in his use of the rhetorical "color" or figure, from the manuals of poetics, called *annominatio:* "It consists of repeating nearly the same word while changing only one or two letters, . . . or again of associating words having the same form but semantically different."[8] Such reproduction of words and sounds is often no more than verbal artifice, something by which Chrétien himself was fascinated; but three passages in *Cligés* reveal a fruitful use of the figure. As Alexander and his companions enter the ship, about to

177

sail for Britain, their relatives and friends climb a hill near the beach
to watch the ship's departure.

> *D'iluec esgardent lor enui*
> *Tant com il le pueent veoir.*
> *Lor enui esgardent por voir;*
> *Que del vaslet mout lor enuie.* (vv. 264-67)

("From here they sadly gaze, as long as their eyes can follow them.
With sorrow indeed, they watch them go, being solicitous for the
youths..., trans. by Comfort, p. 94). Mindful of Wace's manner, the
annominatio is here linked by chiasmus—*esgardent: lor enui: lor enui
esgardent*—as if psychologically bound to the parting emotions of
sadness, worry, and regret. Elsewhere in *Cligés,* Count Angrés and his
knights, surrounded at Windsor, will try a nocturnal sally, hoping to
surprise Arthur's army in the shadows. To punish them, God "illumined
the darkness" and caused the moon to rise.

> *Mout lor est la lune nuisanz,*
> *Qui luist sor les escuz luisanz,*
> *Et li hiaume mout lor renuisent,*
> *Qui contre la lune reluisent.* (vv. 1713-16)

("They are much hampered by the moon, as it shines upon their shields,
and they are handicapped by their helmets, too, as they glitter in the
moonlight," trans. by Comfort, p. 113). Once again, the figure seems
to fit the mood of vexation, an impression confirmed by the third
passage: Cligés, an exile in Britain, hopes in vain to forget Fenice, but
is so preoccupied with memories of her that he decides to return to
Greece:

> *Que trop a fet grant consirree*
> *De vëoir la plus desirree*
> *Qu'onques nus poïst desirrer.*
> *Ne s'en voudra plus consirrer.* (vv. 5077-80)

("...for he has been deprived too long of the sight of the most desired
lady who was ever desired by anyone. He will not prolong this priva-
tion...," trans. by Comfort, p. 157). The disposition and variation of
the rhyme words function here to modulate love's nostalgic obsession.

From the collocation of these three examples, it is quite patent that
Cligés represents a loosening of *annominatio* from its scholarly matrix;
three lines from *Yvain* prove further Chrétien's increasing success in

this regard. A damsel, in search of Yvain, is lost in a deep wood on a
rainy night; she hastens to find shelter:

> *Et la nuiz et li bois li font*
> *Grant enui, mes plus li enuie*
> *Que li bois ne la nuiz, la pluie.* (vv. 4844–46)

("The night and the woods cause her great distress, but she is more
tormented by the rain than by either the woods or the night," trans.
by Comfort, p. 243).

Once again, we have a chiasmus: *la nuiz et li bois: li bois ne la nuiz*.
But the perfection of this *annominatio* may be ascribed to the exquisite
accord of consonants and vowels, suggesting both the dripping rain and
damsel's distress: Chrétien the poet elevates rhetoric to music.

A prestigious storyteller, a talented romancer, he charms us also
with his supple and brilliant versification. Routinely, he uses the broken
couplet, a technique whereby lines connected by rhyme are dissociated
from the same sentence both in syntax and in meaning. This rarely
found freedom—until Chrétien's exercise of it—avoids the monotonous
octosyllabic hum and provides added rhythmical combinations while
inaugurating delicate stops in the narrative. Nor will Chrétien hesitate
to break the unity of the octosyllable, that tenuous line with no caesura,
but upon which he confers rhythm and harmony through expressive
placement of words, through frequent and diverse rests and run-on
lines, which themselves sometimes speed up or decelerate the cadence.
Such graphic little surprises in the verse transmit gestures, intonations,
and movements of thought and of the heart. Meshing with the variety
of rhythms is his art of attuning rhyme, whereby consonants and vowels
are disposed musically. For instance, the reiterated liquids *l* and *r* intensify the freshness and fluidity in the evocative line depicting the spring
beneath the pine tree in the forest of Broceliande: *Ombre li fet li plus
biaus arbres* ("It is shadowed by the fairest tree...," *Yvain*, line 382).
Later, light, sonorous tappings are amplified: *Sonent flaütes et fresteles,
Timbre, tabletes et tabor* ("...flutes and pipes are played, kettle drums,
drums and cymbals...," *Yvain*, vv. 2352–53); or at the entrance of the
lodging, the echoing steps: *Le pont et la porte passames* ("...we crossed
the bridge, and passing through the gate...," *Yvain*, line 210). Elsewhere in *Yvain*, clear vowels harmonize with the calm after the storm:
Et quant je vi l'er cler et pur "And when I saw the air clear and serene...,"

line 455). It would not be difficult to augment this list of paintings in sound. Chrétien is an effortless poet who never sacrifices the meaning or tortures syntax for the sake of homophony. His rapid narrative sometimes permits sufficient, even quite simple rhyme, but he can also, with considerable virtuosity, catch unexpected, rich, yet unforced rhymes. Here and there, dexterity is sprinkled with contrivance, and, like others, Chrétien was also often given to padding, though he seems to excuse himself with good humor. Everything about his style and expression reveals his delight in following the imaginary poetic adventures of his heroes, in immortalizing Yvain, Lancelot, and Perceval.

To measure, insofar as possible, Chrétien's influence would require a long and minute study. Whether he was a leader of a school or not cannot be determined, although his fame appears considerable by the end of the twelfth century and throughout the thirteenth century. His charming stories were appreciated and his stylistic power—even its artifice—admired. Huon de Méri lavishes praise not only upon his expertise with "good French"; he adds the commendation that Chrétien de Troyes "was gifted and reputed for his craft" *(qui tant ot de pris de trover)*—that is, he excelled in literary invention. Huon was particularly impressed with the preciosity of *Cligés:* "Chrétien de Troyes wrote most ineffably of the heart transfixed by the arrow of Love shot through the eyes" *(Chrétien de Troyes dit miex Du cuer navrê, du dart, des iex, Que je ne vos porroie dire).*[9] But the influence of the author, represented here as an imposing master, was felt especially by numerous imitators, verse romancers who, for some fifty years later, all depended upon him directly or indirectly. They may often be unaware of his artful *conjointure,* but still borrow unsubtlely from the elaborate model, myriad characters, situations, motives, and procedures. Whether in romance of adventure, of love, or of morals, or in works mingling, as he did, the marvelous and the real, Chrétien's preponderance is recognizable, even among those, like Jean Renart, phlegmatic toward the *matière de Bretagne.*

However, between *Erec* and *Perceval,* this very matter was so brilliantly ornamented that for two generations Arthurian verse romance flourished. Let us enumerate just a few of the grandiose titles: the *Continuations of the Grail Story*, *Guinglain* or the *Bel Inconnu*, *Chevalier aux deux épées*, *Fergus*, *Durmart le Gallois*, *Meraugis de Portlesguez*, *Vengeance Raguidel*, and *Gliglois*. The vogue continued on up to the fourteenth century, as evidenced by Jean Froissart's *Meliador*. With much banality and few innovations (with the possible exception of Raoul de Houdenc, author of *Meraugis*), this literary tradition follows in Chrétien's footsteps.

Meanwhile, with the Arthurian prose romance, born under a different esthetic star, nurtured around 1220–30, authors will amplify and order the Round Table adventures, progressively, around a central theme—the conflict of the courtly and religious ideals; while it combines within a vast, powerfully original skein the two heterogeneous legends of Lancelot and the Grail, it remains nevertheless largely indebted to Chrétien de Troyes.

The success of the *Prose Lancelot* will soon eclipse the master's reputation, whose work, however, was continuously copied and read in some fifteen manuscripts dating from about 1220 to the 1350s, and later (including four copies of *Erec,* three of *Cligés,* two of *Lancelot,* two of *Yvain,* and eight of *Perceval*). Thereafter, twelfth-century French becomes too difficult to understand, and prose adaptations begin to appear, assuring a momentary revival for *Cligés* and *Erec* (ca. 1454) and for *Perceval* (1530). But after this brief spurt, Chrétien became en-shrouded, like so many others, in the so-called gothic shadows. During the sixteenth century, the erudite curiosities of Etienne Pasquier and Claude Fauchet, then the "troubadour" genre, and later, the popular eighteenth-century romances of chivalry rescued him for a time from neglect. But an enormous critical undertaking was necessary during the second half of the nineteenth century, and it continues today, with the purpose of defining and redefining Chrétien's importance in literary history. And, of course, controversy as to the precise nature of his sources and as to the character of his talent will not end here.

But at a time when romance was only just groping for form, did he not impel this vital genre toward its extraordinary course in modern literature? This particular contribution seems all the more convincing as his work was so soon recognized and imitated beyond the borders of northern France. The *Erec* and *Iwein* of Hartmann von Aue and Wolfram von Eschenbach's *Parzival* comprise indeed the most splendid evidence for the European flowering of the *matière de Bretagne*—as fostered by the French genius, Chrétien de Troyes.

Notes

One: The Background
and the Work

1. For a different view on matters of chronology, see John F. Benton, "The Court of Champagne as a Literary Center," *Spec* 36 (1961): 551-91. For a rebuttal, see A. Fourrier, "Retour au 'terminus'," in *Mélanges Frappier* (Geneva, 1970), pp. 299-311. (Translator's Note.)
2. According to Benton, pp. 553-54, the marriage of Henry I of Champagne and Marie could be dated as early as 1159, not 1164; they were apparently betrothed in 1153, so that the chronology of Chrétien's works proposed here would be moved back by at least five years. (Translator's Note.)
3. M. Bloch, *Feudal Society*, tr. L.A. Manyon (Chicago: Univ. of Chicago Press, 1964), p. 307. (Translator's Note.)
4. A.J. Holden, ed., Wace (de Caen), *Le Roman de Rou*, 3 vols. *SATF* (Paris: A. & J. Picard, 1970-1973). (Translator's Note.)
5. Edmond Faral, ed., *Historia regum Britanniae*, chap. 165, 11.76-86; cf. L. Thorpe, trans., *Geoffrey of Monmouth, The History of the Kings of Britain* (Harmondsworth, 1966), p. 240; and I. Arnold, ed., *Le Roman de Brut de Wace*, 2 vols. *SATF* (Paris, 1938-1940), vv. 11561-92.
6. A. Pauphilet, *Le Legs du Moyen Age* (Melun, 1950), p. 152.
7. J. Loth, ed., *Les Mabinogion*, 2 vols. (Paris, 1913); Gwyn Jones and Thomas Jones, trans., *The Mabinogion* (London, 1949).
8. Jones's translation, replacing Loth's, pp. 97 and 110-11, respectively.
9. See the complete text and prose translation (used here) in B. Woledge, ed., *The Penguin Book of French Verse, I: To the Fifteenth Century* (Harmondsworth, 1961), pp. 63-68. (Translator's Note.)

10. W.W. Comfort, trans., *Cligés*, in *Arthurian Romances by Chrétien de Troyes* (London, 1914), p. 91.

Two: *Early Works*

1. The question is complicated by the fact that midpoint in the fable, line 734, the author of the *Philomena* is called "Chrétien li Gois": *The house was in a woods/Thus relates Chrêtien li Gois*. The enigmatic surname *li Gois* has elicited a number of unconvincing interpretations. In any case, it offers solid proof neither for nor against attribution to our author.
2. This more curious than moving motif seems to derive from a passage in *Brut* (Arnold, ed., vv. 14193-14222), where Brian, nephew of King Cadwalein, cuts a "pound" (*braon*) from his thigh, has it larded and roasted, and, for want of venison, offers it to his sick uncle.

Three: Erec and Enide

1. That is, "'Friend, what a shame it was for you!'" or "'Unfortunate Erec!'" M. Roques, ed., line 2503; Foerster, ed. line 2507: *Con mar i fus!*
2. W.W. Comfort, p. 64; Roques, ed., vv. 4882-4900; Foerster, ed., vv. 490-538.
3. The choice of Nantes perhaps implies an allusion to the court held in that city on Thursday, 25 December 1169, when Henry II Plantagenet came to preside at the investiture of his eleven-year-old son, Geoffrey, as Duke of Brittany.
4. W.W. Comfort, p. 4; Roques, ed., vv. 245-46, 332, 915-16.
5. W.W. Comfort, p. 20; Roques, ed., vv. 1484-91; Foerster, ed., vv. 1504-511.
6. According to the ingenious interpretation by E. Hoepffner, *Archivum Romanicum* 18(1934):433-34, Chrétien designated with the term *premier vers* only the "introduction" of his romance, alluding to the first

vers, that is, the initial stanza which, in a lyric poem, most often celebrated nature's renewal, and which frequently contrasted with a melancholic or mournful tone in the rest of the poem. For R.R. Bezzola,
Le Sens de l'aventure et de l'amour, pp. 87–88, this contrast is found
in *Erec*. M. Roques, ed., *Erec*, p. ix, n. 1, discerns in the expression an
analogous but more discreet meaning: "...one might call the *premier
vers* a pleasing, unemotional debut, filled with anticipation, so to build
suspense about the 'reverse side of the coin,' or to cause the watchful
reader to say 'I can't wait for the end!'" But perhaps it is simply a
popular expression among writers, as suggested by another convincing
example, found at line 11 of the first branch of the *Roman de Renard*,
Martin, ed.: "Thus the story relates in the first verse," a usage that
removes any hint of pedantry or technical inelegance.

7. *Erec and Enide* is most masterfully composed by Chrétien in the form of
a triptych, a structure paralleled in the *Chevalier au Lion*. [See further
Z.P. Zaddy, "The Structure of Chrétien's *Erec*," *MLR* 62(1967): 608–
19; "The Structure of Chrétien's *Yvain*," *MLR* 65(1970): 523–40; cf.
R.J. Cormier, "The Structure of the *Roman d'Eneas*," *Classical Folia*
26(1972).–Translator's Note.]

8. In the *Gereint*, there is no question of a kiss; the day after the marriage,
Enid receives as a gift the head of a hart killed by Arthur, a chivalrous
act whose luster lacks the courtliness favored by Chrétien.

9. G. Cohen, *Littérature française du moyen âge*, 2nd ed. (Paris: Hachette,
1890), p. 95. (Translator's Note.)

10. In the *Gereint*, on the other hand, the hero is in no way concerned
about the fate reserved for Enid if he himself perished, and he orders
her to wear her least beautiful clothing.

11. To the count of Limors, who asks whether she is Erec's wife or mistress,
Enide answers that she is both; Foerster, ed., vv. 4686–89; Roques, ed.,
vv. 4648-51.

Four: Cligés

1. The expression *fine amor*, absent from the *Eneas*, turns up in the *Roman
de Troie* and Thomas's *Tristan*, but Benoît does not always use it mean-

ingfully. Though Chrétien does not use it, he does speak of *fins amanz* (*Cligés*, line 3861) and of *fin amant* (*Lancelot*, line 3980).

2. Foerster, ed., *Cligés*, vv. 3150-64; W.W. Comfort, p. 132.

3. Vv. 475-523; Comfort, p. 97.

4. An interesting use of the word *conscience* appears in line 3826, with the simple psychological meaning, inner "feeling" or "awareness." Face-to-face, Fenice and Cligés dare not reveal to each other their "conscience"—a neologism and a *hapax* in Chrétien's whole work.

Five: Lancelot *or* Le Chevalier de la Charrette

1. The declarations by Godefroi de Lagny (vv. 7120-34) are both explicit and modest. It is with Chrétien's approval that he completed the work, abandoned by Chrétien either for literary reasons (the plot does suffer from banality toward the conclusion) or for some vague material reason lost in his biographical lacunae. But it was not left unfinished because of moral scruples—a reason which certainly would have hindered him much earlier on. Or else, we might assume that he experienced some great aversion the moment it was necessary to cause Lancelot's return to Arthur's court and thus have him fall back into the Tristan situation.

2. It is quite probable, as R.S. Loomis conjectured, that *Gorre* (variant: *Goirre*), the realm of Baudemagus and Meleagant, is a corruption of *Voirre*.

3. It is interesting to note that Hartmann von Aue restores the authentic pattern in his account of the *Lancelot* in his *Iwein* (vv. 4530-726), when Meleagant gains custody of the queen by means of a "rash boon"—perhaps an indication that Chrétien's poem was not Hartmann's only source.

4. Such is by no means the case for Gawain. The nephew of King Arthur remains a paragon of chivalric, courtly elegance, always the representative of the norm. Yet his conduct implies a certain social conformity, faintly disreputable. Though involved in the same quest with Lancelot, he is eclipsed by him, suggesting that Chrétien designed the *Lancelot* in terms of antitheses. For example, the comic lover Kay and the violent,

proud Meleagant serve as psychological foils for Lancelot, sublimely extravagant. King Baudemagus is the picture of generosity, contrasting with his son's perfidy. Further, accomplished sketches and stunning images—like those of the tournament of Noauz—describe with bemused sympathy the herald or the group of nubile damsels. They all help to fix in our minds certain secondary characters, attesting to the variety of the romance.

Six: Yvain or
Le Chevalier au Lion

1. Jones's translation, pp. 180-81, replacing Loth, 2.43.
2. These two are analogous to the fairy princesses Fann and Líban in the Irish narrative, "The Wasting-Sickness of Cú Chulainn." [Cf. *BBIAS/BBIAS* 23(1971):111.—Translator's Note.]
3. Motifs in the episode of Yvain's first return to the fountain (vv. 3485-769) have been elaborated from the tale of antiquity, *Piramus et Tisbê*: the dialogue through an opening in the wall, the apparent death, and attempted suicide.
4. J. de La Fontaine, *Les Deux Pigeons*, "The Two Doves," in *The Best Fables of La Fontaine*, trans. F. Duke (Charlottesville, Va., 1965), p. 210. (Translator's Note.)
5. She reminds us of Erec, while Yvain, complemented by his symbolic doublet, the lion, seems to take after Enide's patience and devotion. We may perhaps infer that, within the two romances, Chrétien set forth an amusing psychological chiasm between his male and female personages.

Seven: Perceval or
Le Conte du Graal

1. The word "book" does not necessarily mean a work written in Latin, for Chrétien himself called his *Lancelot* a "book," line 25.
2. The theme of Perceval's mysterious *enfances* may be compared to tradi-

tions in both Irish (in the heroic narratives, the "boyhood deeds" of Cú Chulainn and of Finn) and Welsh (those of Pryderi).

3. The young girl is precise (vv. 3507-27) about the fact that, during a battle, the Fisher King was wounded by a javelin "through the two hips" (variants: "through the two legs," "through the two thighs"), and that since then he has been unable to walk or ride, so that for diversion, unable to hunt, he has himself placed on board a "ship" and fishes with a hook: "Therefore he is called the Fisher King."

4. The conjunction of snow, of blood, of the bird, and of the beloved appears to be a motif of Celtic origin, but it has been artfully reworked by Chrétien.

5. *The Medieval French Roman d'Alexandre, III. Version of Alexandre de Paris, Variants and Notes to Branch I*, edited by A. Foulet (Princeton, 1949); cf. p. 91, line 601, 611, and commentary, p. 92.

6. W. Roach, ed., 1:9648-50, 2:13430-32, 3:1.268, 269.

7. Whether the *graal* is mounted on a pedestal or not cannot be determined. Nor is it clear how the damsel in the procession holds it "between her two hands" (line 3220), an expression which is ambiguous, although "between" suggests more or less that the damsel's hands are parted to hold the *graal* at opposite ends.

8. Cf. "*La lance dont la pointe lerme/Del sanc tot cler que ele plore*" (vv. 6166-67); "*la lance dont la pointe verse des larmes de sang*" is L. Foulet's version. Would Chrétien have used the expression "*lerme del sanc*" and a collective verb like *plorer* if he meant that the dripping of the lance was caused solely by a "tear of blood"? And the use of the singular elsewhere (*une gote, cele gote*, "a drop," "this drop") may be explained by reference to the single drop which flowed when Perceval observed the lance.

9. Quotations from Mario Roques, "Le Graal de Chrétien et la demoiselle au Graal," *Romania* 76(1955):1-27.

10. Yet it must be noted that a corollary of the interpretation under discussion is the idea that Britain was not yet truly Christianized, a notion nevertheless controverted by several passages. The same objection can be made to the hypothesis which claims that the procession would merely be "an imaginary vision granted to Perceval."

11. The allegorical maze misled U.T. Holmes to discern in *The Story of the Grail* a *figura* of the ancient Mosaic law and of the prophecy that it would be superseded by the new law of Christ, that is, a *figura* for the

conversion of the Jews. The theory claims that the *graal* contains *manna*; the lance represents Aaron's rod; the Grail castle is to be identified with Solomon's temple; the Fisher King is no other than Jacob. Holmes maintains that Chrétien himself may have been a converted Jew. Sister M. Amelia Klenke, O.P., goes even farther: the father of the Fisher King would be the prophet Elias, or rather Melchisedech; the hermit is Saint John the Baptist; the damsel of the tent would be the Virgin Mary; Blancheflor personifies chastity. Sister Klenke also believes the damsel of the Grail to be *Ecclesia*.

12. To choose only one example, the Church is always designated as *dame* in the *Queste del Saint Graal* (*Quest of the Holy Grail*), Pauphilet, ed., pp. 168–85, while *Synagoga*, usually also a *dame*, is nevertheless named once with the less dignified title "damsel," ibid., p. 173, line 4.

13. On the Celtic hypothesis, see Helaine Newstead, "Recent Perspectives on Arthurian Literature," in *Mélanges Frappier* (Geneva, 1970), pp. 877–83; R.J. Cormier, "Tradition and Sources: The Jackson-Loomis Controversy Re-Examined," *Folklore* (London), 83(1972), 101–21. (Translator's Note.)

14. One stylistic detail expresses discreetly the progressive symbolism of the *graal*: in the procession the damsel bears *a* grail (line 3220); later the hermit declares, "'So sacred a thing is *the* grail'" (line 6425). This grammatical slip from the indefinite to the definite article carries us from the secular to the spiritual plane. The definite article used by the hermit doubtless refers to *this grail* (line 6423) in which one brings the wafer to the old king; however, it confers upon the object in addition an exceptional and unique value (this grail, no other, is a *sacred* thing), thus making the somewhat sententious line, though here latent and unspecific, almost prophetic of the later fixed expression: *the* Holy Grail.

Eight: Originality and Influence

1. Voltaire, *Le Taureau Blanc*, ["The White Bull"], in *The Complete Romances of Voltaire*, trans. G.W. Black (New York, 1927), p. 114.

2. *Erec et Enide*, ed. Foerster, vv. 5898–905; ed. Roques, vv. 5847–55.

3. The term *chevalier errant*, "knight-errant," occurs in fact in *Yvain*, line 259.
4. Along these lines, see the penetrating observations of L. Foulet, *Rom*, 71(1950), 19-23.
5. In spite of medieval and modern temporal and esthetic differences, J. Bédier's remarks on this issue are still convincing (*Les Légendes épiques*, 4 vols. [Paris, 1926-29], 1.335): "Twelfth-century logic was no less demanding than today's. To prove this we only need point out that the courtly romances of the twelfth century, like the *Eneas, Erec*, or *Lancelot*, are as rigorously constructed as Benjamin Constant's *Adolphe*, or the *Dominique* by Fromentin; like those in the modern novel, lapses still do occur. But the real inconsistencies belong to epic."
6. See P. Imbs, *Les Propositions temporelles en ancien français* (Paris, 1956), pp. 301, 325-28, 550.
7. Cf. Tatiana Fotitch, *The Narrative Tenses in Chrétien de Troyes* (Washington, D.C., 1950).
8. Edmond Faral, *Les Arts poétiques du XIIe et du XIIIe siècle* (Paris, 1923), pp. 94-96.
9. G. Wimmer, ed., Huon de Méri: *Le Tornoiemenz Antecrist* (Marburg, 1888), p. 62.

Bibliography
(Revised 1978)

List of Abbreviations

AnBret	Annales de Bretagne
ARom	Archivum Romanicum
ASNSP	Annali delli R. Scuola Superiore di Pisa
BBSIA/BBIAS	Bulletin Bibliographique de la Société International Arthurienne/Bibliographical Bulletin of the International Arthurian Society
BEC	Bibliothèque de l'Ecole des Chartes
CCM	Cahiers de civilisation médiévale
CFMA	Classiques français du moyen âge
CL	Comparative Literature
CLS	Comparative Literature Studies
CN	Cultura Neolatina
Dvj	Deutsche Vierteljahrsschrift fűr Literaturwissenschaft und Geistesgeschichte
EC	Etudes celtiques
EL	Etudes littéraires
Esp	Esprit Créateur
FMLS	Forum for Modern Language Studies
FR	French Review
FRom	Filologia Romanza
GRM	Germanisch-romanische Monatsschrift
HSNPL	Harvard Studies and Notes in Philology and Literature

HumB	Humanitas
JEGP	Journal of English and Germanic Philology
KRQ	Kentucky Romance Quarterly
LR	Les Lettres romanes
MA	Moyen Age
Med. Aev.	Medium Aevum
M&H	Medievalia et Humanistica
MLN	Modern Language Notes
MLQ	Modern Language Quarterly
MLR	Modern Language Review
MP	Modern Philology
MRom	Marche romane (Liège)
MS	Mediaeval Studies
Neophil	Neophilologus
NMS	Nottingham Medieval Studies
PMLA	Publications of the Modern Language Association
PRF	Publications romanes et françaises
RBC	Research Bibliographies and Checklists
RBPH	Revue belge de philologie et d'histoire
RC	Revue celtique
RF	Romanische Forschungen
RLC	Revue de littérature comparée
RLMC	Rivista di letterature moderne e comparate
Rom	Romania
RomN	Romance Notes
RPh	Romance Philology
RR	Romanic Review
RS	Research Studies
RSH	Revue des Sciences Humaines
SATF	Société des Anciens Textes français
SF	Studi francesi
SMed	Studi medievali
SMV	Studi mediolatini e volgari
SP	Studies in Philology
Spec	Speculum
StC	Studia Celtica
Symp	Symposium

TLF	Textes littéraires français
TLL	Travaux de linguistique et de littérature, U. Strasbourg
Trad	Traditio
TWAS	Twayne World Authors Series
UCPMP	University of California Publications in Modern Philology
UNCSRLL	University of North Carolina Studies in Romance Languages and Literatures
VR	Vox Romanica
YFS	Yale French Studies
ZfSL	Zeitschrift für französische Sprache und Literatur
ZrP	Zeitschrift für romanische Philologie

Without further indication, all references are to W. Foerster's editions of *Guillaume d'Angleterre, Erec et Enide, Cligés, Chevalier de la Charrette, Chevalier au Lion*; to A. Hilka's edition of the *Conte du Graal*; and to Charles de Boer's edition of *Philomena*. English translations of *Erec et Enide, Cligés, Yvain*, and *Lancelot* are taken from W.W. Comfort, *Arthurian Romances by Chrétien de Troyes*, London, 1914; for the *Perceval*, translations are from Roger Sherman Loomis and Laura Hibbard Loomis, eds., *Medieval Romances*, New York, 1957. A large number of post-1972 items are included, though it is our wish to retain the canonical contours of Professor Frappier's original bibliographies (1957; rev. 1968); his latest authorized update reached us in the summer of 1972.–Translator's Note.

I. Bibliographies

Among the numerous studies devoted to Chrétien's works, we list only the most important and the most useful ones for the preparation of this book. Additional information will be found in the following reference works.

BBSIA/BBIAS. Edited by Ch. Foulon (Rennes). 1949 to date. (Comprehensive yearly listing of all Arthurian research, with abstracts.)

Bossuat, R. *Manuel bibliographique de la littérature française du Moyen Age*. Melun, 1951.

_____. _____. *Supplément (1949-50)*. Paris, 1955.

_____. _____. *Supplément (1950-60)*. Paris, 1961.

Cabeen, D.C. *Critical Bibliographies of French Literature*. The Medieval Period, edited by Urban T. Holmes, Jr., Vol. 1. Syracuse, 1947; 2d ed., 1952.

Encomia: Bibliographical Bulletin of the International Courtly Literature Society. Edited by F.R.P. Akehurst. Minnesota, 1975 to date.

Fisher, J.H., ed. *The Medieval Literature of Western Europe: A Review of Research, Mainly 1930-1960*. New York, London, 1966.

Kellerman, W. "Wege und Ziele der neueren Chrestien de Troyes-Forschung." *GRM* 23 (1935):204-28.

Kelly, Douglas. *Chrétien de Troyes: An Analytic Bibliography*. RBC 17. London: Grant & Cutler, 1976. (Indispensable research tool.)

Modern Language Association of America. *International Bibliography*. New York, 1921 to date. (Vol. 2 includes foreign languages and literatures; vol. 1 includes Celtic and medieval Latin subjects.)

Parry, J.J. and Brown, P.A. "A Bibliography of Critical Arthurian Literature." *MLQ* 1940-55. (Annual, June issue.)

Reinhard, J.R. *Chrétien de Troyes: A Bibliographical Essay*. Ann Arbor, Mich., 1932.

II. Manuscript Tradition

(See the various editions of Chrétien's works.)

Flutre, L.F. "Nouveaux fragments du manuscrit dit d'Annonay des oeuvres de Chrétien de Troyes." *Rom* 75 (1954):1-21.

Jodogne, O. "Fragments de Mons. I. *Erec et Enide* de Chrétien de Troyes." *LR* 4 (1950):311-30.

Micha, A. *La Tradition manuscrite des romans de Chrétien de Troyes*. PRF 90. Paris, 1939; 2d ed., Geneva, 1966.

Misrahi, J. "Fragments of *Erec et Enide* and Their Relation to the Manuscript Tradition." *PMLA* 56 (1951):951-61.

Pauphilet, A., ed. *Chrétien de Troyes: Le Manuscrit d'Annonay*. Paris, 1934. [Reprinted, 1966.]

_____. "Nouveax fragments manuscrits de Chrétien de Troyes."
Rom 63 (1937):310-23.

Reid, T.B.W. "Chrétien de Troyes and the Scribe Guiot." *Med. Aev.*
45 (1976):1-19.

Roques, M. "Le Manuscrit français 794 de la Bibliothèque nationale et
le scribe Guiot." *Rom* 73 (1952):177-99.

III. General Studies

Arthurian Literature in the Middle Ages. Edited by Roger S. Loomis.
Oxford, 1959; 2d ed., 1961. Reviewed by J. Marx, *EC* 9 (1960):
253-59.

Bednar, J. *La Spiritualité et le symbolisme dans les oeuvres de Chrétien
de Troyes.* Paris, 1974.

Benton, John F. "The Court of Champagne as a Literary Center."
Spec 36 (1961):551-91.

Bezzola, Reto R. *Le Sens de l'aventure et de l'amour: Chrétien de
Troyes et son oeuvre.* Paris, 1947. Reviewed by J. Misrahi, *RPh* 4
(1950-51):348-61.

Bruce, J.D. *The Evolution of Arthurian Romance.* 2 vols. Baltimore,
Göttingen, 1923; 2d ed., 1927. (1:100-128; bibliography: 2:380-
412, 445-60.)

Bruckner, Matilda T. *Narrative Invention in Twelfth-Century Romance:
The Convention of Hospitality (1160-1200).* French Forum Monographs, 17. Lexington, Ky., 1979.

Carasso-Bulow, Lucienne. *The Merveilleux in Chrétien de Troyes's
Romances.* Geneva, 1976.

Cohen, Gustave. *Un grand romancier d'amour et d'aventure au XIIe
siècle: Chrétien de Troyes et son oeuvre.* Paris, 1931; 2d ed., 1948.
Reviewed by E. Hoepffner, *Rom* 57 (1931):579-85.

Cormier, R.J. "A propos de quelques ouvrages récents sur Chrétien de
Troyes" (forthcoming).

Ferrante, J.M. and Economou, G.D. eds. *In Pursuit of Perfection:
Courtly Love in Medieval Literature.* Port Washington, New York,
London, 1975.

Chrétien de Troyes

Foerster, W. *Kristian von Troyes: Wörterbuch zu seinen sämtlichen Werken*. Halle, 1914; 2d ed., edited by H. Breuer 1933. (Especially Introduction.)

Frappier, J. "Jeunesse de Chrétien de Troyes." *Bulletin de l'Académie royale de Belgique* (Classe des lettres et des sciences morales et politiques, Brussels), 5th series, 54 (1968):574-91.

_____.. "Le Concept de l'amour dans les romans arthuriens." *BBSIA/ BBIAS* 22(1970):119-36. [Reprinted *Amour courtois et Table Ronde*. Geneva, 1973.]

Gallien, Simone. *La Conception sentimentale de Chrétien de Troyes*. Paris, 1975.

Gröber, G. *Grundriss der romanischen Philologie*. Strasbourg, 1893-1902. (Especially 2:1, 497-506.)

Grundriss der romanischen Literaturen des Mittelalters. Heidelberg, 1968 to date. (Chrétien appears in vol. 4, A4.)

Hanning, R.W. *The Individual in Twelfth-Century Romance*. New Haven, London, 1977. Reviewed by R.J. Cormier, *FR* 52(1979): 921-23.

Hofer, Stefan. *Chrétien de Troyes: Leben und Werke des altfranzösischen Epikers*. Graz, Cologne, 1954. Reviewed by H. Newstead, *RPh* 10 (1956-57):56-61.

Holmes, Urban T., Jr. Chrétien de Troyes. *TWAS*. New York, 1970.

Köhler, Erich. *Ideal und Wirklichkeit in der höfischen Epik: Studien zur Form der Frühen Artus und Graldichtung*. Tübingen, 1956. Translated by Elaine Kaufholz. *L'Aventure chevaleresque*. Paris, 1970.

Leclercq, J. "Modern Psychology and the Interpretation of Medieval Texts." *Spec* 48 (1973):476-90.

Lot-Borodine, Myrrha. *La Femme et l'amour au XIIe d'après les poémes de Chrétien de Troyes*. Paris, 1909. Reviewed by M. Roques, *Rom* 39 (1910):337-83.

Maillet, G. *L'Influence des légendes sur le cadre social: La Légende chevaleresque et sociale*. Travaux du Comité de Folklore Champenois 4. Châlons-sur-Marne, [1972].

Maranini, L. *Personaggi e immagini nell'opera di Chrétien de Troyes*. Milan, Varese, 1966. (Consists of previously published articles; see "Motivi cortesi e anticortesi"; "I motivi psicologici"; "Cavalleria,

196

amore conjugale"; "'Quest'e amore cortese"; and "Educazione dell'uomo.")

_____. *"Cavalleria e Cavalieri* nel mondo di Chrétien de Troyes." In *Mélanges Jean Frappier*, 2:737-55. Geneva, 1970.

Ménard, Philippe "Le Chevalier errant dans la littérature arthurienne: Recherches sur les raisons du départ et de l'errance." *Senefiance* 2 (1976):289-311.

_____. *Le Rire et le sourire dans le roman courtois en France au Moyen Age. PRF* 105. Geneva, 1969. Reviewed by R.J. Cormier, *Spec* 46 (1971):168-72.

Micha, A. "Temps et conscience chez Chrétien de Troyes." In *Mélanges Pierre Le Gentil*, pp. 253-60. Paris, 1973.

Morris, C. *The Discovery of the Individual 1050-1200*. London, 1972. (Especially pp. 133-38.)

Pauphilet, A. *Le Legs du Moyen Age*, pp. 348-61. Melun, 1950.

The Romances of Chrétien de Troyes. Edited by Douglas Kelly. The E.C. Armstrong Monographs in Medieval Literature. Lawrence, Kansas (forthcoming).

Sargent, B.N. "'L'Autre' chez Chrétien de Troyes." *CCM* 10 (1967): 199-205.

_____. "Old and New in the Character-Drawing of Chrétien de Troyes." In *Innovation in Medieval Literature: Essays Alan Markman*, edited by D. Radcliff-Umstead, pp. 35-48. Pittsburgh, 1971.

Thomov, T.S. *Thèmes et problèmes dans les romans de Chrétien de Troyes*. Sofia, Bulgaria, 1936.

Topsfield, L.T. *Chrétien de Troyes: A Study of the Arthurian Romances*. Cambridge, 1981.

Zumthor, Paul. *Parler du Moyen Age*. Paris, 1980.

IV. Background

A. Chronology

Fourrier, A. "Encore la chronologie des oeuvres de Chrétien de Troyes." *BBSIA/BBIAS* 2 (1950):69-88.

————. "Remarques sur la date du *Conte del Graal.*" *BBSIA/BBIAS*
7 (1955):89-110; 10 (1958):73-85.

————. "Retour au 'terminus'." In *Mélanges Jean Frappier*, 1:299-
311. Geneva, 1970.

Hofer, S. "Streitfragen zu Kristian." *ZfSL* 60 (1936-37):335-43.

Hunt, T. "Redating Chrestien de Troyes." *BBSIA/BBIAS* 30 (1978):
209-37.

Lejeune, Rita. "La Date du *Conte del Graal.*" *MA* 60 (1954):51-79.

————. "Encore la date du *Conte del Graal* de Chrétien de Troyes."
BBSIA/BBIAS 9 (1957):85-100. (Cf. Fourrier, "Remarques.")

Ménard, Philippe. "Note sur la date du *Chevalier de la Charrette.*" *Rom*
92 (1971):118-26.

Misrahi, J. "More Light on the Chronology of Chrétien de Troyes?"
BBSIA/BBIAS 11 (1959):89-120. (Cf. Fourrier, "Encore.")

B. The Humanist Tradition, artes poeticae, and the Nature, Structure, and Rise of Romance

Altieri, Marcelle. *Les Romans de Chrétien de Troyes: Leur perspective
proverbiale et gnomique*. Paris, 1976. (Cf. M.-L. Ollier, *RSH*, 1976,
pp. 311-430.)

Arbusow, L. *Colores rhetorici*. Göttingen, 1948.

Bruyne, E. de. *Etudes d'esthétique médiévale*. 3 vols. Bruges, 1946.
(See especially "L'époque romane," 2:14-49.)

Curtius, E.R. *Europäische Literatur und lateinisches Mittelalter*. Bern,
1948; 2d ed. 1955. Translated by Willard R. Trask. *European Literature and the Latin Middle Ages*. New York, 1953. Bréjoux, J. *La
Littérature européenne et le Moyen Age latin*. Paris, 1956. Reviewed
by J. Frappier, *Revue de Paris* (September 1957), pp. 148-52;
reprinted in *Histoire, mythes et symboles*. Geneva, 1976.

Faral, Edmond. *Les Arts poétiques du XIIe et XIIIe siècle*. Paris, 1923.

————. *Recherches sur les sources latines des contes et des romans
courtois du Moyen Age*. Paris, 1913. [Reprinted, New York, 1975.]

Gallais, P. "Littérature et médiatisation: Réflexions sur la genèse du genre romanesque." *EL* 4 (1971):39-73.

Gilson, E. *Les Idées et les lettres*. Paris, 1932. ("Humanisme médiéval et Renaissance," pp. 171-96.)

Hunt, T. "The Rhetorical Background to the Arthurian Prologue: Tradition and the Old French Vernacular Prologues." *FMLS* 6 (1970):1-23.

_____. "The Structure of Medieval Narrative." *Journal of European Studies* 3 (1973):295-328.

Jackson, W.T.H. "The Nature of Romance." *YFS* 51 (1974):12-25.

Kelly, D. "Theory of Composition in Medieval Narrative Poetry and Geoffrey of Vinsauf's *Poetria Nova.*" *MS* 31 (1969):117-48.

_____. "Topical Invention in Medieval French Literature." *Medieval Eloquence*, edited by J.J. Murphy, pp. 231-51. Berkeley, Los Angeles, London, 1978.

Knapp, F.P. *Similitudo: Stil- und Erzählfunktion von Vergleich und Exempel in der lateinischen, französischen und deutschen Grossepik des Hochmittelalters*. Philologica Germanica 2. Vienna, 1975.

Laurie, H.C.R. "Some Experiments in Technique in Early Courtly Romance." *ZrP* 88 (1972):45-68.

Lyons, Faith. "'Entencion' in Chrétien's *Lancelot.*" *SP* 51 (1954): 425-30.

Murphy, J.J. *Rhetoric in the Middle Ages: A History of Rhetorical Theory from Saint Augustine to the Renaissance*. Berkeley, Los Angeles, London, 1974.

Nitze, W. "'Sens et matière' dans les oeuvres de Chrétien de Troyes." *Rom* 44 (1915-17):14-36.

Ollier, M.-L. "Demande sociale et constitution d'un 'genre': La situation dans la France du XIIe siècle." *Mosaic* 8 (1974-75):207-16.

Paquette, J.-M. "Epopée et roman: Continuité ou discontinuité." *EL* 4 (1971):9-38.

Renucci, P. *L'Aventure de l'humanisme européen au Moyen Age IVe-XIVe siècle)*. Paris, 1953.

Ryding, W.W. *Structure in Medieval Narrative*. The Hague, Paris, 1971.

Stevens, J. *Medieval Romance: Themes and Approaches*. London, 1973.

Trimpi, W. "The Quality of Fiction: The Rhetorical Transmission of Literary Theory." *Trad* 30 (1974):1-118.

Vinaver, E. *The Rise of Romance*. Oxford, 1971.
Zaddy, Z.P. *Chrétien Studies: Problems of Form and Meaning in Erec, Yvain, Cligés and the Charrette*. Glasgow, 1973.
Zumthor, P. "Le Roman courtois: Essai de définition." *EL* 4 (1971): 75-90.

C. Influence of Classical Antiquity

Cormier, Raymond J. *One Heart One Mind: The Rebirth of Virgil's Hero in Medieval French Romance*. Romance Monographs 3. University, MS, 1973. Reviewed by D. Poirion, *RBPH* 55 (1977):545-47.
————. "The Present State of Studies on the *Roman d'Eneas*. *CN* 31 (1971):7-39.
Guyer, F.E. *Romance in the Making: Chrétien de Troyes and the Earliest French Romances*. New York, 1954. Reviewed by F.A.G. Cowper, *RR* 47 (1956):39-41.
————. "The Influence of Ovid on Chrétien de Troyes." *RR* 12 (1921):97-134; 216-47.
Jones, R. *The Theme of Love in the Romans d'antiquité*. Dissertation Series of the Modern Humanities Research Association 5. London, 1972.
Lewis, C.B. *Classical Mythology and Arthurian Romance: A Study of the Sources of Chrestien de Troyes, Yvain and other Arthurian Romances*. London, 1932. (Numerous conjectures.)
Yunck, J.A., trans. *Eneas: A Twelfth-Century French Romance*. New York, London, 1974. (Good introduction and bibliography.)
Ziltener, W. *Chrétien und die Aeneis*. Graz, Cologne, 1957. Reviewed by J. Frappier, *RPh* 13 (1959-60):50-59.

D. Origins of the matière de Bretagne

1. The "Learned" Tradition

Arnold, I., ed. *Le Roman de Brut de Wace*. 2 vols., *SATF*. Paris, 1938-40. Translated by E. Mason, *Arthurian Chronicles* [by Wace and

Layaman] ; introduction by G. Jones. London, 1976 (original edition, 1912). [A new translation by R.J. Cormier, et al. is in preparation.]

Brault, G.J. *Early Blazon: Heraldic Terminology in the Twelfth and Thirteenth Centuries with Special Reference to Arthurian Literature.* Oxford, 1972.

Chambers, E.K. *Arthur of Britain*. London, 1927.

Chotzen, Thomas M. "Le 'Livre de Gautier d'Oxford,' l' 'Historia regum Britanniae,' les 'Bruts' gallois et l'épisode de Lludd et Llevellys." *EC* 4 (1948):221-54.

Delbouille, M. "Le Témoignage de Wace sur la légende arthurienne." *Rom* 74 (1953):172-99.

Faral, Edmond. *La Légende arthurienne: Etudes et documents*. 3 vols. Paris, 1929. (1: "Des origines à Geoffroy de Monmouth"; 2: "Geoffroy de Monmouth. La Légende arthurienne à Glastonbury"; 3: "Documents. Editions of *Historia Britonum, Historia regum Britanniae*, and the *Vita Merlini*.") Reviewed by J. Loth, *MA* 41 (1931): 289-331; and by J. Vendryes, *RC* 46 (1931):401-13.

Griscom, A., ed. *Historia regum Britanniae*. New York, 1929. Translated by Lewis Thorpe. *The History of the Kings of Britain*. 4th ed. Harmondsworth, 1976.

Hammer, J., ed. *Historia regum Britanniae: Variant Version*. Cambridge, Mass., 1951.

Jones, Thomas. "The Early Evolution of the Legend of Arthur." *NMS* 8 (1964):3-21.

Lot, F. *Nennius et l'Historia Britonum*. 2 vols. Paris, 1934.

Pelan, Margaret. *L'Influence du Brut de Wace sur les romans français de son temps*. Paris, 1931. Reviewed by E. Hoepffner, *Rom* 58 (1932): 292-300.

Tatlock, J.S.P. *The Legendary History of Britain*. Berkeley, Los Angeles, 1950. Reviewed by J. Marx, *EC* 6 (1953-54):377-79.

Wetherbee, W. *Platonism and Poetry in the Twelfth Century: The Literary Influence of the School of Chartres*. Princeton, 1972.

2. The Celtic Hypothesis

Bromwich, Rachel. "Concepts of Arthur." *StC* 10/11 (1975-76):163-81.

Chotzen, Thomas M. "Emain Ablach, Ynis Awallach, Insula Avallonis, Isle d'Avalon." *EC* 4 (1948):255-74.

Cormier, R.J. "Tradition and Sources: The Jackson-Loomis Controversy Re-examined." *Folklore* 83 (1972):101-21.

Dillon, Myles. "Les Sources irlandaises des romans arthuriens." *LR* 9 (1955):143-59.

Dottin, G. *Les Littératures celtiques*. Paris, 1924.

Fourquet, J. "Le Rapport entre l'oeuvre et la source chez Chrétien de Troyes et la problème des sources bretonnes." *RPh* 9 (1955-56): 298-312.

Frappier, J. "Le Motif du 'don contraignant' dans la littérature du Moyen Age." *TLL* 7, 3 (1969):7-47.

_____. *Le Roman breton: Introduction. Des origines à Chrétien de Troyes*. Paris, 1950.

Hubert, H. *Les Celtes depuis l'époque de la Tène et la civilisation celtique*, pp. 318-26. Paris, 1932.

Loomis, Roger S. "The Arthurian Legend before 1139." *RR* 22 (1941): 3-38.

_____. *Arthurian Tradition and Chrétien de Troyes*. New York, 1949. Reviewed by J. Frappier, *Rom* 72 (1951):118-27; by J. Marx, *EC* 5 (1950-51):456-59; and by H. Newstead, *Spec* 24 (1949): 591-98.

Les Mabinogion. Translated by J. Loth. 2 vols. 2d ed. Paris, 1913. Translated by Gwyn Jones and Thomas Jones. London, 1949. Translated by Patrick K. Ford. *The Mabinogi and Other Medieval Welsh Tales*. Berkeley, Los Angeles, London, 1977. Translated by Jeffrey Gantz. *The Mabinogion*. Harmondsworth, 1976.

Markale, Jean. *L'Epopée celtique d'Irlande*. Paris, 1971.

_____. *L'Epopée celtique en Bretagne*. Paris, 1971.

Marx, J. *La Légende arthurienne et le Graal*. Paris, 1952. Reviewed by R. Bossuat, *BEC* 110 (1952):282-87; by E. Faral, *Rom* 73 (1952): 262-71; and by J. Frappier, *Rom* 73 (1952):248-62. (Cf. *Rom* 73 (1952):531-35—"Correspondance" between J. Marx and Edmond Faral.)

Newstead, Helaine. *Bran the Blessed in Arthurian Romance*. New York, 1939.

_____. "Recent Perspectives on Arthurian Literature." *Mélanges Jean Frappier*, 2:877-83. Geneva, 1970.

Rivoallan, A. *Présence des Celtes*. Paris, 1957.

Sjoestedt, Marie-Louise. *Dieux et héros des Celtes*. Paris, 1940. Translated by M. Dillon. *Gods and Heroes of the Celts*. London, 1949.

Stiennon, Jacques, and Lejeune, Rita. "La Légende arthurienne dans la sculpture de la cathédrale de Modène." *CCM* 6 (1963):291-96.

Vendryes, J. "Les Eléments celtiques de la légende du Graal." *EC* 5 (1949):1-50.

Webster, K.G.T. *Guinevere: A Study of Her Abductions*. Milton, Mass., 1951. Reviewed by J. Frappier, *RLC* 27 (1953):101-3 and by H. Newstead, *JEGP* 52 (1953):250-53.

V. Early Works

A. Philomena

De Boer, C., ed. *Philomena: Conte raconté d'après Ovide par Chrétien de Troyes*. Paris, 1909. Translated by R.J. Cormier in "After Ovid: Three Tales of Antiquity Translated from the Old French." New York, forthcoming.

_____. "Chrétien de Troyes auteur de *Philomena*." *Rom* 41 (1912): 94-100.

Hoepffner, E. "Le *Philomena* de Chrétien de Troyes." *Rom* 57 (1931): 13-74.

Levy, R. "Old French *Goz* and Chrestiens li Gois." *PMLA* 46 (1931): 312-30.

_____. "Etat présent des études sur l'attribution de *Philomena*." *LR* 5 (1951):46-52.

Zaman, F. *L'Attribution de 'Philomena' à Chrétien de Troyes*. Amsterdam, 1928.

B. Two Love Poems

Foerster, W. (See Foerster, *Kristian von Troyes*, pp. 202-209: edition of the two poems attributed to Chrétien.)

Roncaglia, A. "Carestia." *CN* 18 (1958):1-17.

Zai, Marie-Claire. *Les Chansons courtoises de Chrétien de Troyes.* Bern: H. Lang, 1974. Edition critique avec introduction, notes et commentaire. 'Publicatio Universitatis Europensis, Série 13: Langue et littérature française 27.

C. *Guillaume d'Angleterre*

1. Editions

Foerster, W., ed. *Kristian von Troyes: Sämtliche erhaltene Werke.* 4: 253-475. Halle, 1884-99. ["Grosse Ausgabe."]
_____. Romanische Bibliothek 20. Halle, 1911. ["Kleine Ausgabe."]
Wilmotte, M., ed. *CFMA* 55. Paris, 1927. Translated by J. Trotin. *Guillaume d'Angleterre.* Paris, 1974.

2. Studies

Danelon, Franca. "Sull'ispirazione del *Guillaume d'Angleterre.*" *CN* 11 (1951):49-67. (Defends attribution to Chrétien.)
Foulon, C. "Les Tendances aristocratiques dans le roman de *Guillaume d'Angleterre.*" *Rom* 71(1950):222-37.
Francis, E.A. "Guillaume d'Angleterre." In *Studies Presented to R.L.G. Ritchie*, pp. 63-76. Cambridge, 1949.
Lonigan, P.R. "The Authorship of the *Guillaume d'Angleterre*: A New Approach." *SF* no. 47-48 (1972):308-14.
Tanquerey, F.J. "Chrétien de Troyes est-il l'auteur de Guillaume d'Angleterre?" *Rom* 57 (1931):75-116. (Against attribution; cf. Philip-August Becker, *ZrP* 55 [1935]:423-45.)
Wilmotte, M. "Chrétien de Troyes et le conte de *Guillaume d'Angleterre.*" *Rom* 46 (1920):1-38.

D. *Others*

Two Old French Gauvain Romances: 'Le Chevalier à l'épée' and 'La Mule sans frein.' Edited by R.C. Johnston and D.D.R. Owen. Edinburgh, London, 1972, (Two romances, heretofore considered anonymous, ascribed to Chrétien by the editors; cf. Owen, *Rom* 92 [1971]: 246-60.)

VI. Erec et Enide

A. Editions

Foerster, W. (See Foerster, *Kristian von Troyes*, vol. 3; Foerster, Romanische Bibliothek 20, vol. 13, 1896; 2d ed., 1909; 3d ed., 1934. Translated by W.W. Comfort. *Arthurian Romances by Chrétien de Troyes*. London, 1914. Translated by M. Borodine. In *Poèmes et récits de la vieille France*. Vol. 4. Paris, 1924.

Roques, M. *Les Romans de Chrétien de Troyes édités d'après la copie de Guiot* (Bibliothèque Nationale, manuscrit français 794). *I.* CFMA 80. Paris, 1952. Reviewed by H.F. Williams, *RPh* 9 (1955-56):457-60. Translated by René Louis, Paris, 1954.

B. Studies

Brault, G.J. "Isolt and Guenevere: Two Twelfth-Century Views of Woman." In *The Role of Woman in the Middle Ages*, edited by R.T. Morewedge, pp. 41-64. Albany, 1975.

Brogyanyi, G.J. "Motivation in *Erec et Enide*: An Interpretation of the Romance." *KRQ* 19 (1972):407-31.

Delbouille, M. "A propos de la patrie et de la date de *Floire et Blanchefleur*." In *Mélanges Mario Roques*, 4:53-98. Paris, 1952.

_____. "Le 'Draco Normannicus,' source d'*Erec et Enide*." In *Mélanges Pierre Le Gentil*, pp. 181-98. Paris, 1973.

Ferrante, J.M. *Woman as Image in Medieval Literature: From the Twelfth Century to Dante*. New York, 1975.

Frappier, J. "Pour le commentaire d'Erec et Enide: Notes de lecture. I: Bilis, Le roi d'Antipodes. II: Les Offrandes d'Erec et d'Enide au 'moutier' de Carmant. III: Erec revêt son armure d'emmener Enide 'en aventure'." *MRom* 20,4 (1970):15-30. [Reprinted in *Histoire, mythes et symboles.* Geneva, 1976.]

Hoepffner, E. "'Matière et sens' dans le roman d'*Erec et Enide*." *ARom* 18 (1934):433-50.

Kelly, Douglas. "La Forme et le sens de la quête dans l'*Erec et Enide* de Chrétien de Troyes." *Rom* 92 (1971):326-58.

————. "The Source and Meaning of *conjointure* in Chrétien's *Erec* 14." *Viator* 1 (1970):179-200.

Lacy, N.J. "Narrative Point of View and the Problem of Erec's Motivation." *KRQ* 18 (1971):355-62.

Lot, F. "Les Noces d'Erec et d'Enide." *Rom* 46 (1920):42-45.

Luttrell, C. *The Creation of the First Arthurian Romance: A Quest.* Evanston, London, 1974. Reviewed by R.J. Cormier, *RBPH* 57, 1 (1979):86-88.

Maddox, Donald. *Structure and Sacring: The Systematic Kingdom in Chrétien's Erec et Enide.* French Forum Monographs, 8. Lexington, KY, 1978.

Maranini, Lorenza. "Motivi cortesi e anticortesi nell'*Erec et Enide*." *Saggia di Umanismo Cristiano* 3 (1947):3-20.

————. "Motivi lirici e psicologici dell'amore nell'*Erec et Enide*." *Saggia di Umanismo Cristiano* 4 (1947):3-22.

Meyer-Lübke, W. "Chrestien von Troyes: Erec und Enide." *ZfSL* 44 (1917):129-88.

Mickel, E.J. "A Reconsideration of Chrétien's *Erec*." *RF* 84 (1972): 18-44.

Newstead, H. *Bran the Blessed in Arthurian Romance*, pp. 106-20.

Niemeyer, K.H. "The Writer's Craft: 'La Joie de la cort'." *Esp* 9 (1969): 286-92.

Nitze, W.A. "The Romance of Erec, Son of Lac." *MP* 10 (1912-13): 445-89.

————. "Erec's Treatment of Enide." *RR* 10 (1919):26-37.

Pagani, W. "Ancora sul prologo dell'*Erec et Enide*." *SMV* 24 (1976): 141-52.

Philipot, E. "Un épisode d'Erec et Enide: La Joie de la Cour, Mabon l'Enchanteur." *Rom* 25 (1896):258-94.

Pickens, R.T. "*Estoire, lai* and Romance: Chrétien's *Erec et Enide* and *Cligés*." *RR* 46 (1975):247-62.

Press, A.R. "Le Comportement d'Erec envers Enide dans le roman de Chrétien de Troyes." *Rom* 90 (1969):529-38.

Sargent, Barbara N. "Petite histoire de Maboagrain (à propos d'un article récent)." *Rom* 93 (1972):87-96.

Schleiner, W. "Rank and Marriage: A Study of the Motif of 'Woman Willfully Tested.'" *CLS* 9 (1972):365-75.

Sheldon, E.S. "Why Does Chrétien's Erec Treat Enide so Harshly?" *RR* 5 (1914):115-26.

Shippey, T.A. "The Uses of Chivalry: *Erec* and *Gawain*." *MLR* 46 (1971):241-50.

Spensley, R.M. "Allusion as a Structural Device in Three Old French Romances." *RomN* 15 (1973):349-54.

Thiébaux, M. *The Stag of Love: The Chase in Medieval Literature.* Ithaca, 1974.

West, G.D. *An Index of Proper Names in French Arthurian Verse Romances, 1150-1300.* Toronto, 1969.

Wittig, J.S. "The Aeneas-Dido Allusion in Chrétien's *Erec et Enide*." *CL* 22 (1970):237-53.

VII. Cligés

A. Editions

Foerster, *Kristian von Troyes*, vol. 1; Foerster, Romanische Bibliothek 20, vol. 1, 1888; 2d ed., 1901; 3d ed., 1921. Translated by W.W. Comfort. *Arthurian Romances by Chrétien de Troyes*. London, 1914. Translated by A. Mary. *La Loge de feuillage*, pp. 67-134. Paris, 1928.

Micha, A., ed. Roques, *Les Romans de Chrétien*, vol. 2. *CFMA* 84. Paris, 1957. Translated by A. Micha. Paris, 1957.

B. Studies

Bertolucci, Valeria. "Commento retorico all'*Erec* e al *Cligés*." *SMV* 8 (1960):9-51.

_____. "Di nuovo su *Cligés* e *Tristan*." *SF* 18 (1962):401-13.

Favati, G. "Le *Cligés* de Chrétien de Troyes dans les éditions critiques et dans les manuscrits." *CCM* 10 (1967):385-407.

Fourrier, A. *Le Courant réaliste dans le roman courtois en France au Moyen Age: Les Débuts (XII$_e$ siècle)*, pp. 111-18. Paris, 1960.

Frappier, J. *Le Roman breton: Chrétien de Troyes. Cligés.* Paris, 1951.

Freeman, Michelle A. *The Poetics of Translatio Studii and Conjointure: Chrétien de Troyes's Cligés.* French Forum Monographs, 12. Lexington, Ky., 1979.

Guiette, R. "Sur quelques vers de *Cligés*." *Rom* 91(1970):75-82.

Haidu, P. *Aesthetic Distance in Chrétien de Troyes: Irony and Comedy in "Cligés" and "Perceval."* Geneva, 1968.

Hauvette, H. *La 'Morte vivante,'* pp. 100-108. Paris, 1933.

Hoepffner, E. "Chrétien de Troyes et Thomas d'Angleterre." *Rom* 55 (1929):1-16. (Defends the theory that *Cligés* and the *Lancelot* are earlier than the *Tristan* of Thomas.)

Laurie, Helen C.R. *Two Studies in Chrétien de Troyes.* (From *Erec* to *Cligés. Yvain* and the Romantic Tradition.) Geneva, 1972.

Lefay-Toury, M.-N. "Roman breton et mythes courtois: L'Evolution du personnage féminin dans les romans de Chrétien de Troyes." *CCM* 15 (1972):193-204, 283-93.

Lonigan, P.R. "The *Cligés* and the Tristan Legend." *SF* 18 (1974):201-12.

Lyons, Faith. "La Fausse mort dans le *Cligés* de Chrétien de Troyes." *Mélanges Mario Roques*, 1:167-77. Paris and Baden, 1950.

Maddox, D.L. "Kinship Alliances in the *Cligés* of Chrétien de Troyes." *Esp* 12 (1972):3-12.

Maranini, Lorenza. "I motivi psicologici di un Anti-Tristano nel 'Cligés'." *ASNSP* 12 (1943):13-26.

Micha, A. "Enéas et Cligés." In *Mélanges E. Hoepffner*, pp. 237-43. Paris, 1949.

_____. "Tristan et Cligés." *Neophil* 36 (1952):1-10. (Argues that Chrétien composed *Cligés* while thinking mainly about the *Tristan* which he supposedly wrote under the title, *Del roi Marc et d'Iseut la blonde*, a hypothesis with very little supporting evidence.)

Newman, F.X., ed. *The Meaning of Courtly Love.* Albany, 1968. Reviewed by J. Frappier, "Sur un procès fait à l'amour courtois," *Rom*

93 (1972):145-93. [Reprinted in *Amour courtois et Table Ronde*. Geneva, 1973].

Nolan, E.P. "Mythopoetic Evolution: Chrétien de Troyes's *Erec et Enide, Cligés* and *Yvain*." *Symp* 25 (1971):139-61.

Paris, G. "Cligés." *Journal des Savants*, 1902. Reprinted in *Mélanges de littérature française au Moyen Age*, pp. 229-322. Paris, 1910.

Payen, J.-C. "Figures féminines dans le roman médiéval français." In *Entretiens sur la renaissance du XII$_e$ siècle*, edited by M. de Gandillac and E. Jeauneau, pp. 407-28. Paris, The Hague, 1968.

Robertson, D.W., Jr. "The Idea of Fame in Chrétien's *Cligés*." *SP* 69 (1972):414-33.

Vance, E. "Le Combat érotique chez Chrétien de Troyes: De la figure à la forme." *Poétique* 12 (1972):544-71.

Van Hamel, A.G. "Cligés et Tristan." *Rom* 33 (1904):465-89. (Advances with solid arguments the thesis that *Cligés* postdates the *Tristan* of Thomas.)

VIII. Le Chevalier de la Charrette (Lancelot)

A. Editions

(See Foerster, *Kristian von Troyes*, vol. 4.) Translated by W.W. Comfort. *Arthurian Romances by Chrétien de Troyes*. London, 1914.

Roques, M. (See Roques, *Les Romans de Chrétien*, vol. 3.) *CFMA* 86. Paris, 1958. Translated by J. Frappier. Paris, 1962; 2d ed., 1967.

B. Studies

Adler, A. "A Note on the Composition of Chrétien's *Charrette*." *MLR* 45 (1950):33-39.

Baron, F.X. "Love in Chrétien's *Charrette*: Reversed Values and Isolation." *MLQ* 34 (1973):372-83.

Bogdanow, F. "The Love Theme in Chrétien de Troyes's *Chevalier de la Charrette.*" *MLR* 67 (1972):50-61.

Brand, W. "Die Kompositionelle Einheit von *Lancelot* und *Yvain.*" *RF* 85 (1973):330-40.

Brault, G.J. "Chrétien de Troyes's *Lancelot*: The Eye and the Heart." *BBSIA/BBIAS* 24 (1972):142-53.

Chenerie, Marie-Luce. "Ces 'curieux chevaliers tournoyeurs' des fabliaux aux romans." *Rom* 97 (1976):327-68.

Cross, T.P., and Nitze, W.A. *Lancelot and Guenevere: A Study on the Origins of Courtly Love*. Chicago, 1930. (A precise and convincing study of the themes of Celtic origin contained in the *matière* of the romance.)

Frappier, J. "Le Prologue du *Chevalier de la Charrette* et son interprétation." *Rom* 93 (1972):337-77.

Iker-Gittleman, Anne. "Chrétien de Troyes, poète de la cour, dans le *Chevalier de la Charrette.*" *RPh* 39(1976):152-58. [Jean Frappier Memorial Volume.]

Jonin, P. "Le Vasselage de Lancelot dans le conte de la *Charrette.*" *MA* 58 (1952):281-98.

Kelly, Douglas. *Sens et Conjointure in the "Chevalier de la Charrette."* Paris, The Hague, 1966.

Kooijman, J.C. "Le Motif de la charrette dans le *Lancelot* de Chrétien de Troyes." *RF* 87(1975):342-49.

Lazar, M. "Lancelot et la 'mulier mediatrix': La Quête de soi à travers la femme." *Esp* 9 (1969):243-56.

Mandel, J. "Proper Behavior in Chrétien's *Charrette*: The Host-Guest Relationship." *FR* 48 (1974):683-89.

Maranini, Lorenza. "Cavalleria, amore conjugale e amore cortese nel *Chevalier de la Charrette.*" *Saggia di Umanismo Cristiano* 4 (1949): 67-86.

————. "Quest'e amore cortese nel *Chevalier de la Charrette.*" *RLMC* 2 (1951):204-23.

Micha, A. "Sur les sources de la *Charrette.*" *Rom* 71 (1950):345-58. (Attempts to reduce the sources to the influence of a "production hagiographique": *Vita Sancti Gildae*, *Visio* literature, and the *Espurgatoire de Saint Patrice.*)

Noble, P. "The Character of Guinevere in the Arthurian Romances of Chrétien de Troyes." *MLR* 67 (1972):524-35.

Noreiko, S.F. "*Le Chevalier de la Charrette*: Prise de conscience d'un *fin amant*." *Rom* 94 (1973):463-83.

Paris, G. "Le Conte de la *Charrette*." *Rom* 12 (1883):459-534.

————. "Le *Lanzelet* d'Ulrich de Zatzikhoven." *Rom* 10 (1881): 465-96.

Payen, J.-C. "Lancelot contre Tristan: La Conjuration d'un mythe subversif (réflexions sur l'idéologie romanesque au moyen âge)." In *Mélanges Pierre Le Gentil*, pp. 617-32. Paris, 1973.

Radoulet, Carmen. "Intorno al realismo cerimoniale del *Lancelot* di Chrétien de Troyes." *CN* 35 (1975):9-30.

Rychner, J. "Le Prologue du *Chevalier de la Charrette*." *VR* 26 (1967): 2-23.

————. "Le Prologue du *Chevalier de la Charrette* et l'interprétation du roman." In *Mélanges R. Lejeune*, 2:1121-35. Gembloux, 1969.

————. "Le Sujet et la signification du *Chevalier de la Charrette*." *VR* 27 (1968):50-76.

Shirt, D.J. "Chrétien de Troyes and the Cart." In *Studies Frederick Whitehead*, pp. 279-301. Manchester, 1973.

Southward, Elaine. "The Unity of Chrétien's *Lancelot*." In *Mélanges Marie Roques*, 2:281-90. Baden and Paris, 1953.

Zaddy, Z.P. "*Le Chevalier de la Charrette* and the *De amore* of Andreas Capellanus." In *Studies Frederick Whitehead*, pp. 363-99. Manchester, 1973.

Zatzikhoven, Ulrich von. *Lanzelet*. Edited by K.A. Hahn. Frankfurt, 1845. Translated by K.T.G. Webster and R.S. Loomis. *Lanzelet, Translated from the Middle-High German*. New York, 1951.

IX. Le Chevalier au Lion (Yvain)

A. Editions

(See Foerster, *Kristian von Troyes*, vol. 2, 1887; Foerster, Romanische Bibliothek 20, vol. 5, 1891; 2d ed. 1902; 3d ed., 1906; 4th ed. 1912. [Reprinted 1913, 1926.] Translated by W.W. Comfort. *Arthurian*

Romances by Chrétien de Troyes. London, 1914. Translated by A. Mary. Paris, 1923; 2d ed., 1944. Translated by J. Harris. New York, 1963.

Linker, R.W. Chapel Hill, 1940. (Based on Bibliothèque Nationale, manuscrit français, 794.)

Reid, T.B.W. Manchester, 1942; 2d ed. 1948. (Reproduces Foerster's excellent 1912 edition of *Yvain.* English Glossary. [See preceding Foerster entry.]

Roques, M. (See Roques, *Les Romans de Chrétien*, vol. 4.) *CFMA* 89. Paris, 1960. Translated by R.H. Cline. *Yvain* or, *The Knight With the Lion.* Athens, Ga., 1975. Translated by Claude Buridant and J. Trotin. *Le Chevalier au Lion.* Paris, 1972.

B.   Studies

Adler, A. "Sovereignty in Chrétien's *Yvain*." *PMLA* 62 (1947):281-305.

Brown, A.C.L. "Chrétien's *Ivain*." *MP* 9 (1911-12):109-28.

_____. "Iwain: A Study in the Origins of Arthurian Romance." *HSNPL* 8 (1903):1-147.

_____. "The Knight of the Lion." *PMLA* 20 (1904):673-706.

Brugger, E. "Yvain and His Lion." *MP* 28 (1941):267-87.

Chaitin, G.D. "Celtic Tradition and Psychological Truth in Chrétien's *Chevalier au lion*." *Sub-stance* 2 (1972):63-76.

Chotzen, Thomas M. "Le Lion d'Owein et ses prototypes celtiques." *Neophil* 18 (1932):51-58, 131-36.

Combellack, C.R.B. "The Entrapment of Yvain." *MS* 37 (1975):524-30.

_____. "Yvain's Guilt." *SP* 68 (1971):10-25.

Cook, R.G. "The Structure of Romance in Chrétien's *Erec* and *Yvain*." *MP* 71 (1973-74):128-43.

Cormier, R.J. "Cú Chulainn and Yvain: The Love Hero in Early Irish and Old French Literature." *SP* 72 (1975):115-39.

Diverres, A.H. "Chivalry and *fin'amor* in *Le Chevalier au Lion*." In *Studies Frederick Whitehead*, pp. 91-116. Manchester, 1973.

Frappier, J. *Etude sur 'Yvain' ou 'Le Chevalier au Lion' de Chrétien de Troyes.* Paris, 1969. (Revision and expansion of Frappier, *Le Roman breton.*)

————. *Le Roman breton: Yvain ou le chevalier au Lion.* Paris, 1952.

Haidu, P. *Lion-queue-coupée: L'Ecart symbolique chez Chrétien de Troyes.* Geneva, 1972.

Imbs, P. "La Reine Guenièvre dans *Le Chevalier au Lion.*" In *Etudes Félix Lecoy*, pp. 235-60. Paris, 1973.

Laurie, Helen C.R. (See Laurie, *Two Studies*.)

Lewis, C.B. "The Function of the Gong in the Source of Chrétien de Troyes's *Yvain.*" *ZrP* 47 (1927):254-70.

Lonigan, Paul R. "Calogrenant's Journey and the Mood of the *Yvain.*" *SF* 58 (1976):1-20.

Loomis, R.S. "Calogrenanz and Chrétien's Originality." *MLN* 43 (1928):215-23.

Lozachmeur, Jean-Claude. "Le Motif du *Passage périlleux* dans les romans arthuriens et dans la littérature orale bretonne." *EC* 15 (1976):289-99.

Murtaugh, D.M. "*Oïr et entandre*: Figuralism and Narrative Structure in Chrétien's *Yvain.*" *RR* 44 (1973):161-74.

Newstead, H. "Narrative Techniques in Chrétien's *Yvain.*" *RPh* 30 (1977):431-41.

Nitze, W.A. "The Fountain Defended." *MP* 7 (1909):146-64.

————. "Yvain and the Myth of the Fountain." *Spec* 30 (1955): 170-79.

Nolting-Hauff, I. "Märchen und Märchenroman: Zur Beziehung zwischen einfacher Form und narrativer Grossform in der Literatur." *Poetica* 6(1974):129-78.

Pensom, R. "Rapports du symbole et de la narration dans *Yvain* et dans *La Mort Artu.*" *Rom* 94 (1973):398-407.

Philipot, E. "Le Roman du *Chevalier au Lion* de Chrétien de Troyes: Etude littéraire." *AnBret* 8 (1892-93):33-83, 321-45, 455-79.

Schweitzer, E.C. "Pattern and Theme in Chrétien's *Yvain.*" *Trad* 30 (1974):145-89.

Thoss, D. *Studien zum 'locus amoenus' im Mittelalter.* Wiener romanistische Arbeiten 10. Vienna, Stuttgart, 1972.

Uitti, K.D. "Chrétien de Troyes's *Yvain*: Fiction and Sense." *RPh* 22 (1968-69):471-83.

Whitehead, F. "Yvain's Wooing." In *Medieval Miscellany Eugène Vinaver*, pp. 321-36. Manchester, 1965.

X. Le Conte du Graal (Perceval)

A. Editions

Baist, G. Freiburg, 1912. (Based on Bibliothèque Nationale, manuscrit français 794.)

Hilka, A. Vol. 5 of the Foerster edition, Halle, 1932. (Text of the *Perceval en prose*, pp. 483–614.) Translated in part by R.S. and L.H. Loomis. *Medieval Romances*. New York, 1957. Foulet, *Perceval le Gallois*. Préface by M. Roques. Paris, 1947. [Reprinted, 1970.]

Potvin, Charles. *Perceval le Gallois ou le Conte du Graal publié d'après les manuscrits originaux*. 6 vols. Mons, 1865–71. (Vol. 1: *Perlevaus*; vols. 2–3: *Conte du Graal*; vols. 3–4: *Continuations du Conte du Graal*.)

Roach, W. *TLF* 71. Geneva, Lille, 1956; 2d ed., Geneva, Paris, 1959. (Based on Bibliothèque Nationale, manuscrit français 12576.)

B. Studies

Nelli, René, ed. *Lumière du Graal: Etudes et textes*. Cahiers du Sud. Paris, 1951.

Les Romans du Graal dans la littérature des XIIe et XIIIe siècles. Colloque de Strasbourg, 1954. Paris, 1956.

1. Origins of the Grail Legend

For the ritualistic origins based on the vegetation and fertility cults, see:

Weston, Jessie. *The Legend of Sir Perceval*. 2 vols. London, 1906–09. [Reprinted, 1969.]

————. *From Ritual to Romance*. Cambridge, 1920. [Reprinted, New York, 1957.] (The lance and the grail are viewed as sexual symbols.)

For the Christian origin (liturgical, biblical, allegorical), see:

Adolf, H. *Visio Pacis: Holy City and Grail*. University Park, Pa., 1960.
_____. "G.W.F. Hegel, die Kreuzzüge und Chrétiens *Conte del graal*." *Dvj* 49 (1975):32-42.
Anitchkof, E. "Le Saint Graal et les rites eucharistiques." *Rom* 55 (1929):174-94.
Bruce, J.D. *The Evolution of Arthurian Romance*. 1:219-68. (See Bruce, *Evolution*.)
Burdach, K. Der Graal, *Forschungen über seinen Ursprung und seinen Zusammenhang mit der Longinus Legende*. Stuttgart, 1938.
Carmody, F.J. *Perceval le gallois: Roman du douzième siècle*. Berkeley, 1970.
Holmes, U.T., Jr. *A New Interpretation of Chrétien's "Conte del Graal."* *UNCSRLL* 8. Chapel Hill, 1948. (Associates the Grail legend with Hebrew traditions.)
Imbs, P. "Perceval et le Graal chez Chrétien de Troyes." *Bulletin de la société académique du Bas-Rhin* 72-74 (1950):38-79.
Klenke, Sister M. Amelia. *Liturgy and Allegory in Chrétien's 'Perceval.'* *UNCSRLL* 14. Chapel Hill, 1951.
_____. "Chrétien's Symbolism and Cathedral Art." *PMLA* 70 (1955):223-43.
_____. "The Spiritual Ascent of Perceval." *SP* 53 (1956):1-21.
Lot-Borodine, Myrrha. "Le *Conte del Graal* de Chrétien de Troyes et sa présentation symbolique." *Rom* 77 (1956):235-88.
Micha, A. "Deux études sur le Graal," I. "Le Graal et la lance." *Rom* 73(1952):462-79. (The Grail is interpreted as a pyx.)
Peebles, Rose J. *The Legend of Longinus and Its Connection with the Grail*. Baltimore, 1911.
Riquer, M. de. "Interpretación cristiana de *Li Contes del Graal*." In *Miscelanea dedicada a Mons. A. Griera*, pp. 209-83. Barcelona, 1960.
Roques, M. "Le Graal de Chrétien et la demoiselle au Graal." *Rom* 76 (1955):1-27. (The damsel of the Grail interpreted as *Ecclesia*.)
Weinraub, Eugene T. *Chrétien's Jewish Grail: A New Investigation of the Imagery and Significance of Chrétien de Troyes's Grail Episode Based Upon Medieval Hebraic Sources*. Chapel Hill, 1976.

On the Celtic origins and a progressive Christianization
of the legend, see:

Brown, A.C.L. *The Origin of the Grail Legend*. Cambridge, Mass., 1943.

Delbouille, M. "Réalité du château du Roi Pécheur dans le *Conte du Graal*." In *Mélanges René Crozet*, 2:903-13. Poitiers, 1966.

Frappier, J. "Du 'graal trestot descovert' à la forme du graal chez Chrétien de Troyes." *Rom* 73 (1952):82-92.

————. "Du 'graal trestot descovert' à l'origine de la légende." *Rom* 74 (1953):358-75.

————. "Le Conte du Graal' est-il une allégorie judéo-chrétienne?" *RPh* 16 (1962-63):179-213; 20 (1966):1-31.

———— *Chrétien de Troyes et le mythe du Graal: Etude sur "Perceval" ou le "Conte du Graal."* Paris, 1972 (Revision and expansion of Frappier, *Le Roman breton*.) Reviewed by B.N. Sargent. *RPh* 30 (1976):278-83.

————. "Le Graal et l'hostie." In *Les Romans du Graal*, pp. 63-81.

Jackson, K. "Les Sources celtiques du *Roman du graal*." (See *Les Romans du Graal*, pp. 213-17; denies Celtic origins as presented by most Arthurian scholars; cf. Cormier, "Tradition and Sources.")

Lejeune, Rita, "Préfiguration du Graal." *SMed* 17 (1951):1-26.

Loomis, R.S. (See *Arthurian Tradition*, pp. 333-459.)

————. "Grail Problems." *RR* 45 (1954):12-17.

————. "The Grail Story of Chrétien de Troyes as Ritual and Symbolism." *PMLA* 71 (1956):840-52. (Replies to Sister A.M. Klenke.)

Marx, J. "Le Cortège du 'Château des Merveilles' dans le roman gallois de *Peredur*." *EC* 9(1960):92-105.

————. "Le 'Bruiden' celtique et le château de Graal." *Rom* 75 (1954):231-40, 512-20.

————. "Quelques remarques au sujet de travaux récents sur l'origine du Graal." *MA* 63 (1957):469-80.

Nitze, W.A. "The Fisher King and the Grail in Retrospect." *RPh* 69 (1952-53):14-22.

2. *On the Structure and Literary Import of the* Conte du Graal

Frappier, J. *Le Roman breton: Chrétien de Troyes. Perceval ou le Conte du Graal*. Paris, 1953.

_____. "Le Graal et la chevalerie." *Rom* 75 (1954):165-210.

_____. "Féerie du château du Roi Pêcheur dans le *Conte du Graal.*" In *Mélanges Jean Fourquet*, pp. 101-17. Paris, 1969.

_____. "Le Graal et ses feux divergents." *RPh* 24 (1970-71):373-440.

Kellermann, W. *Aufbaustil und Weltbild Chrestiens von Troyes im Percevalroman*. Halle, 1936.

Maranini, Lorenza. "Educazione dell'uomo e amore materno nel 'conte del Graal'." *HumB* 1 (1946):1164-76.

Roques, M. "Chrétien de Troyes: Le Conte du Graal." In *Etudes de littérature française*, pp. 29-42. Lille, Geneva, 1949.

3. Other Studies

Armstrong, G. "The Scene of the Blood Drops on the Snow: A Crucial Narrative Moment in the *Conte du Graal.*" *KRQ* 19 (1972):127-47.

Dragonetti, Roger. *La Vie de la lettre au Moyen Age (Le Conte du Graal)*. Paris, 1980.

Gallais, P. *Perceval et l'initiation: Essais sur le dernier roman de Chrétien de Troyes, ses correspondances 'orientales' et sa signification anthropologique*. Paris, 1972. Reviewed by D. Poirion, *Spec* 50 (1975):306-9.

Golther, W. *Parzival und die Gral in der Dichtung des Mittelalters und der Neuzeit*. Stuttgart, 1925.

Gouttebroze, J.-G. "L'Arrière-plan psychique et mythique de l'itinéraire de Perceval dans le *Conte du Graal.*" *Senefiance* 2 (1976):339-51.

Grisward, J. "*Com ces trois goutes de sanc furent, Qui sor le blance noif parurent*: Note sur un motif littéraire." In *Etudes Félix Lecoy*, pp. 157-64. Paris, 1973.

Haidu, P. (See Haidu, *Aesthetic Distance*.)

Heinzel, R. "Uber die franz. Gralromane." *Denkschriften der Wiener Akademie der Wissenschaften* 40, 3 (1892). (Especially pp. 3-25.)

Hoggan, D.G. "Le Péché de Perceval: Pour l'authenticité de l'épisode de l'ermite dans le *Conte du Graal* de Chrétien de Troyes." *Rom* 93(1972):50-76; 244-75.

Le Rider, Paule. *Le Chevalier dans Le Conte du Graal de Chrétien de Troyes*. Paris, 1978.

Méla, Charles. *Blanchefleur et le saint homme ou la semblance des reliques: Etude de littérature médiévale*. Paris, 1979.

Nitze, W.A., and Williams, H.F. *Perceval and the Holy Grail: An Essay on the Romance of Chrétien de Troyes*, pp. 281-332. *UCPMP* 28, 5. Berkeley, Los Angeles, 1949.

_____. *Arthurian Names in the Perceval of Chrétien de Troyes: Analysis and Commentary*, pp. 265-97. *UCPMP* 38, 2. Berkeley, Los Angeles, 1955.

Olschki, L. "Il Castello del Re Pescatore e i suoi misteri nel *Conte del Graal* di Chrétien de Troyes." *Atti dell' Accademica Nazionale del Lincei* 10, 3 (1961):101-59. Translated by J.A. Scott. *The Grail Castle and Its Mysteries*. Foreword by E. Vinaver. Manchester, Berkeley, 1966.

Owen, D.D.R. *The Evolution of the Grail Legend*. Edinburgh, London, 1968.

Pauphilet, A. "Perceval et le Graal." (See Pauphilet, *Le Legs*, pp. 169-209.)

Payen, J.-C. *Le Motif du repentir dans la littérature française médiévale. (Des origines à 1230.)* *PRF* 98. Geneva, 1967. (Especially pp. 391-400.) Reviewed by P. Gallais, *CCM* 15 (1972):61-74.

Poirion, D. "Du sang sur la neige: Nature et fonction de l'image dans le *Conte du Graal*." In *Essays J.D. Powell and R. Hodgins*, edited by R.J. Cormier, pp. 143-65. Philadelphia, 1977.

_____. "L'Ombre mythique de Perceval dans le *Conte du Graal*." *CCM* 16 (1973):191-98.

Pollmann, Leo, *Chrétien de Troyes und der Conte del Graal*. Tübingen, 1965.

Reiss, E. "The Birth of the Grail Quest." In *Innovation in Medieval Literature: Essays Alan Markman*, edited by D. Radcliff-Umstead, pp. 20-34. Pittsburgh, 1971.

Roloff, V. *Reden und Schweigen: Zur Tradition eines mittelalterlichen Themas in der französischen Literatur*. (Münchener romanistische Arbeiten 34.) Munich, 1973. (Especially pp. 117-64.)

Spensley, R.M. "Gauvain's Castle of Marvels Adventure in the *Conte del Graal*." *Med. Aev.* 42 (1973):32-37.

Suard, F. "Place et signification de l'épisode Blanchefleur dans le *Conte du Graal* de Chrétien de Troyes." In *Mélanges Pierre Le Gentil*, pp. 803-10. Paris, 1973.

4. On the Debate Over the Unity or Bipartition of the Conte du Graal

Frappier, J. "Sur la composition du *'Conte du Graal'*." *MA* 65 (1958): 67-102. (Defends the thesis of unity.)

_____. "Note complémentaire sur la composition du 'Conte du Graal'." *Rom* 81 (1960):308-37.

Köhler, E. "Zur Diskussion über die Einheit von Chrestiens 'Li Conte del Graal'." *ZrP* 75(1959):523-39.

Riquer M. de. "La Composición de 'Li contes del Graal' y el 'Guiromelant'." *Boletin de la Real Academia de Buenas Letras de Barcelona* 27 (1957-58):279-320.

_____. "Perceval y Gauvain en 'Li contes del Graal'." *FRom* 4 (1957):119-47. (Supports with new arguments the thesis of bipartition.)

XI. Language and Expression

A. Glossaries

Foerster, W. Wörterbuch…(See reference on p. 196.)
Roach, W., ed. *Première continuation de Perceval*. Philadelphia, 1955. (Very useful glossary prepared by L. Foulet.)

B. Other Studies

Bianchini, S. "I pronomi allocutivi in Chrétien de Troyes." *CN* 31 (1971):69-114.

Biller, G. *Etude sur le style des premiers romans français en vers*. Goteborg, 1916.

Burgess, G.S. "*Orgueil* and *Fierté* in Twelfth-Century French." *ZrP* 89 (1973):103-22.

Colby, Alice M. *The Portrait in Twelfth-Century French Literature: An Example of the Stylistic Originality of Chrétien de Troyes.* Geneva, 1965. Reviewed by J. Frappier, *CCM* 9 (1966):71–73.

Dubois, C., M. Dubois-Stasse, and G. Lavis. *Chrétien de Troyes: Philomena. Concordances et index établis d'après l'édition C. De Boer.* Publications de l'institut de lexicologie français. Liège, [n.d.]

Dubois-Stasse, M., and Fontaine-Lanve, A., eds. *Chrétien de Troyes: Guillaume d'Angleterre, I, II. Concordances et index établis d'après l'édition de M. Wilmotte.* Publications de l'institut de lexicologie française. Liège, [n.d.]

Fotitch, Tatiana. *The Narrative Tenses in Chrétien de Troyes: A Study in Syntax and Stylistics.* Washington, 1950.

Frappier, J. "Le Tour 'je me sui' chez Chrétien de Troyes." *RPh* 9 (1955–56):126–33.

————. "Sur la versification de Chrétien de Troyes: L'Enjambement dans *Erec et Enide*." *RS* 32 (1964):41–49.

————. "La Brisure du couplet dans *Erec et Enide*." *Rom* 86 (1965): 1–21.

Getzler, Adele. "Beiträge zur Kenntnis der Sprache Christians von Troyes." *ZrP* 51 (1931):226–48.

Gsteiger, M. *Die Landschaftsschilderungen in den Romanen Chrestiens de Troyes.* Berne, 1958.

Hilka, A. *Die direkte Rede als stilistisches Kunstmittel in den Romanen des Kristian von Troyes.* Halle, 1903.

Imbs, P. *Les Propositions temporelles en ancien français.* Paris, 1956.

Johnston, R.C. "Sound-Related Couplets in Old French." *FMLS* 12 (1976):194–205.

Koenig, D. *'Sen'/'sens' et 'savoir' et leur synonymes dans quelques romans courtois du 12e et du début du 13e siècle.* Bern, Frankfurt, 1973.

C. Narrativity

Beatie, B.A. "Patterns of Myth in Medieval Narrative." *Symp* 25 (1971):101–22.

Brand, W. *Chrétien de Troyes: Zur Dichtungstechnik seiner Romane.*

Freiburger Schriften zur romanischen Philologie 19. Munich, 1972.

Brogyanyi, G.J. "Plot Structure and Motivation in Chrétien's Romances." *VR* 31 (1972):272-86.

Chaurand, J. "Quelques réflexions sur l'hyperbole dans *Le Chevalier de la Charrette*." In *Etudes Félix Lecoy*, pp. 43-53. Paris, 1973.

Delbouille, M. "A propos des rimes familières à Chrétien de Troyes et à Gautier d'Arras (signification de la fréquence relative des 'rimes répétées')." In *Etudes Félix Lecoy*, pp. 55-65. Paris, 1973.

Dembowski, P.F. "Monologue, Author's Monologue and Related Problems in the Romances of Chrétien de Troyes." *YFS* 51 (1974): 102-14.

Duplat, A. "Etude stylistique des apostrophes adressées aux personnages féminins dans les romans de Chrétien de Troyes." *CCM* 17 (1974):129-52.

Gallais, P. "Hexagonal and Spiral Structure in Medieval Narrative." *YFS* 51 (1974):115-32.

————. "L'Hexagone logique et le roman médiéval." *CCM* 18 (1975): 1-14, 133-48.

————. "Recherches sur la mentalité des romanciers français du moyen âge: Les Formules et le vocabulaire des prologues. I." *CCM* 7 (1964):479-93; ibid., 13 (1970):333-47.

Green, D.H. "Irony and Medieval Romance." *FMLS* 6 (1970):49-64.

Haidu, P. "Humor and the Aesthetics of Medieval Romance." *RR* 64 (1973):54-68.

————. "Narrative Structure in *Floire et Blancheflor:* A Comparison with Two Romances of Chrétien de Troyes." *RomN* 14 (1972-73): 383-88.

————. "Narrativity and Language in Some Twelfth-Century Romances." *YFS* 51 (1974):133-46.

Haug, W. "Struktur und Geschichte: Ein literaturtheoretisches Experiment an mittelalterlichen Texten." *GRM* 23 (1973):129-52.

Hunt, T. "Tradition and Originality in the Prologues of Chrestien de Troyes." *FMLS* 8 (1972):320-44.

Jodogne, O. "Le Personnalité de l'écrivain d'oïl du XIIe au XIVe siècle." In *L'Humanisme médiéval dans les littératures romanes du XIIe au XIVe siècle*, edited by A. Fourrier, pp. 87-104. Paris, 1964.

Lacy, N.J. *The Craft of Chrétien de Troyes: An Essay in Narrative Art.* Leiden, 1980.

Ménard, Ph. "La Déclaration amoureuse dans la littérature arthurienne au XIIe siècle." *CCM* 13 (1970):33-42.

Micha, H. "Structure et regard romanesques dans l'oeuvre de Chrétien de Troyes." *CCM* 13 (1970):323-32.

Nykrog, P. "Two Creators of Narrative Form in Twelfth-Century France: Gautier d'Arras–Chrétien de Troyes." *Spec* 48 (1973):258-76.

Ollier, M.-L. "Le Discours en 'abyme' ou la narration équivoque." *Medioevo Romanzo* 1 (1974):351-64.

_____. "The Author in the Text: The Prologues of Chrétien de Troyes." *YFS* 51 (1974):26-41.

Uitti, K.D. "Remarks on Old French Narrative: Courtly Love and Poetic Form." *RPh* 26 (1972-73):77-93; 28 (1974-75):190-99.

_____. *Story, Myth, and Celebration in Old French Narrative Poetry 1050-1200.* Princeton, 1973. Especially pp. 128-231. Reviewed by E. von Richthofen, *Spec* 51 (1976):362-63.

Völker, W. *Märchenhafte Elemente bei Chrétien de Troyes.* (Romanistische Versuche und Vorarbeiten 39.) Bonn, 1972.

Zumthor, P. *Essai de poétique médiévale.* Paris, 1972.

_____. *Langue texte énigme.* Paris, 1975.

_____. "Le Texte médiéval et l'histoire: Propositions méthodologiques." RR 44 (1973):5-15.

[A forthcoming collected volume of interest, "La Réception critique des oeuvres de Chrétien de Troyes," *Oeuvres et critiques*, 5, 2, fasc. 9 (Paris, 1981), coordinated by R.J. Cormier, will include: K.D. Uitti, "Nouvelle critique et Chrétien de Troyes: Quelques perspectives"; R. Jones, "Chrétien devant la critique anglaise contemporaine: Questions de structure"; Claude Luttrell, "The Arthurian Traditionalist's Approach to the Composer of Romance: R.S. Loomis on Chrétien de Troyes"; D. Kelly, "Psychologie/pathologie et parole dans Chrétien de Troyes"; F. Lyons, "Interprétations critiques au XXe siècle du prologue de *Cligés: La Translatio Studii* selon les historiens, les philosophes et les philologues"; J.-C. Payen, "Une approche classiciste du roman médiéval: Jean Frappier, lecteur de Chrétien de Troyes"; A.A. Rutledge, "Perceval's Sin: Critical Perspectives"; S. Sturm-Maddox, "*Hortus non con-*

clusus: Critics and the *Joie de la Cort*"; L. Thorpe, "L'*Yvain* de Chrétien de Troyes et le jeu des topoi"; L.D. Wolfgang, "Prologues to the *Perceval* and Perceval's Father: The First Literary Critics of Chrétien were the Grail Authors Themselves"; D. Maddox, "Trois sur deux: Théories de bipartition et de tripartition des oeuvres de Chrétien de Troyes"; J. Ribard, "Ecriture symbolique et visée allégorique dans *Le Conte du Graal*"; D.P. Schenck, "Des vues sur le temps et l'espace chez Chrétien de Troyes"; H.F. Williams, "*Le Conte du Graal* de Chrétien de Troyes: Positions critiques et nouvelles perspectives"; M. Freeman, "Jean Frappier et le mythe du Graal"; and F.P. Sweetser, "La Réincarnation de Lancelot dans le roman en prose."]

Index

Modern critics marked*

Aaron, 189*n*
Abduction: of Queen Guenevere, 35; story of, 101, 102; theme, 103
Abel, 120
Acre, 3, 127
Adolphe, 190*n*
Adonis, 142
Adventure, 110, 165; of the tomb, 108
Adventure tale. *See* Tale of adventure
Aelis de Blois, 8
Aeneid, 19
Aithed, "elopement," 101, 103
Alexander, 80, 81, 86, 87, 89, 165, 168, 169, 171, 174, 175
Alexander the Great, 128
Alier, 113
Alis, 81, 83, 85, 86, 174
Allegorical interpretation, 189*n*
Alliteration, 179, 180
Amer, l', 84
"*Amors tançon et bataille*," 53
Amour lointain, "distant" love, 8
Andreas Capellanus, 106
Anglo-Norman, 42
Anglo-Saxon *Brut* by Layamon, 21
Angrès, 81, 83, 178
Anguingueron, 133
Angusel (Anguisseaus), King of Scotland, 32

Annominatio, 177, 178
Antiquity: legacy from, 12, 13
Apollonius of Tyre, 58
Ariosto, 111
Aristocracy: 40, 159; civilization, 76; morality of, 59
Armorica, 35, 39, 87. *See also* Breton; Brittany
*Arnold, I., 183
Ars amandi (Art of Love), 5
Ars amatoria (Ovid), 5, 168
Art d'amors, L' (Chrétien de Troyes), 5
Artes poeticae (manuals of poetics and rhetoric), xviii, 171
Arthur (King Arthur), 14, 15, 24, 63, 81, 90, 95, 98, 100, 102, 106, 110, 111, 113, 115, 117, 121, 131, 154, 155, 165, 166, 169, 178, 185*n*; battles. See Battles; betrayed by Guenevere, 18: betrayed by Mordred, 18; Celtic hero, 27; conquests. See Conquests; his betrayal, 18; his mortal wound, 18; his return (myth), 20; reversal of his fortune, 18; his magical birth, 15; of Britain, 14, 15; son of Pendragon (Utherpendragon) and Ygerna, 15
Arthurian: early legends and fables, 22; hero, versus epic hero, 9; legend, origins of, 24; legends, 28; romance, 9; romance, contrasted with epic,

179-80; *annominatio* in,
178-79; *Chastel de Pesme*
Aventure episode, 69; date of,
6; fountain motif in, 23;
moral of, 125
Yvain: son of Urien, hero of
Yvain romance, 30, 111, 112,

113, 115, 117, 120, 121-24,
125, 160, 165, 166, 167, 172,
175, 180, 187n
Yvain li Avoutre, the "Bastard,"
30

*Zaddy, Z.P., 185n